WHAT LIFE HAS TAUGHT ME

LIFE LESSONS WORTH LEARNING

ANTHONY EKANEM

To my beloved mother, whose unwavering love and guidance inspire me daily. This book is a testament to your strength and the lessons you imparted to me and my siblings. Although you are no longer with us, your spirit lives on in every word I write.

I also dedicate this work to my beloved wife, Victoria, whose unwavering love and support inspire me every day, and to our wonderful children, Idara, Emmanuella, and Confidence, whose laughter fills my heart with joy. This journey is for you, a testament to the love and strength we share as a family.

Contents

Contents

Ephigraph

"Life is a teacher. The more you live, the more you learn."

Foreword

It is both a privilege and an honour to introduce What Life Has Taught Me, a profoundly personal and thought-provoking book by Anthony Ekanem. In this captivating work, Anthony opens a window into his life, sharing his experiences and the wisdom he gained along the way. These lessons – shaped by resilience, courage, and a profound sense of purpose – resonate deeply with the universal journey of self-discovery and growth.

This book is more than an autobiography; it is a tapestry of insights woven from the highs and lows of a life fully lived. Anthony invites readers to walk alongside him, experiencing his triumphs, challenges, and moments of quiet reflection. What sets What Life Has Taught Me apart is its ability to transcend the personal narrative and speak to human experience at large. Through his vulnerability and honesty, Anthony offers a guide to navigating life's unpredictable terrain with grace and determination.

Anthony's story is not merely a recounting of events but a reflection on how those events shaped his understanding of himself and the world around him. He shows us that even in our darkest hours, there is room for growth and transformation. Each chapter reads like a conversation with a trusted mentor – one who has weathered life's storms and emerged with wisdom and compassion to share. His journey reminds us that resilience is not the absence of struggle but the ability to rise, time and time again, in the face of adversity.

What makes this book particularly inspiring is its relevance to everyone, no matter where they are in their life's journey. Anthony's insights will resonate whether you are at the beginning of your path, grappling with challenges, or reflecting on past experiences. His reflections on setbacks and personal growth are not abstract musings but lessons drawn from real-life encounters. His story is a testament to the power of perseverance and self-belief, even when the odds seem insurmountable.

Anthony's ability to find meaning in every experience is a recurring theme throughout this book. He invites readers to see their struggles not as burdens but as opportunities for growth. Through his eyes, we come to understand that life's greatest lessons often emerge from the most unexpected places. It is a reminder that within each of us lies the potential to transform pain into purpose and obstacles into steppingstones.

In a world where it is easy to feel overwhelmed, What Life Has Taught Me offers a beacon of clarity and hope. Anthony's words encourage us to embrace our imperfections, to view setbacks as temporary, and to trust in our ability to chart a new course. He reminds us that life's journey is as much about the lessons learnt from failure as it is about the joy found in success.

Whether you are a student, a professional, or someone searching for a deeper understanding of your life's path, this book has something for you. It is not just Anthony's story – it is a universal story of growth, resilience, and the power of embracing life's lessons. It challenges us to look inwards, reflect on our life's journey, and find the courage to keep moving forwards.

Anthony Ekanem's What Life Has Taught Me is a testament to the strength of the human spirit and the transformative power of introspection. I have no doubt that as you turn the pages of this book, you will be inspired to view your life through a renewed lens.

Imo O. Imo, PhD

Author, *Essentials of Reinsurance: Principles & Applications*

Preface

Life is an extraordinary journey filled with lessons, experiences, and reflections that shape who we are. In writing *What Life Has Taught Me*, I seek to share the insights I have gained through my path, filled with unique challenges and triumphs. This book is a compendium of life lessons and wisdom, which illustrates how life's moments, both big and small, have contributed to my understanding of resilience, love, and the importance of human relationships. Each chapter draws upon memories that have had a profound impact on my life, serving as reminders of the beauty and complexity of human experience.

As I navigated my struggles, doubts, and triumphs, I discovered the invaluable lessons that come from personal experiences and the experiences of people around me. I dedicate these pages to those who have taught me, supported me, and inspired me along the way.

Life is a great teacher; the more you live, the more you learn. This saying captures a deep truth about human life, highlighting that our existence involves ongoing learning from both positive and negative experiences. With all its complexities, life serves as an unmatched teacher, imparting valuable lessons through the various challenges, opportunities, trials, and triumphs we encounter. *What Life Has Taught Me* delves into the notion that life, with all its complex realities, teaches us profound and invaluable lessons across all aspects of our lives.

Life offers us a series of valuable learning moments. From the innocence of childhood to the challenges of adulthood, each phase of life provides lessons that shape our understanding of ourselves, our environment, and the world. In childhood, we learnt important values such as honesty, respect, and the importance of relationships. These early experiences are critical as they lay the foundation for future interactions and decisions. For example, the act of sharing toys may seem unimportant, but it teaches the value of collaboration and the essence of community. These formative experiences establish the basis for social behaviour and emotional intelligence which are essential for personal growth and development.

As young children transition into adolescence, life presents more intricate lessons that challenge existing beliefs and ideals. The teenage years are often filled with confusion and self-discovery, where lessons range from academic to existential. The pressures of fitting in and finding one's identity often lead to a struggle between societal expectations and personal desires. Navigating this tumultuous terrain provides insights into self-acceptance, the significance of authenticity, and the power of choice – lessons that are beneficial not just for personal growth but also for nurturing healthy relationships. The challenges encountered during this critical stage serve as a training ground for resilience, preparing the young ones for the life ahead.

Building on the lessons learnt in youth, adulthood often brings significant responsibilities and challenges. Whether in career, relationships, or parenthood, adult life demands a higher level of emotional maturity and resilience. Within this context, life teaches important lessons about perseverance and the ability to adapt. Facing setbacks, whether in professional pursuits or personal aspirations, encourages us to cultivate perseverance and determination. The failures experienced along the way are crucial, as they provide valuable lessons about humility, the necessity of hard work, and the recognition of our limitations. Perhaps, the most enlightening aspect of these experiences is the understanding that failure is not the opposite of success; instead, it is an integral part of the journey towards achievement.

Furthermore, life serves as a teacher of empathy and compassion, urging us to develop a nuanced understanding of human experience. Through our interactions with others and the shared experience of suffering and joy, we learn that appreciating diverse perspectives and backgrounds often comes from personal suffering or witnessing the struggles of others, which teaches us empathy. Experiencing a loss deepens our understanding of grief and fosters compassion for those going through similar situations. Interacting with others helps us recognise the interconnectedness of humanity, which enriches our moral and ethical values.

Life lessons are not limited to personal experiences; they are also influenced by the broader societal context. Historical events, cultural changes, and collective experiences shape our worldviews and values. Learning from history, both successes and tragedies, provides insights into the consequences of our actions. Examining historical precedents teaches us about justice, fairness, and the importance of safeguarding everyone's rights. Humanity's collective memory reminds us that learning is a shared journey marked by communal growth and understanding.

The idea that life is a great teacher strongly resonates with human existence. Life imparts lessons that promote personal growth, resilience, empathy, and an understanding of our place in the world. Navigating life's complexities reveals its subtle teachings, showing that every moment, whether joyful or painful, offers opportunities for reflection and learning. Embracing life as a teacher not only enriches our individual experiences but also nurtures a deeper appreciation for the shared human experience, fostering a society rooted in understanding and compassion. Recognising life's instructive nature allows us to thrive, adapt, and make positive contributions to the world.

I invite you to join me on this reflective journey - a journey of self-discovery and growth. May these reflections resonate with your own experiences and ignite the spark of contemplation underlining what life's lessons mean to you. We all have stories to tell, and together, they create a tapestry of shared understanding.

Thank you for allowing me to share these life lessons with you.

Happy reading.

Anthony Ekanem

Acknowledgements

As I reflect on the journey of writing What Life Has Taught Me, I am grateful to everyone who supported me directly or indirectly.

First and foremost, I would like to thank my family for their unwavering love and encouragement. Your belief in my dreams has been the foundation that sustained me through the highs and lows of this endeavour.

To my friends, thank you for your understanding when I was lost in my thoughts or too absorbed in my writing. Your insights and heartfelt conversations inspired many ideas that find their way into this book.

I extend my deepest gratitude to my mentors and teachers, who have imparted wisdom and guidance to my life. Your wisdom and advice resonate within these pages and have shaped not only my writing but also the person I have become.

I must also acknowledge you, my readers. Your curiosity and desire to understand life better fuelled my passion for sharing these experiences and insights. I hope this book sparks conversation and reflection in your own lives.

Lastly, I would like to thank anyone who believed in the power of stories. Every person who has shared their experiences has contributed to my understanding of life; this book is as much yours as it is mine.

CHAPTER ONE

LIFE IS NOT FAIR

Life is often seen through a lens of fairness and justice, instilled in us from a young age through parental guidance, education, and societal norms. This strong expectation of fairness provides a sense of security in a world that is inherently unpredictable and imbalanced. As we go through life, it becomes clear that life is not always fair. This lesson will explore the different aspects of this concept, drawing from personal experiences, societal observations, and philosophical considerations about fairness in life.

Fairness is based on the principles of equal treatment and justice, but what seems fair in one context may be deeply unjust in another. This shows that our experiences and expectations shape our perceptions of fairness. For example, in education, ideally, every student would have equal access to quality education, allowing them to thrive based on their potential. However, disparities in wealth, geography, and resources often lead to inequalities in educational opportunities. A gifted child born into poverty may struggle to receive the necessary support and resources to excel academically compared to a less capable peer from a privileged background. This highlights that life's inequities are often due to societal imbalances rather than individual effort or worth.

Beyond education, the professional landscape also highlights life's unjust nature. We may dedicate ourselves to our careers but find ourselves overlooked for promotions or opportunities due to factors like favouritism, gender bias, or racial discrimination. This leads to frustration as hardworking individuals struggle with the lack of recognition for their efforts. Therefore, fairness is compromised by societal structures that prioritise certain attributes or backgrounds over individual talent and commitment.

Personal Reflections on Fairness

Personal experiences further illustrate the complex understanding of fairness and unfairness. There are instances where individuals strive towards specific goals, but external factors hinder their aspirations. For example, an individual pursuing a career in the arts may face financial constraints, a lack of networking opportunities, or the unpredictable tastes of the industry, stifling their potential despite their talent and work ethic. These narratives of unfulfilled potential highlight the unpredictable nature of success, often influenced more by circumstance than merit.

In addition, experiencing life's inherent unfairness can lead to feelings of bitterness, resentment, or despair. When expectations of fairness are not fulfilled, we may struggle with a deep sense of disillusionment, causing us to question our beliefs about the intrinsic fairness of life. The shattering of these ideals can have wide-ranging effects, impacting not only our mental wellbeing but also our relationships and worldview. Therefore, it is crucial to develop resilience and adaptability in the face of life's inequities, acknowledging that while we may seek fairness, the outcomes may often deviate from expectations.

The Philosophical Perspective

From a philosophical standpoint, acknowledging life's lack of fairness encourages deeper contemplation about the nature of existence itself. Numerous existential and philosophical theories delve into the randomness of life's events and the inherent chaos that characterises human experience. The concept of absurdism, particularly as expounded by philosophers like Albert Camus, suggests that the pursuit of meaning in a capricious world often leads to conflict and disillusionment. Embracing the absurdity of existence, according to Camus, can free us from the constraints of expectation and empower us to carve our paths, regardless of societal measures of success or fairness. This perspective presents a route to resilience, prompting us to discern our purpose beyond the bounds of fairness or justice.

Furthermore, delving into the philosophical aspects of fairness prompts a reconsideration of how society constructs ideas of equity. While laws and societal norms aim to achieve justice, the reality is that human biases and limitations often undermine these well-intentioned efforts. Consequently, examining systemic injustices requires collective responsibility and a dedication to promoting social change. It entails actively engaging with concepts of equity, advocating for marginalised communities, and the imperative to dismantle the structures perpetuating inequality.

Defining Fairness and Unfairness

Fairness can be likened to a unicorn - frequently discussed but elusive in real life. On the other hand, unfairness seems to have a talent for appearing uninvited. It is when we play by the rules, but the game is rigged against us. Life is not always fair, but understanding this can help navigate its twists and turns. By acknowledging this lesson, we can live more fully because we are aware that nothing is perfect in life. Many people feel as if the world owes them something, but the reality is that we must carve our path in life. Although life has the best intentions for us, one of the valuable life lessons you will learn is that life does not always go as planned.

Recognising Systemic Inequities

Recognising systemic inequities is like noticing weeds in a garden - they grow unnoticed until they start suffocating everything around them. Acknowledging these deeply rooted issues is the first step towards eradicating them. It is not just about pointing out unfairness; it is about dismantling the structures that perpetuate it.

Embracing Acceptance in Unfair Situations

Embracing acceptance in unjust situations is like befriending a school bully – it is not about surrendering, but about discovering serenity amidst turmoil. Acceptance does not entail giving up; it involves recognising reality and choosing how to respond with poise and honour. Developing coping strategies for resilience is like possessing a versatile tool for life's obstacles. It is about discovering what works for us – whether it is writing in a journal or confiding in a friend. Building resilience can help us in enduring the challenges that life throws our way.

Cultivating Inner Strength and Wellness

Cultivating inner strength and emotional wellbeing is comparable to nurturing a garden during a storm – it is challenging but necessary for personal development. Prioritising mental and emotional health is like securing our oxygen mask before assisting others; it is not self-centred but essential for survival. Creating a support network and seeking assistance is like forming a team of superheroes for the obstacles ahead. No one can go through it alone, and asking for help demonstrates strength, not weakness. Whether it is friends, family, or a therapist, having a team in our corner can make a significant difference.

Practising Gratitude and Optimism

Practising gratitude and optimism is like adding sprinkles to a cupcake – it enhances life's sweetness. It does not entail disregarding challenges but choosing to concentrate on the positive aspects. Gratitude is like a muscle – the more we use it, the stronger it becomes. Transforming setbacks into opportunities for growth is like turning lemons into a lemonade stand – it is all about perspective and a touch of creativity. Setbacks do not block our path but redirect us to unexpected destinations. Embracing change and learning from failures can pave the way for greater success.

Seeking Justice and Equity

Advocating for fairness and equality is like being the hero in our narrative, fighting for what is just. Whether it involves standing up against discrimination or advocating for equal opportunities, taking a stand can have a significant impact on our lives and wellbeing.

Embracing Growth Through Life's Inequities

Life's inequities can feel like a blow to the stomach, but they also impart valuable lessons. Learning from unjust experiences is like turning lemons into lemonade – it is about discovering the positive side. Channelling adversity into personal growth is like fueling our inner fire, igniting growth and resilience in the face of challenges.

Building Empathy and Compassion

When life presents unfairness, it is easy to feel resentful and disillusioned. However, developing empathy and compassion can be transformative. Cultivating understanding and empathy towards others is like stepping into someone else's shoes and experiencing their journey. Demonstrating kindness and compassion in the face of injustice is like sprinkling goodness into a world that greatly needs it.

Conclusion

As we navigate life's highs and lows, it is essential to remember that while fairness may not always be guaranteed, our responses to adversity can shape our journey. By embracing resilience, seeking justice, and nurturing empathy, we can discover strength and growth in the face of life's trials. Keep in mind that we can rise above injustice with grace and compassion, defining our character and shaping our paths forwards. Let us embrace the journey, learn from unfairness, and let it fuel our determination to create a more just and compassionate world for ourselves and others.

Acknowledging that life is not always fair is crucial to understanding the complexities of human existence. Personal stories, societal observations, and philosophical inquiries all point to the fact that fairness is often a subjective notion influenced by circumstances, privilege, and systemic inequalities. While striving for justice and equality is important, it is necessary to reconcile these goals with the unpredictable nature of life. Embracing the absence of fairness can lead to the development of resilience, empathy, and a deeper comprehension of human experience, guiding us to engage with a world marked by inherent disparities meaningfully. Recognising that although life may not always be fair, it presents abundant opportunities for growth, learning, and transformation is essential as we navigate this journey.

CHAPTER TWO

WE DON'T ALWAYS GET WHAT WE WANT

Life has taught me that you cannot always get what you want. This is deeply ingrained in our shared consciousness, serving not just as a warning but as a profound contemplation of human experience. While this idea may initially bring about feelings of letdown, upon closer examination, it reveals profound insights into resilience, acceptance, and the complex nature of human existence.

Human beings are taught from a young age to aspire and dream. The environment fosters a constant pursuit of objectives, from simple wishes for a toy or a favourite snack to more significant aspirations related to careers and personal relationships. These desires serve as a driving force, compelling us to utilise our abilities and determination in the pursuit of fulfilment. However, the continuum of human longing often collides with the harsh reality of limitations – financial constraints, societal expectations, personal setbacks, and various unforeseen circumstances pose formidable obstacles. The struggle to achieve these desires can lead to deep disappointment, resulting in feelings of frustration and helplessness.

The Role of Expectations in Disappointment

Expectations play a central role in disappointment. Expectations are inherently connected to desires and shape our perceptions of what should happen in our lives. When there is a gap between expectation and reality, disappointment inevitably follows. For example, a person who works hard for a promotion may face rejection despite their sincere efforts, leading to feelings of despair. Similarly, the unexpected loss of a job, a failed relationship, or a missed opportunity can directly contrast with our envisioned path.

This phenomenon is not confined to personal failures; it also extends to broader societal structures. For instance, economic downturns and shifting social dynamics can thwart the aspirations of entire communities. The collective yearning for a better future can turn into disillusionment when the anticipated improvements fail to materialise. Such occurrences intensify the notion that desires often go unfulfilled in life.

Resilience in the Face of Disappointment

Amidst the inevitability of unmet desires lies the potential for resilience. The ability to adapt to disappointment is a characteristic of the human spirit. It is through facing unfulfilled desires that we often develop our capacity for resilience. When confronted with adversity, we frequently find the strength to reassess our goals, explore alternative paths, and sometimes even discover new passions that were previously obscured by our singular focus.

Consider the story of J. K. Rowling, the author of the *Harry Potter* series. Before her success, she faced significant hardships, including a period of unemployment and rejection from multiple publishers. Her unwavering perseverance in the face of adversity not only led to her triumph but also gave rise to a cultural phenomenon that has transcended generations. Rowling's journey underscores the notion that unmet desires may redirect us towards unforeseen opportunities and greater achievements.

Contextualising Disappointment

From a philosophical perspective, the idea that we don't always get what we want invites contemplation of the nature of happiness itself. Many cultures advocate the belief that happiness is not dependent on the fulfilment of desires but rather on the acceptance of life's uncertainties. Eastern philosophies, particularly Buddhism, emphasise the transient nature of desire and the significance of detachment from it. The pursuit of desires, when taken to an extreme, can lead to suffering; therefore, embracing impermanence often serves as a pathway to inner peace.

Furthermore, the Stoics underscore the significance of rationality and the acceptance of fate, arguing that we should concentrate on what is within our control while embracing what is not. This philosophical framework encourages a mindset where unfulfilled desires do not govern our emotional state, nurturing a sense of resilience and contentment rooted in acceptance rather than relentless pursuit.

Embracing Life's Uncertainties

Embracing the uncertainties of life, that we cannot always get what we want encapsulates a fundamental aspect of human existence. While unmet desires may result in disappointment, they also serve as catalysts for personal growth, resilience, and self-examination. The inevitability of life's unpredictability urges us to adapt, reassess our goals, and sometimes discover new paths filled with opportunities. Recognising that life may not unfold according to our plans encourages a broader perspective – one that values adaptability, acceptance, and a deeper appreciation for the unpredictable journey of existence. Ultimately, it is through grappling with unmet desires that we may uncover a more profound sense of purpose, leading to a richer and more fulfilling life experience.

Understanding the Nature of Desires

Have you ever found yourself eyeing a tempting snack, even after having quality food for lunch? Understanding the psychology behind desires can explain why we crave certain things, whether it is food, experiences, or even a new gadget everyone is talking about. From social media influencers endorsing the latest fashion trends to societal norms defining success through material possessions, it is challenging to evade the influence of society and culture on our desires. Exploring how these external factors shape what we want can assist us in navigating our values and priorities.

How Expectations Impact Our Desires

Expectations can function as the covert puppeteer manipulating our desires. Whether it is expecting a promotion at work or anticipating a flawless vacation, our expectations play a significant role in shaping what we yearn for. Understanding this dynamic can help us align our desires with reality. Expectations can greatly influence our desires by setting the framework for what we believe we should accomplish or obtain. When our expectations are not met, it can lead to feelings of disappointment and frustration.

Recognising the Power of Perspective

Ever set your heart on something, only to realise it was not all it was said to be? Shifting our perspectives can help us see desires in a new light, guiding us to reassess what truly matters. Embracing different viewpoints can lead to more fulfilling desires that align with our values and aspirations.

Managing Disappointment and Frustration

So, you did not land that dream job, or you missed out on concert tickets. Dealing with disappointment is like weathering a storm – it is about finding refuge in strategies that help you bounce back and move forwards. Learning effective coping mechanisms can turn moments of disappointment into opportunities for growth. Frustration can feel like hitting a roadblock on the way to our desires. But what if frustration is a diversion leading us to growth opportunities? Embracing setbacks as chances to learn, adapt, and evolve can transform moments of frustration into catalysts for personal development and resilience.

Cultivating Gratitude and Acceptance

Cultivating a sense of gratitude can truly transform our perspectives in our world where desires seem endless. Whether it is finding joy in the little things or recognising the impact of those around us, practising gratitude can shift our focus from what we lack to what we already have, nurturing feelings of satisfaction and abundance. This mindset can also help in managing the emotions that arise from unfulfilled desires.

Embracing Acceptance as a Path to Inner Peace

Acceptance can be likened to a comforting ointment for the wounds caused by unmet desires. Embracing acceptance does not mean giving up on our aspirations; rather, it involves making peace with what is and letting go of what is not meant to be. This shift can guide us towards inner peace and a deeper understanding of ourselves.

Navigating the Path to Contentment

Have you ever felt a longing for the latest gadget or fashion trend, only to feel a pain of disappointment when it is out of reach? You are not alone! In a world driven by material desires, it is easy to feel like we are constantly pursuing unattainable goals. However, genuine contentment is not found in the next big purchase, but in life's simple pleasures. Let us embark on a journey to uncover fulfilment beyond our material cravings.

Finding Fulfillment Beyond Material Desires

Imagine this: a steaming cup of coffee on a rainy day, a heartfelt conversation with a loved one, or a tranquil moment of solitude in nature. These are the intangible things that money cannot buy, yet they hold the key to authentic happiness. By shifting our focus from what we desire to what we already have, we can unlock a trove of contentment that transcends material possessions. So, set aside that shopping list and open your heart to the abundance of joy that surrounds you.

Embracing the Journey Towards Contentment

The path to contentment is a journey filled with twists and turns, highs and lows, but it is incredibly rewarding in the end. Embrace each step along the way, savour the small triumphs, and learn from the setbacks. Remember, it is not just about reaching the destination but about relishing the journey and evolving as we progress. Contentment does not depend on fulfilling every desire we have. It springs from acceptance, gratitude, and discovering fulfilment beyond material possessions. By shifting our perspective and embracing life's uncertainties, we can find contentment even when our desires remain unmet.

Embracing Life's Unexpected Twists and Gifts

Life often surprises us, keeping us on our toes. Instead of resisting change or clinging to our plans, let us learn to dance to life's surprises. Embrace the unknown, welcome the unexpected, and marvel at the delightful twists and turns that make each day an adventure. So, release the need for control, raise a toast to life's surprises, and let the journey unfold in all its splendid unpredictability. Prepare yourself for an exciting ride full of surprises. Life has a way of throwing unexpected twists our way and presenting delightful surprises when we least expect them.

Conclusion

As we navigate desires and expectations, it becomes clear that true contentment lies in finding peace and gratitude in the present moment, rather than always getting what we want. By acknowledging the power of perspective, practising acceptance, and embracing life's surprises, we can cultivate a sense of fulfilment beyond material desires. Let us remember that in life, we may not always get what we want, but we have the power to find joy and meaning in what we already have.

CHAPTER THREE

Life Is Not All About Us

In today's interconnected world, shifting our focus from an individual-centric worldview to a more collective perspective is crucial. The idea that life is not all about us reminds us that our personal aspirations must coexist with our roles in a broader societal context. This lesson explores the implications of this statement, emphasising empathy, community engagement, and social responsibility in fostering harmonious coexistence, personal growth, and contributing to a more equitable society.

Beginning with the fundamental aspect of empathy, life has taught me that the ability to understand and share the feelings of others is crucial for human relationships and social interactions. When we prioritise our desires to the exclusion of others, we risk cultivating a narrow worldview that undermines the importance of understanding diverse perspectives. For instance, a student relentlessly pursuing academic excellence without recognising the collaborative nature of learning may find themselves isolated. In contrast, an individual who acknowledges the contributions of others and expresses genuine interest in their experiences is likely to foster deeper connections and mutual support. Recognising that our success is often tangled with the success of others can help us cultivate a sense of community that enhances collective wellbeing.

Furthermore, the idea that life is not all about us extends into the realm of community engagement. A society thrives when its members actively participate in the betterment of their environment and contribute to causes larger than their interests. Volunteering, engaging in local governance, and supporting social initiatives are all manifestations of a commitment to the community. They reflect an understanding that individual welfare is linked to communal welfare.

Urban areas rich in social capital, characterised by active advocates and community organisers, typically witness improved living conditions and greater opportunities for residents. In contrast, apathy and indifference often lead to stagnation and decline. By investing time and energy in community-building endeavours, we not only enhance the quality of our lives but also fortify the social fabric, paving the way for future generations.

Moreover, the shift in perspective towards prioritising the collective, rather than the individual, has significant implications for social responsibility. The pressing global issues we confront, such as climate change, economic inequality, and social injustice, emphasise the critical need for individuals and organisations to operate with high moral consciousness. Ignoring the impact of personal choices on the common good is no longer sustainable. For example, consumer behaviour significantly influences corporate practices, and individuals hold the power to drive substantial change by making conscientious choices, such as supporting ethical brands or reducing waste.

Recognising that life extends beyond personal desires encourages a sense of stewardship towards the planet and its inhabitants. This mindset prompts us to act not solely out of self-interest but with consideration for the broader implications of our actions.

The emotional benefits of adopting a perspective that prioritises the needs of others over our own are also profound. Research suggests that individuals who engage in selfless behaviours and prioritise the needs of others often experience higher levels of happiness and fulfilment. This can be attributed to the positive reinforcement gained from acts of kindness and the intrinsic satisfaction from contributing to something larger. Cultivating gratitude, often a result of recognising the contributions and struggles of others, further enhances emotional wellbeing. By shifting the focus away from self-centred concerns, we open ourselves up to richer, more meaningful experiences that ultimately foster a sense of belonging and purpose.

That life is not all about us captures a crucial ethical principle that promotes self-reflection, empathy, and social engagement. It challenges us to move beyond the limitations of a narrow, self-absorbed viewpoint and embrace a worldview that values the interdependence of humanity. Through fostering empathy, engaging with our community, exercising social responsibility, and promoting collective welfare, we not only enrich our lives but also contribute to the creation of a more just and empathetic society.

In a world marked by division and discord, the shift towards recognising the importance of the collective is not just desirable; it is essential for the advancement and flourishing of humanity. As we navigate the complexities of modern life, may we acknowledge the profound truth that life is not only about us but about the connections we build and the positive impact we create for others.

Self-Centredness and Narcissism

Self-centred behaviour involves prioritising our own needs, desires, and wellbeing over those of others. It entails disregarding how our actions affect the people around us. Narcissism extends beyond self-centeredness and involves an extreme focus on oneself, along with a sense of superiority and entitlement. Signs of narcissism include a constant need for admiration, a lack of empathy, and a belief in one's exceptionalism.

The Impact of Selfish Behaviour

Selfish behaviour undermines trust within relationships since it signifies a lack of concern for other people's feelings and needs. Communication breakdowns often occur when one party consistently prioritises themselves over mutual understanding. Selfish individuals may create emotional distance in relationships, leading to feelings of alienation and resentment. When one person consistently puts their needs above others, it can strain emotional connections and lead to feelings of isolation.

Developing Active Listening Skills

Active listening entails fully concentrating on and understanding what someone is saying without judgment or interruption. By refining this skill, we can better connect with others and demonstrate empathy. Engaging in activities that promote understanding of different perspectives can help in developing empathy and compassion. By gaining insight into others' viewpoints, a deeper connection and comprehension can be fostered.

Finding Fulfilment Through Serving Others

Assisting those in need through volunteering can bring a sense of purpose and fulfilment. Involvement in the community allows for making a positive impact beyond oneself and nurturing stronger connections. Small acts of kindness, whether through gestures or generosity, can significantly affect others' lives. Prioritising the wellbeing of those around us can create a ripple effect of positivity and compassion. It is common to let our egos take control at times, but true happiness often comes from shifting the focus away from our needs and desires.

Letting Go of the Need for Constant Validation

In a world driven by social media validation, it is easy to fall into the trap of seeking approval from external sources. True validation, however, comes from within. Releasing the need for constant approval can lead to a blossoming of self-worth.

Embracing Vulnerability and Authenticity

Being vulnerable can be daunting, yet it is also incredibly liberating. Embracing imperfections, sharing struggles, and presenting ourselves authentically can deepen connections. Life becomes more enriching when we let down our guard and let our true selves shine.

Building Connections Through Selflessness

Life is a team effort, and strong connections are vital. Shifting the focus from ourselves to others can lead to genuinely fulfilling relationships. Empathy is the key ingredient that binds us together. Being there for others not only strengthens bonds but can also bring joy and meaning to our own lives. In a world that often celebrates individual achievement, collaboration can be overlooked. However, we are stronger together. Prioritising the success and wellbeing of those around us leads to thriving for everyone. We rise by lifting others.

Conclusion

In concluding this assertion that life is not all about us, it is evident that shifting our focus from self-centredness to selflessness can result in profound transformations in our relationships, wellbeing, and overall sense of fulfilment. By embracing empathy, compassion, and a genuine desire to serve others, we open ourselves up to a world of connection and meaning that transcends the limitations of ego. Carry forwards the insights gained here to nurture a more compassionate and interconnected existence, where the joy of giving and the beauty of shared experiences become the true essence of our lives.

CHAPTER FOUR

LIVE IS SHORT

Life has taught me that life itself is short! That life is short resonates deeply within human experience, encapsulating the brevity and fleeting nature of human existence. This observation serves as a poignant reminder of the impermanence of life, urging us to cherish our time and engage meaningfully with our environment and the world around us. In examining the implications of this concept, we can uncover profound truths about human purpose, the pursuit of happiness, and the inevitability of death. Ultimately, reflecting on the fleeting essence of life not only fosters a deeper understanding of personal priorities but also encourages a lifestyle filled with intentionality and gratitude.

First and foremost, the acknowledgement that life is short compels us to confront the reality of mortality. From the moment of birth, every person is on a path towards an inevitable end. This recognition can evoke a range of emotions, from fear and anxiety to acceptance and motivation. The temporariness of life serves as a catalyst for introspection, prompting us to examine our values, aspirations, and the legacy we wish to leave behind. Historically, philosophers such as Seneca and Marcus Aurelius have advocated for the contemplation of mortality as a means of living a virtuous life, arguing that awareness of life's limitations fosters a sense of urgency in pursuing fulfilment and meaning.

Moreover, the brevity of life challenges us to prioritise our time and focus on pursuits that evoke genuine joy and satisfaction. In a world increasingly dominated by distractions and obligations, the finite nature of time can easily be overshadowed by the demands of daily living. We often find ourselves rapt in routines that, while necessary for survival, fail to provide a sense of accomplishment or happiness. Recognising that life is a limited resource encourages us to invest our efforts into endeavours that align with our passions and values. Whether nurturing relationships, pursuing hobbies, or engaging in meaningful work, allocating time to what truly matters becomes an essential tenet of a fulfilling life.

In the dynamic fabric of human existence, relationships play a vital role in how we experience life. That life is short serves as a reminder to cherish connections with others, as the bonds formed during our lifetime are invaluable. The relationships we cultivate provide support during challenging times and amplify joy during moments of triumph. They contribute to the fabric of our experiences and construct our sense of identity. When viewed through the lens of life's brevity, the importance of nurturing these bonds becomes increasingly clear. The act of reaching out, expressing love, and showing appreciation for others takes on greater significance, urging us to create lasting memories and foster a sense of community that will transcend the limitations of time.

Furthermore, the pursuit of happiness in the context of life's shortness invites us to embrace new experiences with an open heart and mind. Life offers many opportunities for exploration and growth; however, many are often impeded by fear and complacency. The notion that life is short encourages a mindset of adventure. We are urged to step outside our comfort zones, whether by travelling to new places, trying unfamiliar activities, or engaging with diverse cultures. Each experience serves as a chapter in the story of our lives, enriching it in unforeseen ways. By confronting fear and uncertainty, we can lead a life filled with rich experiences that contribute to a deep sense of satisfaction.

Although the notion that life is short may evoke feelings of sadness or urgency, it also prompts the consideration of our legacy – the impact left behind after departure. We are prompted to contemplate what we will be remembered for, both by our loved ones and society. Acts of kindness, leaving a lasting impression on others, and contributing to the greater good are essential elements of intentional living. We can shape a legacy that mirrors our values and ambitions through mindful daily interactions and decisions. This quest for significance transforms life into a purposeful journey, reinforcing the idea that while life may be short, its essence and impact can endure.

That life is short is laden with inevitability and the urgency to make the most of our time on earth. Recognising life's shortness serves as a reminder to cherish each moment and make meaningful choices that align with our values. As we navigate life's ups and downs, it becomes increasingly clear that time is a limited resource. Contemplating the impermanence of life can inspire us to prioritise what truly matters and let go of insignificant pursuits that do not contribute to our overall wellbeing.

Effect of Embracing Life's Brevity

Embracing the notion that life is short can serve as a catalyst for positive change. It motivates us to live authentically, pursue our passions, and cultivate enriching experiences. This mindset empowers us to make deliberate choices that resonate with our values and bring us closer to leading a purposeful life. In a world filled with distractions and constant busyness, embracing the present moment is an essential act of self-care. Being fully present allows us to relish life's simple pleasures, nurture our relationships, and cultivate contentment.

Benefits Of Living in The Present

Practising mindfulness and living in the present can profoundly impact our mental and emotional wellbeing. It reduces stress, enhances focus, and enables us to appreciate the beauty of every moment. Embracing the present moment offers a sense of calm and clarity that can help us navigate life's challenges with grace. In this fast-paced world, staying present can be challenging. Simple practices such as deep breathing, tuning into our senses, and setting boundaries with technology can help us stay grounded in the present moment. By intentionally creating a space for mindfulness in our daily lives, we can cultivate a deeper connection with ourselves and the world around us.

Leading A Fulfilling and Meaningful Life

Living a meaningful and fulfilling life is a journey of self-discovery and intentional living. Setting meaningful goals, prioritising our values, and nurturing meaningful connections are crucial elements of creating a life that aligns with our authentic selves. Establishing meaningful goals and priorities allows us to focus our energy on what truly matters to us. By clarifying our values and aspirations, we can create a roadmap for achieving our dreams and living a life that is in harmony with our authentic selves.

Fostering Meaningful Connections

Human connections are at the core of a fulfilling life. Nurturing meaningful relationships with loved ones, friends, and community members enriches our lives and provides a sense of belonging. Investing time and energy in building genuine connections can bring immense joy and fulfilment.

Overcoming Obstacles and Guilt

Life presents us with difficulties and regrets, but it is our response that shapes our journey. Confronting fear, embracing forgiveness, and accepting ourselves, are important to moving forward and living without the burden of past regrets. Fear and guilt can hinder us from fully embracing life and pursuing our aspirations. By acknowledging our fears, confronting them with courage, and reframing our regrets as lessons learnt, we can liberate ourselves and be open to new possibilities.

Forgiveness and Acceptance

Forgiveness and acceptance are powerful tools for personal growth and healing. Through self-compassion, forgiving others, and acknowledging our imperfections, we can let go of past mistakes and create room for growth and transformation. Embracing forgiveness and acceptance empowers us to move forwards with renewed purpose and authenticity.

Nurturing Gratitude and Mindfulness

Life is short, so cherish every moment. Cultivating gratitude and mindfulness helps us value the little things and find joy in everyday experiences. Gratitude acts as a shield against negativity and stress. Instead of dwelling on what we lack, practising gratitude shifts our focus to appreciating what we have. Whether it is a sunny day, a kind gesture from a friend, or a delicious meal, taking a moment to be thankful can shift our perspective on life.

Including Mindfulness into Everyday Habits

Mindfulness is about being present in the moment without judgment. It does not have to be complex – simple practices like deep breathing, mindful walking, or savouring a cup of tea or coffee can help us stay grounded in the present. By integrating mindfulness into our daily routines, we can reduce stress, enhance focus, and find moments of peace in our busy lives. So, take a deep breath, observe the world around you, and relish the beauty of the present moment. After all, life is short so make the most of it.

Conclusion

The notion that life is short encompasses many existential themes that deeply resonate with human experience. It prompts reflection on mortality, underscores the importance of relationships, encourages the pursuit of passion and adventure, and emphasises the significance of leaving a legacy. By embracing the fleeting nature of life, we can prioritise what truly matters to us, nurturing connections, embracing experiences, and making meaningful contributions to the world. Ultimately, recognising the brevity of life not only instils a sense of urgency but also inspires a profound appreciation for the beauty and depth of human experience. Life may be brief, but through deliberate living, we can make it rich and meaningful.

As we conclude our exploration of the brevity of life, may we carry forward the wisdom gained from embracing the brevity of our existence. Let us strive to live each day with intention, gratitude, and mindfulness, cherishing the moments we have and making choices that align with our deepest values. By honouring the fleeting nature of life, we can foster a sense of purpose and fulfilment that enriches our journey and leaves behind a legacy of love and meaning. Embrace the present, let go of regrets, and live fully, for life is indeed short, but its possibilities are endless.

CHAPTER FIVE

ACTION IS THE ONLY WAY TO MAKE PROGRESS

Throughout human history, the pursuit of advancement has been the driving force behind societal progress. Whether it is the invention of the wheel or the emergence of the internet, progress has propelled humanity to new heights. However, despite the abundance of knowledge, resources, and technologies, simply thinking about improvement will not lead to significant results. Taking action is the only way to make real progress. This lesson explains the importance of action through different perspectives, including historical context, psychological viewpoints, and the implications for individual and collective responsibility.

To understand the importance of action in the context of progress, we must first look at historical examples. History is full of instances where mere observation or theoretical discussions produced little or no results. The Industrial Revolution is a good example; it was not just the discussions about mechanisation that changed economies and societies, but the bold actions of innovators, entrepreneurs, and workers who utilised new technologies and methods. The development of steam engines and mechanised looms did not happen in isolation; they were the outcomes of dedicated experimentation, trial, and error. Therefore, the progress achieved during that time was directly linked to people taking the initiative and acting on their ideas.

In addition to the historical examples, the psychological aspects of human motivation and behaviour support the idea that action is crucial for progress. The concept of self-efficacy, introduced by psychologist, Albert Bandura, suggests that individuals' belief in their abilities to carry out behaviours necessary to achieve specific goals can significantly influence their actions. When individuals see themselves as capable and are encouraged to act on their visions, they are more likely to pursue and achieve their goals. On the other hand, those who remain passive often find themselves stuck in doubt and stagnation.

Turning aspirations into tangible results requires a proactive approach - one must take deliberate actions to turn dreams into reality. Furthermore, taking action fosters a constructive cycle of feedback and learning, where every step, regardless of its immediate success, provides valuable lessons that improve future efforts.

The implications go beyond personal motivation; collective action plays a vital role in societal progress. For example, social movements throughout history, such as the civil rights movement, women's suffrage, and environmentalism, highlight the power of collective action in driving significant change. These movements were not based on passive agreement with prevailing injustices, but on the passionate mobilisation of individuals who took to the streets, organised campaigns, and demanded accountability. Their actions garnered public support, influenced policy decisions, and ultimately brought about profound changes in societal values and regulations. The lessons from these movements show that meaningful progress arises not only from recognising issues but also from committing to decisive and collaborative action.

Critics may argue that action without thought is futile, and that thorough planning and analysis should precede any attempts at progress. While careful planning is undoubtedly important, excessive deliberation can lead to paralysing over-analysis that stifles innovation and hinders timely progress. The concept of "paralysis by analysis" suggests that individuals or organisations may become immobilised by the desire for complete information or consensus, thus missing crucial opportunities for advancement.

History is full of examples where swift action, although imperfect, has led to progress. The rise of startups in the technology industry is a key example; entrepreneurs often take calculated risks, learning and adjusting their strategies in real time. In this respect, the readiness to embrace uncertainty and take action despite potential setbacks is often a prerequisite for meaningful innovation.

It is important to understand that taking action should be purposeful and well-informed. Taking action should not be an excuse for being careless; instead, it requires a balance of ambition and caution. Furthermore, the type of action needed can vary significantly based on individual circumstances and goals, making it crucial for each person to evaluate their unique situation. Whether it is making small personal changes or making larger, coordinated efforts to impact communities, the call to action remains the same. The dedication to progress, both individually and collectively, is demonstrated through the decisions we make and the responses we create in the face of challenges.

The Impact of Taking Action

Taking action is like pressing the start button for progress. It is about moving forwards, even if it is just a small step. Action generates momentum and produces results. Not taking action is like treading water in a sea of missed opportunities. It keeps you stuck in the same place while time moves forwards. Embracing action means saying goodbye to stagnation. Taking the first step triggers a chain reaction of positive outcomes. It boosts confidence, encourages creativity, and opens doors to new possibilities. So, why wait when you can take charge and make things happen?

Overcoming Procrastination

Procrastination is the enemy of progress. It is sneaky, convincing you that tomorrow is a better day to start. But be aware that tomorrow may never come. Procrastination takes on many forms: distractions, perfectionism, and fear of failure. Recognising these patterns is the first step to defeating procrastination. From breaking tasks into smaller parts to setting deadlines, there are plenty of strategies to outsmart procrastination. Remember, the best time to start anything is always now.

Setting Goals and Executing Plans

Goals are like roadmaps to success. Without them, we are just wandering. But setting goals is just the beginning; executing plans is where the magic happens. Clear goals give us direction and purpose. They act as a guiding light, keeping us on track and focused on what truly matters. So, set those goals high and pursue them with all your might. Plans turn dreams into reality. Break down your goals into actionable steps, set milestones, and be prepared to adapt along the way. A solid plan is your secret weapon against uncertainty. Life is like a rollercoaster full of ups and downs. Perseverance is your seatbelt, keeping you strapped in when things get rough.

Maintaining Motivation During Setbacks

Setbacks are part and parcel of the journey. It is normal to stumble; what matters is how we pick ourselves up and keep going. Remember why you started and let that fuel your fire. Resilience is like a muscle; the more you flex it, the stronger it becomes. Embrace challenges as opportunities to grow, learn from failures, and nurture a spirit of determination. With resilience by our side, no challenge is too great. Change is inevitable, but growth is optional. Embracing change means accepting that things will not always stay the same, which is fine! It is how we learn, evolve, and ultimately make progress in our lives.

Life loves throwing curveballs. Whether it is a sudden job change, a move to a new city, or a global pandemic, we are constantly faced with new situations that challenge us to adapt. The key is to go with the flow, stay flexible, and see change as an opportunity for growth rather than a setback.

The Role of Continuous Learning in Progression

There is a saying that knowledge is power, and that is correct. Continuous learning is not just about hitting the books or attending lectures – it is about staying curious, open-minded, and willing to explore new ideas. Whether it is picking up a new hobby, taking an online course, or simply having a conversation with someone with a different perspective, learning is the fuel that propels us forwards on our journey towards progress.

Conclusion

The notion that taking action is the only way to make progress is substantiated through various lenses: historical context, psychological frameworks, and the significance of collective efforts. Progress cannot materialise through idle speculation or passive acceptance; it demands an informed and proactive approach. While thought and planning are crucial components of the journey, they must ultimately culminate in action to stimulate meaningful change. As we navigate the complexities of the contemporary world, embracing a mindset anchored in action is essential not only for personal development but also for the development of society. Thus, let us heed the call to action and recognise it as the catalyst for progress - one step at a time.

The journey towards progress begins with a single step - the decision to take action. By acknowledging the power we hold to drive change in our lives, we pave the way for growth, resilience, and ultimately, success. Embrace each opportunity to take action, overcome obstacles with determination, and welcome change as a catalyst for advancement.

Remember, it is through our actions that we shape our future and make meaningful strides towards the fulfilment of our aspirations. Keep moving forwards, for taking action is indeed the only way to make progress.

CHAPTER SIX

Every Action Has a Consequence

Life has taught me that every action has a consequence. This resonates across cultures and eras, an enduring reflection on the intricate fabric of human existence. This principle underscores the reality that our decisions – whether grand or seemingly inconsequential - are threaded into the fabric of our lives and the lives of others, forming an interconnected network of cause and effect. As we navigate through various spheres of existence, from personal relationships to broader societal interactions, the acknowledgement of this principle fosters a profound sense of responsibility. The exploration of this tenet illuminates the importance of foresight, ethical considerations, and the recognition of our profound interconnectedness.

At the heart of the notion that every action has a consequence lies the need for foresight. Foresight, or the ability to anticipate the potential outcomes of our actions, is an essential skill that can shape the trajectory of personal and collective experiences. Each decision we make, whether it pertains to our immediate environment, relationships, or societal contributions, is laden with implications that may not be evident in the moment of choice. For instance, an individual may choose to employ deceptive practices in a business setting to gain short-term profit. While this action might yield immediate financial gain, the long-term consequences can be dire, potentially resulting in loss of reputation, legal ramifications, and strained relationships with stakeholders. This example illustrates the importance of considering not only the immediate rewards but also the enduring impact that our actions can have on us and the larger community.

In the realm of ethical considerations, the principle that every action has a consequence further emphasises the necessity of moral responsibility. The decisions we make are often entrenched in ethical frameworks that dictate the appropriateness of our actions. In a world where resources are finite, the allotment, use, and management of these resources can have far-reaching implications for future generations.

The decisions we make today, whether related to environmental practices, economic policies, or social justice initiatives, have long-lasting effects. For instance, exploiting natural resources without considering ecological sustainability can lead to severe environmental degradation, negatively impacting biodiversity and climate conditions. These consequences go beyond the present and affect future generations who will inherit the planet and its resources. Therefore, making ethical decisions is crucial in understanding the impact of our actions. Additionally, the contrast between intention and outcome complicates our understanding of actions and their consequences. While individuals often start endeavours with good intentions, the results may differ significantly from what they initially aimed for. This highlights the unpredictability of human interactions and the intricate web of influences in social dynamics.

A well-intentioned individual may engage in what they believe is nurturing behaviour, only to unintentionally foster dependence instead of empowerment. This difference between intention and consequence reminds us that the effectiveness of our actions should be evaluated not only based on intent but also by examining their impact - a vital consideration in personal relationships, educational settings, and social programmes.

The principle that every action has a consequence also applies to the collective sphere, emphasising the importance of social responsibility. The interconnectedness of modern society, driven by rapid technological advancements and globalisation, magnifies the impact of individual actions. For example, a single social media post can spark widespread discussions, influence public opinion, or even mobilise social movements.

In this digital era, we have unprecedented power, and the consequences of our actions can spread rapidly. A thoughtless comment can escalate into a campaign against an individual or organisation, while a well-thought-out message can inspire positive change. This illustrates the double-edged nature of modern communication: the potential for both harm and healing is closely linked to the choices we make in our interactions with the world.

Considering these factors, it becomes essential to develop a deep awareness of the repercussions of our actions. This awareness is not just a matter of caution but serves as a call to action – a reminder that we are catalysts for change in the constantly evolving world that we live in. Encouraging critical thinking and reflective practice in our personal and public lives creates an environment where individuals can embrace this principle with intention and integrity. By engaging in dialogues that emphasise accountability and encourage ethical decision-making, we strengthen our commitment to responsibly navigating the challenges of existence.

The notion that every action has a consequence serves as a guiding principle for both personal growth and societal progress. By embracing foresight, upholding ethical standards, acknowledging the complexity of intention versus outcome, and promoting social responsibility, we can leverage the power of our actions to create a more just, compassionate, and sustainable world. It is through the conscious recognition of this principle that we can aspire not only to personal development but also to collective wellbeing, ensuring that our legacies make positive contributions to the ongoing narrative of human history. Therefore, as we move forwards, it is crucial to be mindful of our choices, understanding that the ripple effects of our actions extend far beyond our immediate surroundings and shape the future for generations to come.

Understanding Cause and Effect

Understanding cause and effect involves acknowledging the interconnected nature of our actions and their impact on our lives and the world around us. Throughout history, thinkers and philosophers have contemplated the concept of cause and effect, which has been a fundamental principle in understanding the world from ancient times to the present day. Analysing past events allows us to understand how actions have shaped history and learn important lessons for the future.

Cause-and-effect relationships are straightforward yet significant as they illustrate how one action leads to a reaction, creating a cause-and-effect chain. Recognising these connections enables us to make more informed decisions and predict the consequences of our actions. The law of consequences is a universal truth governing our daily lives, emphasising that every action sets off a chain of events leading to specific outcomes. Understanding cause-and-effect relationships increases our awareness of the impact of our choices.

Every decision we make in our daily lives, from hitting the snooze button in the morning to deciding what to have for lunch, carries both immediate and long-term consequences. Whether in personal relationships, health habits, or career choices, our actions shape our reality. Being mindful of these consequences allows us to make choices that align with our goals and values.

The Interconnected Nature of Actions

Our actions are like ripples in a pond, extending outwards and affecting everything they touch. Whether big or small, our actions can have far-reaching consequences that may not be immediately apparent. It is important to consider how our choices not only influence our own lives but also impact others.

Accepting Responsibility for Actions

Taking responsibility for our actions is like admitting when we have made a mistake – it may not always be easy, but it is the mature thing to do. Assuming ownership of our actions is the initial step in handling consequences positively. Recognising our role in a situation empowers us to learn and grow from it.

Mitigating Negative Consequences

To minimise negative consequences, it is important to consider the potential outcomes of our actions in advance. Anticipating and evaluating the impact of our choices can guide us in making more informed decisions. Recognising recurring negative reactions empowers us to break free from harmful patterns. Understanding our typical responses enables us to take steps to change our behaviour.

Tools for Shifting to Positive Responses

Practices such as mindfulness techniques and self-reflection can assist in transforming negative reactions into positive responses. Pausing to consider alternative ways to react can lead to more constructive outcomes. Integrating mindfulness into our decision-making processes can result in more intentional actions. Being present in the moment allows for greater clarity and awareness of our choices.

Benefits of Intentional Actions

Intentional actions bring about a sense of purpose and fulfilment. Aligning our actions with our values and goals leads to a more meaningful and impactful way of living. Our choices not only affect our current circumstances but also play a significant role in shaping our individuality. The decisions we make influence our personal growth and contribute to the development of our character.

How Choices Shape Our Character

Each decision we make reflects our values, beliefs, and priorities, shaping our character over time and defining the kind of person we become. Deliberate and thoughtful decisions enable us to cultivate the traits and qualities that align with our true selves. Self-reflection is a powerful tool for personal growth, providing valuable insights into our past actions and their consequences.

Self-Reflection and Learning from Past Actions

Engaging in self-reflection is a valuable approach to personal development. Analysing past actions and their outcomes provides insights into behavioural patterns and inclinations. Learning from both successes and mistakes enables better decision-making for ongoing personal growth. Individual actions have far-reaching effects on society and the environment, making it crucial to comprehend the social and environmental impacts of our behaviour.

Butterfly Effect: Small Actions, Big Impact

The butterfly effect demonstrates the significance of small actions in shaping significant outcomes. Like how a butterfly's wing flapping can lead to a tornado, seemingly insignificant choices can trigger ripple effects that influence the world. Being mindful of our actions allows for the potential to utilize this influence for positive change.

Environmental Consequences of Our Behaviour

Our actions, from carbon emissions to plastic waste, have significantly affected the environment. Recognising the implications of consumption habits, waste generation, and resource use empowers us to reduce our ecological footprint and safeguard the planet for future generations.

Making Informed Decisions

Decision-making involves assessing potential consequences. Reflecting on the possible outcomes before making a decision can help avoid unexpected results. Considering the long-term effects and seeking advice from various perspectives can lead to a more comprehensive decision-making process.

Accepting Mistakes and Their Consequences

Mistakes are essential for personal growth. Embracing setbacks as opportunities for development adds richness to life experiences. Taking responsibility for mistakes and their repercussions demonstrates strength and character.

Building Accountability and Integrity

Being accountable and acting with integrity sets the stage for success and attracts respect from others. Holding ourselves to high standards is like being a dependable delivery person who is always punctual.

Forgiving Yourself and Others for Past Actions

Forgiveness towards oneself and others for past actions is crucial for moving forwards positively. Letting go of resentment creates space for a brighter future.

Conclusion

Every action, just like tossing a pebble into a pond, has effects that extend beyond immediate visibility. Mindful decision-making can create a ripple effect of positivity and growth. Making thoughtful choices, taking responsibility for mistakes, and understanding the consequences of our actions are all part of embracing a satisfying life. Recognising that every action has consequences empowers us to make informed choices.

Taking responsibility for our decisions and contributing positively to the world around us is crucial. By understanding the impact of our actions, learning from our mistakes, and aiming to create a ripple effect of positivity, we can influence a future filled with growth, understanding, and collective wellbeing.

Moving forwards with mindfulness and purpose, it is important to recognise that our actions have the power to create a brighter tomorrow for ourselves and those around us. Navigating consequences, breaking negative patterns, and cultivating intentional actions all play a role in embracing responsibility in a connected world. Understanding the ripple effects of our actions enables us to strive for a positive impact on ourselves and those around us. Embracing the responsibility that comes with this understanding empowers us to create a more harmonious and intentional existence. May we continue to navigate the intricate dance of cause and effect with compassion, wisdom, and a commitment to fostering a brighter tomorrow for all.

As we conclude our exploration of the interconnected nature of cause and effect, it is important to remember that each decision we make has the potential to shape our future and the world we live in. By cultivating an awareness of our actions and their repercussions, we can strive to make positive contributions to our lives and communities.

CHAPTER SEVEN

LOVE IS NOT ENOUGH

Love is often held as the supreme value in human relationships, revered as the empowering force that can conquer all adversities and bind people together in enduring relationships. While the sentiment of love is both profound and essential, the notion that love alone suffices for a successful relationship is a dangerous generalisation. Life has taught me that love must be complemented by many other factors, including communication, trust, respect, compatibility, and shared goals, which form the bedrock of a healthy, lasting relationship.

The romantic ideal of love is portrayed across various fields, particularly literature, cinema, and music, where it serves as a centrepiece for many narratives. These portrayals often suggest that love is a cure-all; and that once two individuals fall in love, their relationship sails smoothly, unencumbered by issues or challenges. Such representations can lead to unrealistic expectations, hindering the capacity for individuals to nurture their relationships through pragmatic considerations. Love, while a vital element in relationships, is not an all-encompassing solution and can flounder if left unchecked by the realities of human interactions.

This lesson explores the complex dynamics beyond love, highlighting the vital components contributing to a healthy and fulfilling relationship. By delving into the limitations of love and emphasising the importance of respect, humility, finance, communication, trust, compatibility, emotional support, conflict resolution, and personal growth, we reveal the multifaceted nature of relationships and the key factors behind their success.

What Love Is, And What Love Is Not

It is important to understand what love truly means. Love is not just a feeling or an emotion; it is a choice, a commitment, and an action. It goes beyond the initial infatuation and requires effort and dedication to make a relationship thrive. Love is about understanding and accepting our partners for who they are, supporting them through thick and thin, and being there for them in both good times and bad times. However, love is not enough by itself to build a strong and healthy relationship. Other important factors need to be considered, such as respect, humility, and finance.

The Limitations of Love in a Relationship

Love is often romanticised as the magical glue holding a relationship together. However, relying solely on love can lead to unrealistic expectations and disappointments. It is important to recognise that love, while important, is just one piece of the puzzle in a healthy and fulfilling relationship. Relationships are complex webs of emotions, perspectives, and experiences. Love alone cannot address issues such as communication breakdowns, trust issues, or compatibility mismatches. To navigate the complexities of relationships successfully, we must go beyond the surface-level allure of love and delve into the core aspects that truly sustain a relationship.

Communication: The Lifeblood of Relationships

At the core of any successful relationship is effective communication. While love provides the impetus for connection, it is through effective communication that partners articulate their needs, resolve conflicts, express feelings, and reinforce their bond. Misunderstandings and assumptions can develop in the absence of open dialogue, leading to resentment and a gradual erosion of affection. Couples often find that their love wanes not because it was inadequate but because they failed to communicate effectively. Thus, it is evident that love must be nurtured through consistent and respectful communication.

Communication is the lifeline of any relationship. Open, honest, and respectful communication fosters understanding, connection, and intimacy between partners. It is essential to cultivate effective communication skills, such as active listening, expressing emotions constructively, and resolving conflicts peacefully, to nurture a strong and enduring bond. Miscommunication can breed misunderstandings, resentment, and distance in a relationship. When partners fail to communicate effectively, issues can escalate, leading to unnecessary conflicts and emotional distress. By acknowledging the significance of clear and empathetic communication, couples can prevent misinterpretations and strengthen their relationship.

Trust and Respect as Cornerstones of Relationship

Trust and respect are integral components that stabilise the foundation of love. Trust allows us to feel secure and safe within a relationship, facilitating emotional vulnerability. Without trust, doubt creeps in, undermining the very essence of love. Moreover, respect for one another's individuality, desires, and boundaries fosters an environment where love can flourish. When love is void of these crucial elements, it can quickly devolve into jealousy, possessiveness, or even contempt.

Additionally, situations often arise where one partner prioritises love as a sufficing element, neglecting to develop trust and respect. Such negligence can manifest in toxic dynamics in which love is the only glue holding the relationship together, even as resentment brews beneath the surface. We must recognise that while love is a formidable force, it cannot thrive without trust and mutual respect to support its growth. The basis of a healthy relationship is trust, which depends on consistency, honesty, and reliability in actions. Without trust, doubts and insecurities can weaken the foundation of love. Building trust through transparency, dependability, and integrity strengthens the emotional bond between partners and creates a sense of security in the relationship.

Respect is fundamental to a harmonious and respectful relationship. It involves appreciating each other's boundaries, opinions, and autonomy. Mutual respect establishes the groundwork for healthy communication, conflict resolution, and acknowledgement of each other's individuality. Upholding respect as an essential aspect of the relationship allows us to nurture a strong and lasting relationship. It entails treating our partners with consideration, kindness, and courtesy, and valuing their thoughts, opinions, and strengths. When there is respect, partners feel valued and appreciated, leading to greater satisfaction and harmony in the relationship.

Compatibility: Beyond Attraction

Another misconception in discussions about love is the notion that mere attraction or superficial compatibility can sustain a relationship over time. While it is natural to be attracted to one another based on physical or emotional chemistry, deeper compatibility rooted in shared values, beliefs, and lifestyles is crucial for long-term success. Incompatibility on important matters such as financial management, child-rearing philosophies, sex and sexual orientation, or career aspirations can lead to intractable disagreements.

Successful relationships often involve a convergence of life goals and priorities. Couples must navigate their individual circumstances while aligning their futures. Without this compatibility, love can turn from a source of joy into a battleground of conflicting desires, causing partners to question their commitment to each other.

While love sparks initial attraction, shared values sustain a relationship over time. Compatibility in values, beliefs, and life goals creates a sense of alignment and unity between partners. By prioritizing shared values, couples can overcome challenges, make important decisions, and build a future together based on mutual understanding and agreement.

Differences in compatibility are inevitable in any relationship. It is important to approach these differences with empathy, flexibility, and a willingness to compromise. By embracing and respecting each other's differences, couples can learn and grow together, enriching their relationship with diverse perspectives and experiences. Compatibility goes beyond surface-level similarities and requires a deeper understanding and acceptance of each other's uniqueness.

Shared Goals and Aspirations

Love flourishes when both partners have a clear understanding of their shared goals and aspirations. This alignment serves to strengthen the purpose of the relationship, providing motivation and direction amidst life's challenges. Without common aspirations, each partner risks following different paths, which can lead to disillusionment and eventual drift apart.

It is crucial to understand that love is dynamic and can evolve, but for this evolution to be positive, it is essential that both partners actively engage in discussions about their respective futures. Pursuing common goals does not imply the absence of individuality; instead, it underscores the importance of collaboration in enriching the relationship's depth and meaning.

Love is a wonderful emotion that can bring immense joy and fulfilment in relationships. It is often regarded as the foundation of a strong and enduring partnership. However, love alone is not always sufficient to sustain a relationship in the long term. Several other critical elements play a significant role in maintaining a healthy and fulfilling relationship with our partners.

In the world of relationships, love often takes centre stage, capturing our hearts and fueling the desire for connection. However, beyond the romantic ideals, there is a complex web of elements essential for the sustainability and success of a partnership. While love is important, it alone cannot sustain a relationship. Respect, humility, and understanding of the role of finance are crucial for building a strong and successful relationship.

Nurturing a Healthy Relationship

In relationships, love is often seen as the foundation, but emotional support plays a crucial role in maintaining a strong and lasting union. Building a supportive environment in a relationship involves actively listening, showing empathy, and offering comfort during challenging times. It is about being there for our partner, no matter the situation.

Creating a Supportive Environment

Creating a supportive environment in a relationship means being each other's rock, cheerleader, and confidant. It involves fostering trust, respect, and understanding. By acknowledging your partner's feelings and needs, you create a safe space where both of you feel valued and cherished. Emotional support strengthens the bond between partners and paves the way for a deeper connection.

The Power of Emotional Intimacy

Emotional intimacy goes beyond physical affection. It is about sharing our innermost thoughts, fears, and dreams with our partner. Developing emotional intimacy requires vulnerability and openness. By being emotionally intimate, we create a profound sense of closeness and strengthen the emotional foundation of our relationship.

Managing Conflicts in Relationships

Conflicts are inevitable in any relationship, but how we manage them can make all the difference. Resolving differences constructively involves effective communication, empathy, and a willingness to compromise. By approaching conflicts with an open mind and a desire to understand each other's perspectives, we can navigate disagreements in a way that strengthens our relationship.

Healthy conflict resolution strategies include active listening, expressing thoughts and feelings calmly, and seeking common ground. It is about finding solutions together rather than trying to win the argument. By practising patience and respect during conflicts, you can work towards a resolution that honours both partners' needs and feelings. Conflict, when handled constructively, can be a catalyst for personal and interpersonal growth. It forces both partners to confront their differences, communicate effectively, and find common ground. By turning conflict into a learning opportunity, you can deepen your understanding of each other and emerge stronger as a couple.

Evolving Together in a Relationship

In a healthy relationship, personal growth is not just supported but also celebrated. Encouraging each other's individual growth within a relationship involves respecting each other's ambitions, aspirations, and personal development. It involves creating space for each other to grow and honouring the journey of self-discovery within the context of the relationship. While individual growth is vital, growing together as a couple is equally important. Sharing experiences, setting mutual objectives, and evolving as a team strengthens the bond between partners. By navigating life's challenges and successes together, a deeper connection is formed, creating a shared future founded on a strong base of love, support, and personal growth.

Encouraging Individual Growth in a Partnership

Supporting individual growth within a relationship entails empowering each other to pursue personal interests, passions, and goals. It involves celebrating your partner's accomplishments, providing guidance when necessary, and being a source of encouragement during moments of self-doubt. By fostering individual growth, a relationship dynamic based on mutual support and respect is created.

How Humility Impacts a Relationship

Humility is another crucial aspect of a successful relationship. It involves being humble and setting aside our egos. It means being able to acknowledge when we have made a mistake, apologising when necessary, and being open to compromise. Humility fosters effective communication and prevents conflicts from escalating into destructive arguments. It cultivates an environment of understanding and cooperation, strengthening the bond between partners.

The Financial Aspect of Relationship

Finances can also play a significant role in a relationship. Financial compatibility is important because it impacts various aspects of our shared lives. It involves being aligned when it comes to financial objectives, effectively managing money, and sharing responsibilities. Disagreements about finances can strain the relationship, leading to stress and resentment. Therefore, the ability to work together as a team in financial matters can contribute to a healthier and more secure relationship.

Conclusion

While love is undoubtedly a powerful element in human relationships, it is not enough on its own. Relationships thrive on a combination of communication, trust, respect, compatibility, and shared objectives. Each of these factors works together to create a nurturing environment where love can grow and evolve without falling prey to neglect or unrealistic expectations. The journey of love is beautiful, but it requires dedication, understanding, and commitment to the multifaceted nature of human relationship. As society continues to celebrate love as an essential human experience, it is crucial to recognise that love is just one element in the complex fabric of successful relationships.

As we conclude our exploration of the complexities within relationships, love, while very powerful, is merely one piece of the intricate puzzle. By acknowledging and nurturing the foundations of communication, trust, respect, compatibility, emotional support, conflict resolution, and personal growth, we lay the groundwork for stronger, more resilient relationships. Embracing a holistic approach to relationships empowers us to cultivate bonds that not only stand the test of time but also thrive in the richness of shared experiences and mutual understanding. Love may be the starting point, but it is the culmination of these essential elements that truly sustains and elevates a relationship to its fullest potential.

Love is a strong feeling that serves as the basis of a relationship, but it alone cannot guarantee its longevity. Respect, modesty, and financial compatibility are all essential components that contribute to a healthy and satisfying relationship. By understanding and embracing these factors, couples can collaborate to establish a strong and enduring relationship that can stand the test of time.

CHAPTER EIGHT

LOVE IS MORE THAN A FEELING

Love, a concept deeply entrenched in human existence, goes beyond just being a feeling to embody a deliberate choice that shapes our interactions, commitments, and personal satisfaction. While modern culture often romanticises love as an overpowering emotion – a mysterious magnetic force that sweeps individuals off their feet – this viewpoint overlooks the profound complexity inherent in love as a conscious decision. This lesson explores the complex nature of love, noting that genuine love requires intentionality, commitment, and ethical integrity, ultimately asserting that it is a choice made each day, rather than a fleeting emotion experienced intermittently.

At its core, love is a complex interplay of emotions, thoughts, and actions. Emotions are undeniably a part of love; joy, passion, and connection often accompany romantic relationships, forming the strong essence of initial attraction. However, equating love solely with emotion is a misunderstanding of its true nature. Emotions can be fleeting, influenced by circumstances and individual experiences. Happiness can fluctuate, and passion may diminish as familiarity grows. Therefore, relying solely on emotions to sustain love can lead to unstable relationships based on factors beyond our control.

On the other hand, love as a choice emphasises the role of action and responsibility in nurturing relationships. Choosing to love involves conscious decisions aimed at fostering connection and longevity. This perspective encourages us to engage in intentional acts – whether they are simple gestures, responsible communication, or deep acts of empathy – that signify a commitment to another person. Loving someone requires ongoing effort, often in the face of challenges and discomfort. Moments of dissatisfaction or conflict may arise, yet choosing to love means committing to understanding, forgiveness, and compromise. Thus, true love is rooted in the conscious decisions individuals make amid emotional turbulence, transcending the limitations of mere feeling.

Furthermore, love as a choice underscores the importance of values and principles in guiding our actions. It is crucial to acknowledge that love thrives when nurtured through mutual respect, trust, and shared goals. Embracing love as an intentional act means recognising our values and our alignment with another's. When we choose to love, we are essentially choosing to uphold certain ethical standards - caring for another's wellbeing, prioritising loyalty, and fostering a sense of security. This alignment establishes a strong foundation upon which relationships can operate, perhaps with greater resilience than those based solely on passion or emotional connection.

In addition, love as a choice aligns with the idea of selflessness and sacrifice. The most profound expressions of love often occur when we unconditionally prioritise our partner's needs above our own, establishing a cycle of mutual respect and enduring affection. This selfless act can manifest in various ways, including offering emotional support during challenging times or facilitating personal growth in another. By choosing to engage selflessly with a partner, we not only nurture a deep reservoir of goodwill within the relationship but also create an environment in which both parties feel valued and understood. The choice to love, therefore, encourages the practice of empathy and generosity, further strengthening the bond through shared experiences and mutual support.

Furthermore, highlighting love as a choice underscores its potential to bring about transformation. In various situations, societal expectations, external obstacles, and personal challenges can present significant barriers to maintaining love. In these circumstances, the conscious decision to persist defines the extent of our dedication. Overcoming adversity can fortify relationships, nurturing resilience and unity between partners. Choosing to endure hardships ultimately represents a profound commitment to love, illustrating that genuine affection often develops through shared trials.

Love as an Emotion and a Choice
Love, both as an emotion and a choice, is often depicted as a whirlwind of feelings - from butterflies in the stomach to a racing heart and an overall

feeling of euphoria. But is there more to it than just that? Let us explore the intricate layers of love that extend beyond mere emotions. Love encompasses various forms - from the intense passion of romantic love to the unwavering loyalty of familial love and the comforting companionship of platonic love. It is not just a fleeting emotion but also an intentional choice that demands nurturing and dedication. True love transcends grand gestures and fairy-tale moments; it thrives in the everyday decisions we make to prioritise our loved ones. It involves a willingness to make sacrifices, compromises, and consistently show up for each other, even during challenging times.

Nurturing Love Through Communication

Communication serves as the foundation of any successful relationship, enabling us to openly express our needs, fears, and desires. Empathy and understanding pave the way for deeper connections, bridging gaps, and nurturing a sense of closeness that goes beyond mere words. Love is not just about butterflies in the stomach; it is a full-blown brain celebration! When we fall in love, our brain releases a delightful mix of chemicals like dopamine and oxytocin, creating a warm and fuzzy feeling inside. So, the next time you are head over heels in love with someone, it is all thanks to your brain chemistry!

Health Benefits of Love

Love is not just beneficial for the soul; it is also a powerhouse for our wellbeing! Research indicates that individuals in loving relationships tend to experience lower stress levels, stronger immune systems, and even longer lifespans. So, forget about apples – a daily dose of love might just keep the doctor away!

Building Trust and Intimacy

Trust acts as the adhesive that sustains relationships, while intimacy is like the secret ingredient that enhances its flavour. To cultivate enduring love, generously sprinkle trust and mix in some intimacy and you will have a recipe for relationship success!

Overcoming Challenges and Growing Together

Relationships are not solely about roses and sunshine; they are more like a rollercoaster with twists and turns. However, facing challenges together can fortify your bond and help in your mutual growth as a couple. So, grasp your partner's hand, hold on firmly, and enjoy the journey!

The Power of Generosity and Empathy

Who says grand gestures are the only way to express love? At times, it is the little things that matter – a heartfelt note, a warm embrace, or even doing the dishes without being asked. So, spread kindness and witness your love blossom! Generosity and empathy are like superpowers in a relationship – they can conquer any adversary that threatens your love story. Being generous with your time, attention, and love, and displaying empathy towards your partner's emotions can forge a profound, meaningful relationship that stands the test of time.

Embracing the Complexity of Love

Love cannot be simply categorised; it is a multifaceted and ever-evolving concept. Embrace the unexpected twists, the highs and lows, and the beauty of maturing and growing together. Let us face it, a love story without a few surprises would be dull – so here's to the rollercoaster ride we call love!

Conclusion

Even though love comes with intense emotions, it should not be solely defined by these feelings. Love is a choice that requires individuals to act with purpose, honesty, and bravery. Recognising love as a conscious decision empowers us to thoughtfully shape our relationships, instilling resilience and fostering growth. Choosing love is an ongoing commitment that, when embraced, builds deep connections and enriches the human experience. The true essence of love lies in this choice, revealing its intricate and multifaceted beauty. Love is more than just a feeling; it is the deliberate decision to commit to another person, to show kindness and understanding, and to create a relationship based on respect and mutual fulfilment.

As we conclude this exploration of love, let us remember that love is not just a feeling but a conscious decision and a way of living. By embracing the complexities of love and dedicating ourselves to nurturing and maintaining our relationships with care, communication, and empathy, we can develop profound connections that bring happiness, fulfilment, and meaning to our lives. Love is indeed more than a feeling; it is a transformative force that has the power to shape our world and create endless opportunities for growth and happiness.

CHAPTER NINE

You Can Be Married But Still Single

Life has taught me that, in the intricate dance of love and marriage, it is possible to find oneself in the paradoxical situation of being married but feeling completely isolated. This experience, often characterised by emotional detachment and a sense of solitude in a relationship, can be a bewildering and distressing phenomenon for many couples.

Marriage is traditionally seen as a partnership where two individuals come together to share their lives, dreams, and goals. It typically involves emotional closeness, mutual support, and a deep commitment to each other. However, beneath this seemingly ideal structure lies a complex reality that can lead to emotional detachment, loneliness, and paradoxically, a feeling of being "single" while legally bound to another. This lesson explores the phenomenon where individuals, despite being married, experience emotional isolation, and identifies the underlying factors contributing to this disconnection.

To begin, it is important to define the concept of emotional intimacy, often considered essential for successful marriages. Emotional intimacy involves a profound connection where partners share their innermost thoughts, feelings, and vulnerabilities. This bond is nurtured through effective communication, empathy, and a willingness to support one another. However, many marriages fall short of this ideal. Partners may grow apart due to various factors such as life stressors, differing priorities, and unresolved conflicts, resulting in a marriage lacking genuine emotional connection. Consequently, an individual may find themselves physically present in a marriage yet emotionally distant, resembling a feeling of being single.

A significant factor contributing to this emotional distance is the communication dynamics in a marriage. Open and honest communication is crucial for fostering emotional intimacy; however, many couples struggle with this aspect. Over time, meaningful conversations may be replaced by superficial exchanges, leading to a breakdown in mutual understanding. Partners may excel at managing their daily responsibilities together, such as raising children, handling finances, and fulfilling social obligations, but they often neglect to have meaningful conversations about their emotional needs and personal growth. This lack of depth in communication can lead to individuals feeling unheard and unappreciated, resulting in a sense of loneliness even within the context of a marriage.

Furthermore, societal expectations and traditional gender roles can worsen this issue. In many cultures, people get into marriage with preconceived ideas about their roles in the relationship. Conventional gender roles often come with specific expectations for men and women, which can hinder individuality and restrict emotional expression. For example, a husband might feel compelled to embody a stoic, provider role, discouraging him from expressing his emotions or vulnerabilities. Similarly, a wife might feel obligated to prioritise the family's needs over her own, leading to feelings of resentment and isolation. As these expectations dictate behaviour, partners may find themselves conforming to their roles rather than authentically engaging with each other, perpetuating emotional distance.

In addition to societal expectations, life transitions can place significant strain on marriages. Major life events, such as the birth of a child, career changes, or health crises, can alter the dynamics of a relationship, leaving little room for emotional connection. As partners navigate these transitions, they may unintentionally overlook each other's emotional needs. The demands of daily life can become overwhelming, and the focus on external responsibilities can overshadow the essential act of nurturing the marital bond. Consequently, individuals may feel emotionally isolated and trapped in a relationship that feels more like cohabitation than a mutually supportive relationship.

Another crucial point to consider is the influence of technology on modern relationships. While technology can improve communication, it can also contribute to disconnection. In an era dominated by social media and digital communication, couples may find themselves engaging in superficial interactions rather than fostering genuine emotional connections. Online platforms often create a facade of connectivity, leading individuals to prioritise virtual interactions over face-to-face engagement. The pervasive presence of screens can detract from quality time spent with one's spouse, further fostering feelings of solitude in a marriage - individuals may be physically together but emotionally detached.

Moreover, personal factors such as unresolved trauma, mental health challenges, or differing emotional needs can also contribute to a sense of being married yet feeling alone. Individuals may enter marriage carrying emotional baggage or unaddressed psychological issues, which can hinder their ability to be intimate. If these underlying issues go unacknowledged, they can manifest as emotional withdrawal or detachment, turning the marriage into an environment of solitude rather than connection.

Causes of Emotional Isolation in Marriages

Emotional isolation in marriages is a complex issue that can stem from various underlying factors. Understanding these causes is essential for addressing the decline of emotional intimacy and nurturing healthier relationships. One primary cause of emotional isolation is ineffective communication. When couples fail to openly express their feelings, needs, and concerns, misunderstandings and resentment can accumulate over time, creating a barrier that prevents partners from truly understanding each other, ultimately leading to feelings of loneliness even when physically living together.

Another significant factor is the impact of external stressors. Economic challenges, career pressures, and family obligations can strain a marriage, diverting attention and emotional resources away from the partnership. When individuals are overwhelmed by these stresses, they may withdraw inwardly, prioritising self-preservation over relational engagement, which can aggravate feelings of isolation.

Unresolved conflicts can lead to emotional detachment, as couples may avoid difficult conversations to prevent confrontation, resulting in unaddressed grievances and a persistent emotional gap. Personal issues such as mental health struggles or past traumas can hinder emotional availability, leading to an imbalance in emotional engagement and causing a cycle of isolation.

Effects of Emotional Isolation in Marriages

Emotional isolation, where one partner feels disconnected or unsupported in a relationship, can profoundly and detrimentally affect marriages when individuals fail to communicate their feelings. The lack of emotional support and understanding due to emotional isolation can erode the foundation of trust, intimacy, and companionship essential for a healthy marital union.

When partners feel emotionally isolated, effective communication becomes less likely, leading to misunderstandings and a widening emotional gap, resulting in unresolved issues, frustration, and resentment over time. Emotional isolation can adversely affect mental health, leading to feelings of loneliness, anxiety, and depression, creating a negative atmosphere within the marriage and resulting in heightened tensions.

Emotional and physical intimacy is compromised in scenarios of emotional isolation, leading to a decline in sexual intimacy, a lack of fulfilment, and feelings of disillusionment. Addressing emotional isolation through open conversation and vulnerability is essential in restoring connection and nurturing a resilient marital bond, as the erosion of communication, the toll on mental health, and the decline in intimacy underscore the pervasive impact of this issue.

Nurturing Emotional Intimacy in Marriage

Emotional intimacy serves as the bedrock of a healthy and enduring marriage, fostering deep connections between partners and enabling them to share their thoughts, feelings, and vulnerabilities without fear of judgment. Open and honest communication is crucial in nurturing emotional intimacy, as creating a safe space for meaningful conversations enhances understanding and reinforces trust, allowing both partners to feel valued and heard. Mutual support plays a significant role in strengthening emotional bonds, as couples should strive to be each other's advocate, celebrating successes, and providing comfort during challenges.

In relationships, when partners genuinely show care for each other's wellbeing, they create a sense of safety and comfort. Additionally, participating in shared activities can strengthen emotional closeness. Whether it is through hobbies, mutual interests, or daily routines, spending quality time together nurtures connection. These experiences help couples build a shared history, which is crucial for emotional intimacy. It is important to prioritise these moments as they create opportunities for laughter, joy, and deeper understanding.

Lastly, expressing gratitude and appreciation is essential. Regularly acknowledging each other's efforts and contributions strengthens emotional bonds. Simple acts of kindness or compliments can significantly impact how partners perceive each other, enhancing feelings of love and respect. To nurture emotional intimacy in marriage, intentional efforts in communication, support, shared experiences, and appreciation are necessary. By prioritising these aspects, couples can build a strong and satisfying relationship that can withstand challenges. Ultimately, emotional intimacy enriches the marital bond, fostering a deeply connected and resilient relationship.

Overcoming Feelings of Loneliness and Isolation

Addressing feelings of loneliness and isolation in marriage can be a complex task, despite the union's initial promise of companionship and intimacy. To overcome these emotions, couples must engage in open communication, mutual understanding, and intentional efforts to reconnect.

First and foremost, open communication is crucial in dealing with feelings of loneliness within a marriage. Couples should create a safe space where they can express their thoughts and emotions without fear of judgment. By articulating feelings of isolation, couples gain insight into each other's experiences and can work together to bridge emotional gaps. Regular discussions can provide a platform for both partners to share their feelings, ensuring that issues are addressed promptly.

Furthermore, mutual understanding plays a significant role in fostering emotional connection. Each partner brings unique experiences and expectations to the marriage. Recognising and validating each other's feelings is crucial. Partners must actively listen and seek to understand the underlying factors contributing to their feelings of loneliness. This empathy not only enhances emotional intimacy but also strengthens the bond between spouses, reinforcing a sense of partnership.

Finally, couples must engage in deliberate activities that promote connection. Busy schedules and daily responsibilities can create a divide in relationships, so couples need to prioritise quality time together. Shared activities, whether simple moments like cooking a meal or more elaborate outings, can reignite the spark of companionship. By intentionally investing in time spent together, partners can foster a deeper emotional connection and alleviate feelings of isolation.

Overcoming feelings of loneliness and isolation in marriage requires a proactive approach encompassing open communication, mutual understanding, and intentional connection. By prioritising these elements, couples can cultivate a nurturing relationship that not only alleviates loneliness but also enhances the overall quality of their marriage. In doing so, they not only strengthen their bond but also create a supportive environment where both partners can thrive emotionally.

Conclusion

The experience of feeling married yet single is a complex interplay of communication breakdowns, societal expectations, life transitions, technological impacts, and individual psychological factors. The emotional isolation that transcends marital bonds is an often-overlooked reality that should not be dismissed. To foster genuine emotional intimacy, couples must commit to open communication, challenge societal roles, and prioritise nurturing their relationship amidst the numerous challenges of life.

It is crucial to acknowledge and deal with these concerns in order to turn a marriage into a genuine partnership, ensuring that both partners feel acknowledged, appreciated, and bonded. As the world progresses, our perception of marriage must evolve as well, to fulfil the potential of emotional closeness and connection, going beyond the contradiction of being married yet feeling lonely.

CHAPTER TEN

LONELINESS HAS CONSEQUENCES

In today's ever-changing landscape of modern society, characterised by technological progress and the widespread use of social media, the feeling of loneliness has become a prevalent issue affecting many people. While loneliness is not a new phenomenon, its current widespread occurrence raises important questions about its impact on both individual wellbeing and societal dynamics.

Loneliness is a common human experience that can significantly affect our physical and mental health. In this fast-paced and interconnected world we live in, loneliness and social isolation are increasing, with implications for our overall wellbeing. Understanding the effects of loneliness on different aspects of our lives is crucial in addressing this growing societal problem. This includes its impact on physical health and mental wellbeing, as well as exploring ways to combat loneliness in the digital age.

At its core, loneliness is often described as a subjective feeling of disconnection from the social environment. It is important to distinguish between solitude, which can be a choice and a rejuvenating state, and loneliness, which is often involuntary and distressing. People may feel deeply disconnected even in crowded settings, showing that loneliness is not just about the quantity of social interaction but also the quality and depth of those interactions. Life has taught me that this depth, or lack of it, can have far-reaching consequences.

Psychological Effects of Loneliness

The psychological effects of loneliness are extensive and varied. Research has shown that prolonged experiences of loneliness can lead to various mental health issues, such as depression, anxiety, and increased stress levels. Feeling alone, especially during vulnerable moments, can lead to negative self-talk and further isolation. Over time, these mental health challenges can create a cycle where individuals withdraw from social interactions due to loneliness, leading to worsening mental health and increased isolation.

The Impact of Loneliness on Physical Health

Loneliness has significant implications for physical health. Research has established a connection between loneliness and a higher risk of various health conditions, including cardiovascular diseases, cognitive decline, and weakened immune responses. The underlying physiological mechanisms may involve increased cortisol levels and inflammation. Therefore, addressing loneliness is crucial to mitigating a range of health issues and maintaining overall wellbeing. Additionally, loneliness can impact immune function, making individuals more susceptible to infections and illnesses. Therefore, fostering social connections is important for maintaining heart health. So, the next time you feel lonely, consider reaching out to a friend or loved one to improve your health.

Loneliness and Mental Health

Loneliness and mental health arc closely linked. Studies have demonstrated a strong connection between loneliness and depression, with feelings of isolation worsening symptoms of this common mental health condition. Similarly, loneliness can worsen anxiety disorders, emphasising the importance of addressing feelings of isolation to enhance overall mental wellbeing.

Loneliness and its Effects on Wellbeing

Loneliness has enduring effects on our wellbeing, as chronic loneliness has been linked to cognitive decline, underscoring the importance of social connections for maintaining mental sharpness. Among the elderly, loneliness presents additional health risks, but community programmes and social support can make a significant difference in addressing feelings of isolation.

Loneliness in the Digital Age

In today's digital era, loneliness may paradoxically be increasing despite the prevalence of social media and digital interactions. While social media can worsen feelings of isolation, technology also provides solutions to combat loneliness. By using technology to foster meaningful connections and engage in virtual social interactions, you can combat loneliness and build a supportive network even in the digital age.

Societal Effects of Loneliness

Loneliness is not only an individual experience; its societal impacts are equally significant. The rising rates of loneliness, especially among younger generations who are perceived as more "connected" through digital platforms, have raised concerns about the potential erosion of community bonds and social cohesion. The fabric of society is intricately woven from interpersonal relationships, mutual support, and collective identity. Therefore, widespread loneliness can create divisions within communities, leading to increased social fragmentation and a reduced capacity for collective action. Moreover, as individuals feel isolated and disconnected, the likelihood of social unrest and conflict may rise, emphasising the urgent need for societal intervention.

Addressing the Consequences of Loneliness

Dealing with the consequences of loneliness requires a comprehensive approach that encompasses both individual and collective strategies. At an individual level, raising awareness about the experience of loneliness is crucial. Programmes that promote emotional intelligence and social skills can empower individuals to form deeper connections and seek support when needed. Additionally, creating environments that encourage open discussions about mental health can help reduce the stigma associated with feelings of loneliness, enabling individuals to express their emotions without fear of judgment.

Combating Loneliness

The role of relationships in addressing loneliness is crucial, as strong social connections provide emotional support, foster a sense of belonging, and enhance overall wellbeing, serving as a vital antidote to loneliness. Relationships are essential in providing emotional support during difficult times. Friends and family members offer a listening ear and a comforting presence, which can alleviate feelings of isolation. Sharing experiences and vulnerabilities creates a bond that reinforces the sense of community, instilling hope and promoting resilience.

Participating in social activities fosters a sense of belonging and purpose. Engaging in group activities, clubs, or community service connects individuals with like-minded peers, reducing feelings of loneliness and enriching their social network. These interactions also contribute to personal growth and the development of new skills, creating a support system that you can rely on. Additionally, relationships play a critical role in improving psychological health. Studies have demonstrated that individuals with strong social ties are less likely to experience anxiety and depression. The emotional wellbeing derived from companionship contributes to improved self-esteem and a more positive outlook on life. Prolonged loneliness, on the other hand, can lead to negative health outcomes, including cognitive decline and cardiovascular issues.

The profound and varied impact of relationships in addressing loneliness cannot be overstated. Interpersonal connections act as a shield against isolation by providing emotional support, fostering a sense of belonging, and enhancing psychological wellbeing. Individuals must recognise the importance of nurturing these relationships in order to improve their quality of life and alleviate feelings of loneliness. As society continues to develop, prioritising meaningful relationships will remain essential in tackling this widespread challenge.

Community Support and Loneliness Prevention

Proactive initiatives at the community level play a vital role in combating loneliness. Community programmes and social engagement opportunities create spaces for individuals to connect and establish meaningful relationships. Promoting inclusivity and encouraging participation in social activities can bridge the gap created by loneliness, fostering a sense of belonging and interconnectedness. Additionally, leveraging technology to create virtual support networks can provide a safety net for those who may be unable to engage in traditional forms of social interaction due to mobility or health concerns.

Communities act as a united force in the prevention of loneliness. Joining local clubs, volunteering, or attending community events can help us surround ourselves with people who uplift us. It is important to remember that fighting loneliness requires a collective effort, so allowing the community to serve as a superhero squad is crucial.

The consequences of loneliness are far-reaching and diverse, impacting both individual wellbeing and societal health. In this increasingly isolated world, it is imperative to recognise loneliness not only as a personal struggle but as a collective concern that demands attention and action. Through individual awareness, community initiatives, and societal commitment, it is possible to mitigate the pervasive ramifications of loneliness. In this era marked by remarkable technological connectivity, the challenge lies in fostering genuine human connections that go beyond the superficialities of social media and contribute to the formation of a robust, compassionate society – one that acknowledges and addresses the crucial need for belonging and connection.

Recognising the detrimental effects of loneliness and social isolation is the first step towards creating a more connected and supportive community. By prioritising meaningful relationships, fostering social connections, and utilising technology as a tool for positive interaction, we can combat loneliness and improve our overall wellbeing. Together, we can work towards a society where loneliness has fewer consequences, and everyone feels valued, supported, and connected.

CHAPTER ELEVEN

IT PAYS TO HELP OTHERS

In the intricate fabric of human life, helping others emerges as a foundational element connecting compassion, empathy, and selflessness. This concept goes beyond mere ethical or moral duty, to offer individuals significant personal, societal, and psychological advantages. That it pays to help others reflects a complex reality, indicating that the rewards of selflessness go beyond temporary satisfaction, nurturing an environment for personal growth and societal advancement.

First and foremost, the most immediate and concrete benefit of helping others is the strengthening of social ties and community bonds. In our world, which is increasingly marked by isolation due to technology and fast-paced lifestyles, helping others fosters a sense of belonging and unity. When individuals engage in selfless actions - whether through volunteering, small acts of kindness, or larger charitable endeavours - they help build a supportive community framework. This interconnectedness not only encourages cooperation and trust among community members but also fosters an environment where individuals feel safe, seeking assistance in times of need.

Research suggests that helping others can lead to significant psychological benefits for the helper. Engaging in selfless activities has been linked to increased happiness and overall satisfaction in life. When individuals extend a helping hand, their brain releases endorphins, resulting in what is often called the "helper's high." This biochemical response leads to improved mood, reduced stress levels, and an enhanced sense of purpose. Participating in acts of kindness can lead to a more positive self-image and increased self-esteem, as we derive fulfilment from making a difference in others' lives. In this context, the psychological returns of selflessness go beyond emotional gratification; they establish a deep connection between personal wellbeing and acts of generosity.

Another important aspect to consider is the reciprocal nature of selflessness. The idea that "what goes around comes around" embodies a crucial aspect of human interactions. In communities where individuals actively engage in helping one another, a culture of reciprocity emerges. Those who have received kindness may feel obligated to pay it back, creating a virtuous cycle of assistance and mutual support. This interconnected system reinforces the notion that selflessness benefits the giver as much as it does the receiver, leading to a more robust social fabric and promoting an environment where collective wellbeing is prioritised, fostering resilience and adaptability in the face of challenges.

In the realm of professional relationships, the principle of helping others can have significant implications. In workplace settings, instances of peer support and collaborative efforts can lead to improved team dynamics and productivity. Employees who engage in helping behaviours - such as mentoring colleagues, sharing knowledge, or providing emotional support - tend to create a more cohesive work culture. Such environments not only support individual career advancement but also enhance overall organisational performance. Companies that promote a culture of selflessness often experience lower turnover rates and higher levels of employee engagement, illustrating that fostering generosity correlates positively with economic success.

Furthermore, the impact of helping others extends beyond personal and professional spheres into larger societal frameworks. Communities that prioritise and engage in selfless actions often experience lower crime rates and increased civic participation. When individuals prioritise the wellbeing of others, societal challenges such as poverty, mental health issues, and social injustice are met with collective intervention. This societal obligation fosters a culture of empowerment, guiding marginalised individuals towards opportunities. Therefore, assisting others is a fundamental component of societal advancement and unity.

Understanding Altruism

Altruism is the superhero of human actions. It involves doing things out of the goodness of our heart without expecting anything in return. It is like being a real-life unicorn, spreading positivity wherever we go. Helping people should be a priority, not limited to family and friends. It could be a senior citizen in the parking lot or a single mother on the street. There are numerous ways to help in our communities. Our actions speak louder than our words. Instead of judging others, extend a helping hand. A small gesture can make a significant impact on someone's life.

Conclusion

The idea that it pays to help other people resonates deeply across various aspects of life. The benefits reflect a comprehensive interplay between individual fulfilment and societal progress. As we invest time and energy into helping others, we enrich not only our own lives but also contribute to fostering resilient communities characterised by empathy and unity. Therefore, recognising the importance of helping others becomes crucial, as it paves the way for a brighter, more compassionate future. Embracing the philosophy of altruism not only transforms lives in immediate contexts but also resonates through generations, shaping a world that values kindness and interconnectedness. Thus, indeed, it pays - both literally and metaphorically – to help other people.

The act of helping others not only makes a difference in their lives but also enriches our own lives. Whether it is through a small gesture of kindness or a larger philanthropic endeavour, the rewards of helping other people are undeniable. By nurturing a spirit of generosity and empathy, we not only contribute positively to the world around us but also experience personal growth and fulfilment. Let us continue to embrace the power of helping others, knowing that in doing so, we create a ripple effect of goodness that can truly make the world a better place for all.

CHAPTER TWELVE

It's Good to be Nice to People

Life has taught me that being kind to others is advantageous in today's interconnected and competitive world. Prioritising kindness and respect in human interactions brings benefits to both individuals and society. This lesson explores the numerous advantages of niceness from social, psychological, and economic perspectives, advocating for the widespread adoption of kindness as a fundamental principle in our daily lives.

Niceness promotes social cohesion, fostering a heightened sense of belonging and security in communities. Positive social interactions build trust, which is essential for the development of strong relationships. In the workplace, a culture of kindness and respect among colleagues leads to improved morale and collaboration, reducing hostility and competition. Companies characterised by supportive relationships among employees tend to see increased productivity, lower turnover rates, and enhanced employee satisfaction.

Engaging in acts of kindness has been shown to boost mental health and wellbeing, leading to an elevation in mood and countering feelings of loneliness and depression. Acts of kindness can create a ripple effect, spreading positive behaviour throughout a community. Kindness in the workplace has economic implications, as a positive work environment characterised by kindness can lead to higher profitability and a more robust organisational reputation. Employees who feel valued and respected are more likely to put forth discretionary effort, contributing to the organisation's success.

Moreover, within the business domain, customer service experiences significant improvement when employees adopt a friendly attitude.

Companies that prioritise kindness in their interactions with customers often observe an increase in customer loyalty and satisfaction. Happy customers are more likely to return and recommend the business to others, contributing to its long-term success. Therefore, it can be argued that investing in kindness can lead to substantial economic returns, affirming that kindness brings tangible benefits that go beyond personal interactions.

Establishing a Culture of Kindness

Despite the clear advantages of being nice to others, it is important to acknowledge that societal norms do not always highlight the importance of kindness. In a competitive and individualistic environment, there may be a reluctance to prioritise being nice to others. However, it is crucial to challenge this tendency and actively promote a culture of kindness in our daily interactions. This can start with simple actions such as practising active listening, showing empathy, and acknowledging the inherent value of everyone.

Furthermore, larger institutions such as schools and workplaces should introduce initiatives that promote and recognise kindness. Educational programmes can incorporate social-emotional learning to develop skills like empathy and cooperation among students. Companies can implement policies that reward collaborative behaviours and discourage divisiveness. When kindness becomes ingrained in the system, its benefits are amplified, reaching every level of society.

That it pays to be nice to people encapsulates profound truths about human experience and societal functioning. The benefits of kindness go beyond mere politeness; they encompass social unity, mental wellbeing, and economic prosperity. By actively nurturing a culture of kindness, individuals and organisations can create environments where relationships thrive, mental health improves, and prosperity flourishes. As we navigate the complexities of the modern world, it is our responsibility to recognise that kindness is not just a moral choice but a strategic necessity that enriches our lives and the lives of others. Therefore, let us promote kindness as a fundamental pillar of our social interactions, for indeed, being nice to people pays off - both in tangible and intangible ways.

The Power of Kindness

In a world where you can be anything, be kind. It may sound like a cliché, but there is more truth to it than you might realise. Kindness is not just a concept; it is a powerful force that can shape our interactions, relationships, and even our wellbeing. Let us explore why being nice to people is not just a good idea but a game-changer.

The Importance of Kindness

Kindness is not a passing trend; it is a necessity. In a fast-paced and often disconnected world, small acts of kindness can create ripples of positivity. From brightening someone's day to fostering empathy and compassion, kindness acts like a glue that holds society together. Being nice to people, especially as we progress in life, will help us achieve our goals more easily and quickly. No one knows what life has in store for them. Being kind and supportive to others will go a long way in transforming our lives. One day, we will need kindness from other people, and we will always receive what we have given. This is one of the important life lessons to adopt early in life.

Historical Perspectives on Kindness

Kindness has been esteemed throughout history, appearing in various philosophies, religions, and cultures. From Confucius to the Dalai Lama, the message is clear: kindness is a universal language that surpasses time and boundaries. It is a timeless virtue that speaks volumes about our humanity.

Benefits of Being Nice in Personal Relationships

1. **Enhanced Emotional Wellbeing**

Kindness not only makes others feel good but also has positive effects on our mental wellbeing. Being compassionate and caring can uplift our spirits, reduce stress, and foster a more optimistic perspective on life. It is like a cycle of happiness – what you give, you receive.

2. Strengthening Trust and Connection

Trust is the cornerstone of relationships, and kindness plays a crucial role in building it. By showing kindness and empathy, we create a nurturing environment for trust to develop. Whether it is with friends, family, or partners, kindness lays the foundation for deeper and more meaningful bonds.

Impact of Kindness in the Workplace

Kindness at work is not just a feel-good notion; it has the potential to revolutionise team dynamics and leadership effectiveness. Let us uncover how a touch of kindness can transform our workplace into a hub of productivity.

1. Improved Team Dynamics and Collaboration

Kindness acts as the bond that binds teams together in a world where collaboration is key. By promoting a culture of kindness and mutual respect, we can enhance collaboration, communication, and overall team morale. It is like creating a work family that harmonises well.

2. Enhanced Leadership Effectiveness

Kindness is the new power play in leadership, replacing the tough boss stereotype. Leading with empathy, understanding, and kindness can inspire our team, earn their trust, and drive better results. It is not about being a pushover; it is about leading with heart and humanity.

The Science Behind Acts of Kindness

Kindness is not just a warm and fuzzy feeling; it is supported by scientific evidence. From activating brain regions associated with pleasure to enhancing overall wellbeing, research has shown a lot of benefits of kindness. Acts of kindness light up the brain, triggering the release of feel-good hormones like oxytocin and dopamine, promoting happiness, reducing stress, and even lowering blood pressure. It is like a natural mood booster with a comforting touch. Research has demonstrated that kindness offers a host of health benefits, from improving cardiovascular health to boosting immune function. Studies have also linked acts of kindness to increased longevity, reduced pain, and even enhanced self-esteem.

Building a Culture of Kindness in Society

Creating a culture of kindness in society makes everything a little brighter. Whether through small acts of goodwill or larger community initiatives, spreading kindness can set off a ripple effect that transforms how we engage with one another. Promoting kindness through community initiatives is like giving the soul a warm hug. Whether it is organising food drives, volunteering at shelters, or simply checking in on neighbours, these efforts demonstrate that kindness has no limits. By collaborating, we can create a better and more compassionate world for everyone.

The Role of Education in Fostering Kindness

Education plays a crucial role in nurturing kindness, not only within classrooms but also in the school of life. Teaching empathy, compassion, and the importance of kindness from an early age lays the groundwork for a society that values these qualities. When kindness is integrated into education, we raise a generation that understands the impact of benevolence.

Tips for Incorporating Kindness into Daily Life

Incorporating kindness into our daily lives does not have to be complex. It is like a boomerang that comes back to us. Whether through small gestures or grand acts, every sprinkle of kindness has the power to brighten someone else's day. In a world full of chaos, being kind is like a breath of fresh air. Smiling at strangers, holding the door open, or asking someone about their day - these small acts of kindness can create a ripple effect of positivity that uplifts others and us.

Benefits of Random Acts of Kindness

Random acts of kindness are like little surprises for the soul. From boosting our mood to strengthening social connections, the benefits of spreading kindness are endless. So go ahead, buy that coffee for the person behind you in line or leave an encouraging note for a colleague - you never know how much of a difference it can make.

Overcoming Challenges in Practising Kindness

While spreading kindness is noble, it is not always smooth sailing. Dealing with rejection or unappreciation can sometimes dampen our spirit, but remember, kindness is a gift given freely, regardless of how it is received. Setting boundaries and practising self-care is crucial to ensure that our kindness comes from a place of authenticity, not obligation.

Dealing with Rejection or Unappreciation

Not everyone will respond to our kindness as we hope, and that is fine. Remember that our intentions were pure, and how others receive our kindness is beyond our control. Keep spreading positivity, and the right hearts will appreciate your efforts.

Self-care and Boundaries in Kindness Practices

Kindness should never come at the expense of our wellbeing. Setting boundaries and taking care of ourselves ensures that our acts of kindness come from a place of abundance, not depletion. Remember, you cannot pour from an empty cup, so make sure to fill yours first.

Conclusion

In a world where you can be anything, be kind - because it pays off in ways you might not expect. The simple act of being nice not only brightens someone else's day but also brings a sense of fulfilment and purpose to our lives. So go ahead and show kindness and watch as the world becomes a better and brighter place for everyone. As we navigate the complexities of life, let us remember the transformative power of kindness. By embracing empathy, compassion, and goodwill towards others, we not only create a more positive environment for those around us but also cultivate a sense of fulfilment and joy within ourselves. Let us continue to spread kindness, knowing that by being nice to people, we contribute to a brighter and more harmonious world for all.

CHAPTER THIRTEEN

WE CANNOT SOLVE EVERYONE'S PROBLEMS

In today's world, people often face overwhelming expectations and demands from those around them, whether in personal, professional, or societal contexts. Wanting to ease others' burdens is admirable, but it is important to recognise that it is impossible to solve everyone's problems. This lesson explores the psychological, social, and practical implications of acknowledging our limitations in problem-solving.

In our interconnected society, the pressures of modern life often lead us to take on the role of problem-solvers. While the desire to help others is natural and praiseworthy, life has taught me that it is crucial to understand that believing we can or should solve everyone's problems can have negative emotional and psychological consequences. It is essential to acknowledge that humans are inherently empathetic and feel compelled to respond to others' suffering. While this drives us to offer support and solutions, it also creates the unrealistic expectation that we can fix every problem that arises in the lives of those around us.

We must come to terms with a profound truth - we cannot solve everyone's problems. This understanding requires empathy and humility and emphasises recognising our limitations, setting boundaries, and practising self-care.

The Psychological Dimension

At the core of avoiding the urge to solve everyone's problems is a fundamental psychological truth about human capacity and emotional wellbeing. Everyone has a limited reserve of emotional and cognitive resources and attempting to address the problems of others can lead to emotional burnout, particularly in caregiving professions. This compulsion can also stem from deeper psychological patterns, such as co-dependency, where one's self-worth is tied to another's ability to cope. Prioritising being the problem-solver for others can hinder growth and independence, leading to the necessity of setting boundaries.

The Social Dimension

On a broader societal level, the insistence on solving everyone's problems can create a culture of dependency rather than empowerment. Communities thrive when individuals are encouraged to develop self-efficacy and resilience, and excessive intervention can diminish people's abilities to tackle their challenges. In addition, the desire to solve problems for others may originate from good intentions but can lead to imposing personal values or solutions. This can cause tension and resentment, as those receiving assistance may feel patronised or misunderstood.

Effectively addressing problems in a social context always requires a deep understanding of the perspectives and needs of those involved. Listening is essential; it enables us to express our problems rather than having them defined by an outsider's assumptions. Engaging in open communication and supporting someone's journey towards self-discovery can be much more beneficial than offering potentially flawed solutions.

The Practical Aspect

In practical terms, the inability to solve every person's problem often comes down to constraints of time, capacity, and expertise. Each problem is unique and often demands specialised knowledge, skills, or experiences that not everyone possesses. The idea that we can take on the role of a universal problem-solver disregards the complex realities of individual situations. For example, consider the numerous challenges that professionals in fields like counselling, healthcare, or social work face. While these individuals are trained to help others, they must understand that their role is not to resolve every issue presented to them. Instead, they should strive to provide those seeking help with the tools and frameworks necessary to navigate their challenges. This approach respects the autonomy of the individual facing the problem and nurtures a more sustainable and empowering dynamic.

Adding to this complexity is the concept of the "helper's high," where individuals find fulfilment in helping others. While philanthropy is commendable, we must balance our desire to help with an awareness of our needs and limitations. This balance promotes compassionate engagement rather than an overwhelming burden, allowing us to be present for others while practising self-care.

The Weight of Unsolvable Problems

Each person journeys through life, encountering obstacles as unique as the fingerprints on their fingertips. These obstacles and problems are complex and intertwined with personal histories, emotions, and perspectives. And in the intricate tapestry of life, some knots remain untied, some threads remain unwound.

As much as we wish to be the guiding light in someone else's darkness, to be the balm that soothes their wounds, there are limits to our influence and boundaries to our reach. We are, after all, mere mortals navigating the turbulent waters of existence, grappling with our complexities and uncertainties. Acknowledging our limitations is not a sign of weakness but a testament to our humanity. It is an act of humility that humbles us in the face of life's vastness and unpredictability. In this humility and acceptance, we find the freedom to offer compassion without shouldering the burden of solving every problem that comes our way.

There is a quiet strength in knowing when to listen, when to offer a hand, and when to provide a shoulder to lean on. It is in these moments of presence and understanding that true connection flourishes, transcending the need for solutions and delving deep into the realm of shared experiences. So let us embrace the wisdom that comes with accepting the inherent limitations of our ability to solve everyone's problems. Let us be gentle with ourselves and others, recognising that the beauty of existence lies not in fixing every broken piece but in holding space for the fragile, imperfect, and beautiful tapestry of life to unfold.

In recognising our shared vulnerabilities, we may find comfort in knowing that we are not alone in facing unsolvable problems. Together, we navigate the complexities of existence, finding solace in the truth that sometimes, just being present is sufficient.

The Burden of Trying to Fix Everything

Do you often feel the need to solve everyone's problems? Are you constantly taking on others' burdens, attempting to fix everything for them? It is important to understand that you cannot solve all their problems. Assuming the responsibility of solving everyone's problems places a tremendous amount of pressure on us, like carrying the weight of the world on our shoulders. This can lead to stress, anxiety, and burnout, causing us to neglect our own needs and wellbeing.

Setting Boundaries and Self-Care

Learning to say no is a crucial lesson. We are not obligated to solve everyone's problems. Establishing boundaries is vital for our mental and emotional wellbeing. Prioritising our own needs and responsibilities is essential. Recognising personal limitations is the first and most crucial insight. Everyone's capacity to absorb the emotional weight of others' problems is limited. Engaging deeply with the issues of others has a cumulative effect, which can overwhelm and drain even the most resilient individuals. Psychological literature often emphasises "emotional labour," the process of managing feelings and expressions to meet the emotional needs of a role. This concept vividly illustrates how engaging in the emotional struggles of others can impact our wellbeing.

Attempting to solve everyone's problems can lead to "compassion fatigue," particularly common among caregivers and helping professionals. Continuous exposure to the suffering of others can lead to feelings of hopelessness, reduced empathy, and even symptoms of depression. It highlights the truth that we cannot help others effectively if we are emotionally drained. Prioritising our mental health and emotional stability becomes crucial, not only for ourselves but also for the quality of the help we can provide for others.

Setting boundaries is also crucial in understanding the limits of our ability to help others. Boundaries define the line between one person's difficulties and another's, distinguishing between support and entanglement. In personal relationships, the failure to set and maintain boundaries can lead to co-dependency, where one party becomes overly reliant on the other for emotional support, ultimately leading to resentment and the erosion of both parties' individual identities. In professional contexts, continuous attempts to solve every team's challenge can lead to burnout and reduced productivity. Leaders must learn the art of delegation, providing opportunities for team members to address their issues independently, and fostering growth and ownership.

It is important to note that not all problems need solutions. Sometimes, people simply need the space to express their feelings and thoughts without expecting a resolution. Active listening, for example, can often be more beneficial than trying to fix an issue. Psychotherapist, Carl Rogers, proposed that the therapeutic alliance is based on empathetic understanding rather than problem-solving. The concept applies widely: being there for someone, acknowledging their experiences, and enabling them to handle their challenges can often be a more impactful form of help than imposing solutions.

Additionally, it is essential to acknowledge the inherent value of personal agency. Allowing others to address and work through their problems fosters resilience and self-efficacy. It empowers them to develop their coping mechanisms, problem-solving skills, and ultimately, their capacity for growth. If your role consistently revolves around solving problems, it inadvertently prevents others from exercising their agency in dealing with challenges, hindering their emotional and personal development.

Finally, it is crucial to address the societal pressures that promote self-sacrifice and martyrdom as virtues. Cultural stories often romanticise the idea of the 'selfless hero' – the person who consistently prioritises the needs of others over their own. However, the consequence of such narratives is a distortion of priorities, often causing individuals to neglect their wellbeing for the sake of others. A healthier approach emphasises the importance of self-care, positioning it not as a selfish pursuit but as a fundamental aspect of being effective in supporting others. Acts of self-care – whether through physical activity, pursuing hobbies, seeking therapy, or simply allowing yourself downtime - are crucial for maintaining the stamina necessary for genuinely supportive interactions.

In Setting Boundaries:

1. **Communicate assertively:** Communicate your limits and boundaries to others.
2. **Learn to decline:** It is acceptable to refuse requests that are beyond your capacity.
3. **Prioritise self-care:** Give importance to self-care and ensure your own needs are fulfilled.

Identifying Signs of Boundary Violations

When our boundaries are consistently violated, it can lead to feelings of resentment, burnout, and strained relationships. Learning to assert our limits is crucial for maintaining healthy dynamics.

Self-Care and Making Our Needs a Priority

Contrary to common belief, taking care of ourselves is not selfish – it is strategic. By recharging our energy, we are better equipped to provide genuine and sustainable support to others. Whether it is scheduling a "me time," practising mindfulness, or establishing clear communication channels, prioritising self-care is an ongoing practice that requires conscious effort.

Empowering Others to Solve Their Problems

By constantly attempting to solve everyone's problems, we may inadvertently disempower them. It is important to allow others to take charge of their issues and find their solutions. Offering support and guidance is one thing, but taking over and solving everything for them is not sustainable in the long run.

At times, a situation may be beyond our expertise. Recognise when it is time to refer someone to professional help. It shows care and responsibility in ensuring they receive the support they need. There are various resources available for additional support, from therapy to support groups. Encourage others to seek help when needed and provide them with information on where to find resources that suit their needs.

Empower others by fostering independence and resilience. Encourage them to solve their problems and offer guidance and support along the way. Building resilience helps them navigate challenges effectively. Support others in their journey towards personal growth and self-efficacy. Acknowledge their strengths and capabilities and encourage them to realise their potential. Empowering others leads to long-lasting positive outcomes.

Steps to Empower Others:

1. **Listen actively:** Demonstrate that you are supportive and ready to help but let them take the lead.
2. **Encourage problem-solving:** Pose open-ended questions to help them consider potential solutions.
3. **Provide guidance:** Offer resources or suggestions but leave the decision-making to them.

Support and Enabling: The Distinction

Providing valuable support in someone's life involves offering a listening ear, a shoulder to lean on, and guidance while empowering them to find their solutions. On the other hand, enabling often involves unintentionally perpetuating unhealthy patterns by intervening to shield others from facing consequences or taking responsibility, potentially hindering their growth and fostering dependence. It is essential to recognise that even superheroes need to take a break. By establishing boundaries, prioritising self-care, and grasping the nuances of support, we can navigate the delicate balance of helping others without losing sight of our wellbeing.

Focusing on What We Can Influence

It is crucial to acknowledge that not everything is within our control. Some situations will be beyond our capacity to resolve. Accepting this reality is liberating and allows us to concentrate on what we can change or influence.

Questions to Reflect On:

1. What aspects are within my control?
2. Am I taking on responsibilities that are not mine?
3. How can I prioritise my wellbeing?

Remember, the journey of balancing support for others and self-care is ongoing. It is important to prioritise our wellbeing while being there for others. By maintaining healthy boundaries, we can continue to support others effectively while taking care of ourselves. That is what life has taught me.

Conclusion

Recognising that we cannot solve everyone's problems is not just an acknowledgement of personal limitations; it is a fundamental aspect of fostering autonomy, resilience, and healthy relationships, both personally and socially. Embracing this perspective allows us to cultivate a more balanced approach to problem-solving that prioritises empowerment over dependency, understanding over assumptions, and empathy over intervention.

Instead of trying to solve every distressing situation, it is more productive to offer guidance and encouragement, supporting others to navigate their challenges. This approach ensures the wellbeing of those we care for and promotes our mental wellness, enriching our lives through the meaningful connections we foster along the way. In a world full of complexities, understanding this principle is essential for nurturing healthy and fulfilling relationships.

While the instinct to help others solve their problems is human, it is critical to recognise the limitations of such an endeavour. We must learn to navigate the delicate balance between offering help and respecting boundaries for our own mental and emotional health.

Not all problems can or should be addressed by an external source; many require personal engagement from the individuals involved. Promoting resilience, recognising our limits, setting boundaries, and embracing self-care are essential for personal wellbeing and the ability to support others effectively. Ultimately, understanding that we cannot solve everyone's problems is not a statement of defeat but an affirmation of the complexities of human relationships and the value of nurturing both ourselves and others within those dynamics.

CHAPTER FOURTEEN

WE CANNOT PLEASE EVERYONE

In the intricate web of human relationships, the pursuit of universal approval often emerges as a fundamental aspiration for many individuals. However, as we navigate the multifaceted realms of personal and social interactions, it becomes increasingly evident that the notion of pleasing everyone is not only a difficult task but also an inherently unattainable one. Life has taught me that we cannot please everyone regardless of how hard we try, and this epitomises the challenges of individuality, diversity, and the pressures of societal norms.

This lesson delves into the complexities of this concept, examining the consequences of seeking universal approval, the importance of self-identity, and the significance of embracing a more nuanced understanding of acceptance and rejection.

At the core of the idea that pleasing everyone is impossible is the inherent diversity of human perspectives. Each person is influenced by a multitude of factors such as personal experiences, cultural backgrounds, socio-economic status, and psychological tendencies. This diversity leads to a wide range of opinions, beliefs, and preferences. As a result, an action or decision that one person finds favourable may be viewed as unfavourable or objectionable by another. For example, in a professional environment, a manager may introduce a new policy aimed at improving productivity. While some employees may welcome the change, others may see it as disruptive or counterproductive. These examples demonstrate the limitations of pursuing a universally acceptable approach - what benefits one group may alienate another at the same time.

Furthermore, striving for universal approval can result in a dilution of individual authenticity. When individuals prioritise external validation over their intrinsic values and beliefs, they risk compromising their unique identities. This is particularly evident today, where social media platforms amplify the voices of many, creating an environment filled with scrutiny and judgment. The constant pursuit of likes, shares, and positive comments can foster a culture of conformity, where the fear of negative feedback hampers authentic self-expression. This is especially noticeable among public figures and influencers, who often feel pressured to tailor their content to match their audience's preferences, sacrificing their narratives in the process. These dynamics highlight the irony that in trying to please everyone, we may ultimately lose our true essence.

The implications of this quest for approval extend beyond individuals and permeate the collective consciousness of society. A culture fixated on collective validation can create environments that discourage dissent and alternative viewpoints. The fear of repercussions for expressing differing opinions often leads to echo chambers, where individuals only engage with ideas that echo their own. This phenomenon stifles creativity and innovation, as the potential for constructive discourse diminishes in an environment characterised by groupthink. A prominent example is observed in the political sphere, where partisanship often hinders productive dialogue.

Rather than collaboratively seeking solutions that may involve compromise, individuals tend to align themselves with party ideologies, forgoing the opportunity for a more nuanced understanding of complex issues. Thus, the pursuit of pleasing everyone can inadvertently contribute to societal polarisation and stagnation. However, it is important to acknowledge that recognising the impossibility of pleasing everyone does not mean rejecting the need for empathy and understanding. On the contrary, this realisation can foster a greater appreciation for the diversity of thought and experience that enrich our interactions. Embracing the idea that differing opinions are an integral part of humanity enables us to take a more gracious approach to disagreement and dissent. It promotes resilience in the face of criticism and the ability to discern constructive feedback from mere negativity. Moreover, by understanding that one cannot fulfil every desire, we can redirect our focus towards building genuine relationships based on mutual respect and shared values, rather than a superficial need for approval.

In various aspects of life, from leadership to personal relationships, the courage to stand by our beliefs while acknowledging the potential for disagreement is crucial. In many cases, leaders must prioritise the common good, even if it does not please everyone in their community. The ability to communicate these decisions honestly and considerately builds trust and respect, even in disagreement. In personal relationships, developing a sense of self-worth, independent of others' opinions, fosters genuine connections and a deeper understanding of each other's complexities.

That we cannot please everyone reminds us of the complexities of human relationships and the diversity of human experiences. Seeking universal approval is not only unrealistic but can also dilute individual authenticity and encourage conformity that stifles creativity and discussion. Embracing the idea that disagreement is inevitable allows us to build a stronger sense of self while fostering meaningful relationships based on respect and understanding. Ultimately, authenticity is not achieved by seeking universal approval but by staying true to ourselves amidst diverse opinions and perspectives. By appreciating individuality, we create a more inclusive and enriched societal landscape.

The Paradox of Trying to Please Everyone

In a world where everyone has different preferences and opinions, trying to please everyone is an impossible task. Understanding that universal approval is unattainable can relieve us from the burden of unrealistic expectations. No matter how hard we try, there will always be someone who disagrees with us or criticizes our choices. Realizing that we cannot control others' perceptions enables us to focus on being authentic. The desire to please others often arises from a deep-seated need for validation and acceptance. Exploring the reasons behind our people-pleasing tendencies can help us break free from this cycle.

The Impact of Seeking Approval from Others

Relying on external validation for our self-worth can have significant effects on our mental and emotional wellbeing. Understanding the effects of seeking approval from others is essential for cultivating a healthy sense of self. Constantly seeking approval from others can undermine our self-esteem and lead to feelings of inadequacy. By placing our self-worth in the hands of others, we relinquish our power to define ourselves.

Giving priority to others' approval over our own needs can lead to neglecting our wellbeing and authenticity. It is important to find a balance between seeking external validation and honouring our values and desires.

Cultivating self-acceptance and authenticity is crucial to break free from the trap of people-pleasing. By embracing who we are and validating ourselves from within, we can live a more fulfilling and genuine life. Developing self-awareness and accepting our strengths and weaknesses are crucial steps towards self-validation. Embracing our authentic selves allows us to let go of the need for constant external approval.

Practising Self-Compassion and Inner Validation

Learning to be kind and compassionate towards ourselves is crucial for nurturing inner validation. By treating ourselves with the same empathy and understanding we offer others, we can cultivate a deep sense of self-worth.

Setting Boundaries and Prioritising Self-Care

Establishing healthy boundaries and prioritising self-care is essential for maintaining our wellbeing and sense of self. By respecting our limits and practising self-care, we can protect ourselves from the pitfalls of people-pleasing. Setting boundaries is a form of self-respect that allows us to protect our time, energy, and emotions.

Setting clear boundaries and effectively communicating them to others is crucial for maintaining healthy relationships. Balancing the needs of others with prioritising our wellbeing involves establishing boundaries, practising self-care, and developing self-awareness. It is important to understand that sacrificing our own needs for external validation can have negative effects on our mental and emotional wellbeing.

Nurturing Mental and Emotional Wellbeing

Taking care of our mental and emotional health should be a top priority to counteract the adverse effects of seeking external validation. Engaging in activities that bring us happiness, relaxation, and a sense of fulfilment can help us reconnect with ourselves and build a strong sense of self-worth.

Navigating Conflict and Handling Criticism

Managing conflicts and handling criticism gracefully is like juggling oranges – it may be messy, but it can be managed. In a world where opinions are freely expressed and differences are inevitable, knowing how to navigate through challenging conversations and feedback is essential for maintaining our sanity and relationships.

When faced with disagreements, remember that effective communication is key. Actively listen, express yourself clearly, and show empathy. Resist the temptation to become aggressive or passive-aggressive. Instead, aim for a balance of assertiveness and understanding. Keep in mind that the goal is not to win the argument but to find a common ground.

Handling Criticisms Constructively

Receiving and processing criticisms constructively is important. While criticism can be hurtful, it does not have to leave a lasting impact. When receiving feedback, take a deep breath and avoid becoming defensive. View criticism as an opportunity for personal growth. Reflect on the feedback, sift through the valid points, and use it as a steppingstone for self-improvement. Embrace criticism as you would a well-meaning but occasionally annoying relative. Gracefully handling criticism and conflicts involves effective communication, active listening, and maintaining a sense of self-worth. By staying true to our values and beliefs while being open to constructive feedback, we can navigate disagreements with integrity and authenticity.

Conclusion

Learning to let go of the need to please everyone is a powerful act of self-love and liberation. By embracing authenticity, setting boundaries, and prioritising self-care, we can cultivate inner peace and self-acceptance. Navigating conflicts and handling criticism with grace and resilience becomes more manageable when we shift our focus from seeking external validation to nurturing internal strength. Remember, it is fine to prioritise our wellbeing and happiness, even if it means not pleasing everyone around us.

CHAPTER FIFTEEN

OUR HEALTH IS OUR MOST VALUABLE ASSET

In today's competitive environment and the relentless pursuit of wealth and recognition, the value of health is often overlooked. Life has taught me that health is not just one aspect of life but the very foundation upon which everything else rests. That our health is our most valuable asset holds great significance as it captures the essence of human existence. Without good health, the ability to fully engage in life diminishes significantly. This lesson explores the multifaceted nature of health, highlighting its importance as a personal asset and a societal necessity, and advocating for a shift in our perception and prioritisation of our health.

It is crucial to start by understanding the definition of health. The World Health Organization defines health as "the complete physical, mental, and social wellbeing, not merely the absence of a disease". This comprehensive definition invites a broader discussion that includes not only physical health but also mental and social aspects. Our health affects our productivity, decision-making, and ability to participate in relationships and community activities. Therefore, health is connected with every aspect of human endeavour, serving as a prerequisite for success and fulfilment in personal and professional spheres.

One of the most convincing arguments for the importance of health as an asset is the economic impact of poor health. Individuals dealing with health issues often face medical expenses, reduced earning potential, and increased absenteeism from work. Numerous studies have shown that poor health is linked to decreased productivity and economic strain, affecting not only individuals but also families and communities. For example, in many countries, chronic diseases like diabetes and heart problems significantly increase healthcare costs and reduce workforce participation. Therefore, neglecting health has detrimental economic consequences, emphasising the need to prioritise wellbeing as a crucial asset.

Furthermore, the psychological aspect of health demonstrates a deep connection between mental wellbeing and overall life satisfaction. In a time where mental health disorders are increasingly common, maintaining psychological wellbeing is crucial. Mental health is a vital part of overall health and directly impacts emotional resilience, social relationships, and the ability to adapt to life's challenges. Those lacking mental wellness may experience impaired judgment, lack of motivation, and reduced quality of life. On the other hand, individuals who invest in their mental health through mindfulness, therapy, and social engagement are better equipped to tackle challenges, benefiting not only themselves but also those around them. The essential role of mental health in achieving a balanced and fulfilling life reinforces the argument that our health must be seen as an invaluable asset.

Additionally, the societal aspect of health further supports this idea. Countries that prioritise the health and wellbeing of their citizens often experience improved economic growth, better educational outcomes, and greater social stability. Investing in public health initiatives such as immunisation programmes, access to mental health resources, and fitness initiatives leads to significant returns, resulting in a more productive workforce and reduced healthcare expenses in the long term. Moreover, societies that create an environment for health awareness and the promotion of preventive measures lead to a reduction in health disparities and an improvement in the overall quality of life for the population. This emphasises the significant impact of individual wellbeing on societal structure and function, characterising health as a collective asset.

Despite the paramount importance of health, many individuals tend to prioritise short-term gains and immediate gratification, often neglecting their wellbeing. In a society driven by instant access to information and rapid responses, the focus on long-term health perspectives is often neglected. The fast-paced lifestyle, which prioritises convenience over nourishment, results in unhealthy habits such as poor diet, lack of exercise, and insufficient sleep. Consequently, chronic health issues are on the rise, leading to a compromised state of societal health in favour of productivity. We must shift our mindset, acknowledging that health should be viewed with a perspective that values its long-term importance rather than just short-lived choices.

That our health is our most valuable asset embodies a profound truth that extends beyond individual experiences and resonates within broader society. Health forms the foundation for personal fulfilment, productivity, and social cohesion. As we navigate the complexities of modern life, it is essential to deeply value health, not just as a series of medical check-ups or diet plans, but as a lasting asset that enriches our lives and empowers us to pursue our aspirations. Therefore, advocating for a holistic approach to health that recognises its multifaceted nature and prioritises wellbeing as a fundamental principle for leading a prosperous and meaningful life is crucial. In doing so, we reclaim the true essence of our most valuable asset: our health.

The Importance of Prioritising Our Health

In a world filled with distractions and obligations, it is easy to overlook our most valuable possession – our health. Prioritising our health goes beyond physical appearance or fitness goals; it involves investing in our long-term wellbeing and quality of life. Prioritising our health is critical as it influences every aspect of our lives. By taking care of our physical and mental wellbeing, we can enhance our quality of life, boost our energy levels, and reduce the risk of developing chronic ailments.

Health as Our Most Precious Asset

Our health is like a VIP ticket to a fulfilling and joyful life. Without it, all the wealth, success, and material possessions lose their significance. Once you recognise the inherent value of your health, you will begin making decisions that respect and preserve it at all costs.

Healthy Habits and Lifestyle Choices

Establishing a strong foundation for good health begins with developing healthy habits and making mindful lifestyle choices. It is not about perfection but progress – small, consistent steps that contribute to significant enhancements in our overall wellbeing. We can initiate healthier lifestyle choices by setting attainable health objectives, integrating regular exercise into our routine, prioritising nutritious food options, staying hydrated, getting sufficient sleep, and effectively managing stress. Minor changes can lead to substantial enhancements in our overall health.

Establishing a Balanced Routine

Balancing work, social life, and personal time may be challenging, but prioritising our health involves finding equilibrium in our daily schedule. Whether it is scheduling regular exercise, preparing nutritious meals in advance, or setting aside time for relaxation, a balanced routine is essential for maintaining our health.

Establishing Achievable Health Objectives

Instead of striving for unattainable standards or quick solutions, set realistic health goals that are consistent with your values and priorities. Whether it is increasing water intake, lowering stress levels, or exercising once a week, setting attainable goals positions us for success and long-term wellness.

Caring for Our Body and Wellbeing

Our body is sacred, and prioritising its care should be a top concern. Nurturing our physical health goes beyond appearance – it is about feeling strong, energised, and resilient in the face of life's challenges.

Recognising the Importance of Regular Exercise

Exercise acts like a wonder drug for our body and mind. From boosting our mood to enhancing our cardiovascular health, regular physical activity is essential when it comes to prioritising our health. Discover activities you enjoy and incorporate them into your routine.

Ensuring Adequate Rest

Sleep is not a luxury, but a necessity for optimal health. Strive for seven to nine hours of quality sleep each night to rejuvenate your body, support brain function, and improve your overall wellbeing. Make good sleep habits a priority to ensure you get the rest you need.

Fostering Mindfulness and Emotional Wellbeing

True health encompasses not only our physical wellbeing but also our mental and emotional state. Fostering mindfulness and emotional wellbeing is crucial for a well-rounded and satisfying life.

Implementing Stress Management Techniques

In a world filled with constant stressors, learning how to manage and reduce stress is a critical skill for maintaining our mental health. Whether it is through meditation, deep breathing exercises, or engaging in enjoyable hobbies, find strategies that help you effectively cope with stress.

Prioritising Self-care Practices

Self-care is not selfish; it is an essential practice for preserving our mental health and emotional wellbeing. Prioritise activities that nourish your spirit, whether it is taking a leisurely nature walk, indulging in a relaxing bath, or simply disconnecting from technology. Remember, you cannot pour from an empty cup, so take care of yourself first.

Preventative Care and Regular Check-ups

Our health is like a garden - it requires regular maintenance to thrive. Investing in preventative care and keeping up with regular check-ups establishes a strong foundation for overall wellbeing. Do not wait for the flowers to wilt before watering them! Preventative care, such as regular check-ups, screenings, and vaccinations, can help identify and prevent potential health issues before they escalate. By being proactive with our healthcare and following our doctor's advice, we can identify any concerns early and take action to address them promptly.

Sustaining Optimal Health

Just like a well-maintained machine, our bodies flourish with good nutrition and regular activity. Develop a well-rounded diet plan that nourishes you from the inside out and find ways to incorporate physical activity into your daily routine. Your body will thank you for being a source of energy and vitality!

Balancing Work and Life for Overall Wellbeing

Life can sometimes feel like a balancing act but finding the right equilibrium between work and personal time is crucial for our overall wellbeing. Implement strategies that help you navigate this delicate balance, and remember, it is fine to say no sometimes. Our mental health deserves top-notch treatment too! Balancing work and personal life is essential for our mental health and overall wellbeing. Setting boundaries, prioritising self-care, delegating tasks, and practising stress management techniques can help us achieve a healthier balance and reduce burnout. Remember that taking care of ourselves is just as important as our work responsibilities.

Health Risks and Prevention Methods

Understanding potential health risks and prevention methods is crucial for taking control of your wellbeing. Embrace healthy ageing practices to support your long-term health and remember that age is just a number – it is how you feel inside that truly counts.

Conclusion

Always remember that our health is priceless and requires our full attention and care. By integrating the concepts discussed in this lesson into our everyday lives, we can empower ourselves to live a healthier and more fulfilling life. Prioritise self-care, make well-informed decisions, and seek assistance when necessary to ensure you are taking proactive steps towards maintaining your wellbeing. Our health is truly our most valuable asset - cherish it, nurture it, and let it lead you towards a vibrant and fulfilling future.

CHAPTER SIXTEEN

Work-Life Balance Is Important

Life has taught me that in today's world, achieving a balance between work and personal life is crucial for both individual satisfaction and professional success. This balance involves managing the demands of our job and personal commitments to maintain overall wellbeing. Striking this equilibrium is not only beneficial for personal happiness but also for organisational productivity. This lesson explores the complex nature of work-life balance, its impact on employees and employers, and the methods for creating an environment that supports this balance.

Maintaining work-life balance is like juggling multiple tasks while navigating a challenging path – it is difficult but necessary to prevent exhaustion and maintain overall wellness. This concept revolves around balancing work responsibilities and personal life to avoid burnout and promote wellbeing. The importance of work-life balance is evident in its profound effects on mental and physical health. The boundaries between work and personal life have become increasingly blurred in today's fast-paced and technology-driven world. With remote work and digitalisation becoming more common, we often struggle to disconnect from work even outside official hours. This constant connectivity can lead to heightened stress, burnout, and various health issues, including anxiety and depression. Studies consistently show that employees experiencing high work-related stress are more likely to have reduced performance, lower job satisfaction, and increased intentions to leave their jobs. On the other hand, maintaining a healthy work-life balance is linked to improved mental resilience, better physical health, and greater overall life satisfaction.

From an organisational standpoint, fostering a culture that prioritises work-life balance can yield significant benefits. Companies that value their employees' wellbeing often report increased productivity, higher job satisfaction, and reduced absenteeism. When employees feel that their personal lives are respected as much as their professional contributions, they are more likely to stay loyal to the organisation, leading to lower turnover rates. Moreover, a commitment to work-life balance can enhance an organisation's reputation, making it more appealing to potential talent, especially among younger generations who prioritise holistic wellbeing. In today's competitive job market, organisations that actively promote work-life balance can gain a significant advantage in attracting and retaining skilled workers.

The importance of work-life balance extends beyond the individual and the organisation to society at large. A population that maintains a balanced lifestyle is likely to be more engaged in community activities and civic duties. Individuals who experience less work-related stress can dedicate more time and energy to their families, hobbies, and social interactions, ultimately enriching society. Additionally, promoting work-life balance can contribute to broader issues such as gender equality and diversity in the workplace. By implementing flexible work arrangements, organisations create an environment that accommodates diverse needs, allowing individuals from various backgrounds to succeed professionally without sacrificing personal aspirations.

To achieve work-life balance, various strategies can be implemented at both the individual and organisational levels. We can benefit from setting clear boundaries between work and personal life, which may involve establishing specific work hours and creating a dedicated workspace. Effective time management techniques, such as prioritising tasks and scheduling breaks, can improve efficiency and create time for personal pursuits. Practising mindfulness, such as meditation or exercise, can help reduce stress and enhance overall wellbeing.

In terms of organisation, effective leadership is crucial in setting an example and encouraging a healthy work-life balance. Businesses should support flexible work options, such as telecommuting, condensed workweeks, and the ability to tailor schedules to individual needs. Creating a results-driven work environment that prioritises productivity over the number of hours spent in the office can empower employees to manage their workloads more efficiently. Offering resources such as employee assistance programmes, wellness initiatives, and opportunities for professional development can further assist individuals in achieving life balance.

Achieving a harmonious work-life balance is a vital aspect of contemporary life that deeply impacts both personal and organisational success. As the boundaries between professional and personal lives become increasingly blurred, the importance of attaining a well-rounded equilibrium cannot be overstated. The advantages of work-life balance go beyond the individual, benefiting organisations and society. Through deliberate efforts to establish boundaries, encourage flexibility, and foster a supportive culture, both individuals and organisations can navigate the complexities of the modern workplace while nurturing a fulfilling life outside work. In this pursuit of balance, the potential for improved wellbeing, productivity, and overall life satisfaction is not only achievable but essential for thriving in today's dynamic work landscape.

Impact of Imbalance on Health and Wellbeing

When work dominates our lives, stress and burnout can become unwelcome companions. Feeling overwhelmed and exhausted can lead to a downward spiral in both our work performance and personal happiness. Neglecting our personal lives in favour of work can have consequences that make us feel like we have been hit by a double-decker bus. From an increased risk of heart disease to mental health challenges like anxiety and depression, the toll on our health can be significant.

Strategies for Achieving Work-Life Balance

Mastering time management is like having a magic wand that allows us to create more hours in the day. By prioritising tasks, setting achievable goals, and minimising distractions, we can make the most of our time at work and home. Establishing boundaries is crucial to prevent work from intruding on our personal lives. By setting clear priorities and learning to say no, when necessary, we can protect our time and focus on what truly matters.

Benefits of Prioritising Work-Life Balance

Achieving work-life balance is like hitting the bullseye in a game of darts – it leads to enhanced productivity and job satisfaction. By taking care of ourselves and finding harmony between work and personal life, we can perform better on the job and feel more fulfilled in our careers. Prioritising work-life balance can boost our relationships and overall wellbeing. By nurturing personal connections, making time for self-care, and finding joy outside work, we can lead a more fulfilling and balanced life.

Overcoming Challenges to Work-Life Balance

Finding balance can be challenging when the workplace culture encourages overwork. It is like trying to juggle while someone keeps handing you more balls. Sometimes the biggest obstacle to work-life balance is staring back at us in the mirror. Take a good hard look, maybe even a selfie, and ask yourself, "Am I living my best life?"

Set boundaries like they are hot! Let your coworkers know when you are off the clock. Get a neon sign if you must. Your phone does not need to be glued to your hand like a permanent appendage. Let those work emails marinate until tomorrow. Your mental health will thank you.

Conclusion

In the ongoing struggle between work and personal life, always remember that you are the hero of your own story. Establish clear boundaries, and conquer the world, or at least strive for equilibrium. Prioritising work-life balance is not just a luxury but a necessity for maintaining overall wellbeing and happiness. By acknowledging the significance of setting boundaries, managing time efficiently, and engaging in self-care, we can navigate the complexities of modern life with greater ease and fulfilment.

Adopting a balanced approach to work and personal life not only boosts productivity and job satisfaction but also nurtures stronger relationships, improved health, and a greater sense of contentment. Making work-life balance a priority is a journey worth pursuing for a more sustainable and fulfilling lifestyle.

CHAPTER SEVENTEEN

SETTING BOUNDARIES IS LIBERATING

Setting boundaries has become increasingly important today, where people are constantly connected and have many commitments. Boundaries refer to the limits we set to protect our emotional, mental, and physical wellbeing. They are crucial for creating a framework in which we can thrive, maintain healthy relationships, and cultivate self-respect and autonomy. This lesson explores the various benefits of establishing boundaries, including their positive impacts on personal effectiveness, interpersonal relationships, and overall mental health.

It is important to understand the complex relationship between self-identity and boundaries. In a world that often requires conformity and compliance with external expectations, we may compromise our values and desires. By setting personal boundaries, we can clearly articulate our needs and preferences. This not only strengthens personal identity but also promotes authenticity. For example, an employee who communicates their limits regarding work hours fosters a professional environment where their personal life is respected. This proactive approach leads to a deeper understanding of our capabilities and aspirations, ultimately contributing to personal growth and satisfaction.

Setting boundaries is crucial for improving productivity and efficiency. In both professional and personal spheres, we often face demands that can overwhelm our capacity to function effectively. By establishing clear boundaries related to time management, task delegation, and disengagement from excessive obligations, we can optimise our focus and energy. For instance, a student who sets specific hours for study, free from distractions such as social media and personal interactions, is likely to achieve greater academic success. Boundaries foster a distraction-free environment and encourage us to allocate our resources more judiciously, giving us a sense of control over our pursuits.

Boundaries play a significant role in nurturing healthy relationships. Effective communication of limits can prevent misunderstandings and foster mutual respect among individuals. Whether in friendships, familial ties, or romantic relationships, clearly defined boundaries establish expectations that contribute to harmony and understanding. For example, if a friend repeatedly imposes on our time without regard for our commitments, the lack of boundaries can lead to resentment and conflict. By addressing the situation and expressing the need for personal space and time, we can reinforce the importance of mutual respect, thereby strengthening the relationship.

The emotional and psychological benefits of setting boundaries are also crucial. Individuals who practise boundary-setting are often better at safeguarding their emotional health. Establishing limits serves as a protective mechanism against emotional exhaustion, burnout, and stress. When we allow others to dictate the terms of engagement without asserting our needs, we may find ourselves trapped in a cycle of negativity and dissatisfaction. For instance, those in caregiving roles may experience compassion fatigue if they do not establish clear limits on their availability to others. Conversely, by prioritising their wellbeing and communicating their boundaries, caregivers can sustain their capacity to offer support while maintaining their emotional reserves.

Establishing boundaries is vital for combatting the pervasive influence of social media and societal pressures. In an age where digital connectivity blurs the lines between personal and public life, we can easily succumb to the overwhelming demands of online interactions. By setting specific times for engaging with social media, we can reclaim our attention and strive to live more mindfully.

Establishing boundaries empowers us to actively shape our experiences, leading to a healthier relationship with both technology and societal expectations. It is important to note that setting boundaries is not a win-lose situation; rather, it is a skill that can be honed through consistent practice. Many individuals may struggle initially with setting boundaries, viewing it as a rejection of others or a potential source of conflict. However, it is crucial to understand that healthy boundaries do not only promote individual wellbeing but also foster respect and clarity in relationships.

Effective communication is vital in the process, as we must be able to express our limits assertively and kindly. Ultimately, the ability to set and uphold boundaries can result in enriching personal and interpersonal experiences.

The Importance of Setting Boundaries

The importance of setting boundaries goes beyond personal preference; it is a fundamental aspect of wellbeing and fulfilment in our interconnected world. Boundaries contribute to personal identity, boost productivity, nurture healthy relationships, and safeguard emotional health. As society continues to evolve, navigating the intricacies of human interactions requires a deep understanding of the significance of boundaries. By advocating for the practice of setting boundaries, we can cultivate a life characterised by respect, agency, and authenticity. Indeed, setting boundaries pays off, not only for personal growth but also for enhancing the collective human experience.

Setting boundaries is like displaying a "Do Not Disturb" sign on the window of our lives. It delineates where we end and others begin, helping to maintain a sense of self and safeguarding our wellbeing. Boundaries function as invisible fences that demarcate our personal and emotional limits, establishing the rules for how we wish to be treated and what we are willing to accept in our relationships and interactions.

Understanding the Purpose of Boundaries

Boundaries act as a shield, safeguarding our mental and emotional wellbeing. They assist in setting healthy limits, fostering self-respect, and effectively communicating our needs. Setting boundaries is not just about drawing lines in the sand; it is about creating a safe space where we can thrive and grow. By setting boundaries, we reduce stress, anxiety, and overwhelm, gaining a sense of control over our lives, which leads to increased self-esteem and emotional stability. Boundaries are the key to healthy relationships, nurturing respect, trust, and mutual understanding, resulting in more meaningful relationships with others.

Establishing Healthy Boundaries

Setting boundaries is a skill that can be acquired and practised. It is like exercising our assertiveness muscle to create a balanced and fulfilling life. Start by tuning into your own needs and emotions, reflecting on what makes you comfortable or uncomfortable in different situations, and using this self-awareness to define your boundaries. Be specific about your boundaries and communicate them openly. Stand firm in upholding your limits, even if it means saying no or establishing consequences for crossing them.

Overcoming Challenges in Setting Boundaries

Despite the benefits, setting boundaries can feel daunting. However, with a dose of courage and self-compassion, we can navigate the challenges of boundary-setting accurately. It is natural to fear that setting boundaries might lead to conflict or push people away. Remember that healthy boundaries can strengthen relationships by fostering honesty and respect. Guilt may arise when prioritising your own needs over others' needs. Remind yourself that it is acceptable to put yourself first and that setting boundaries is an act of self-care, not selfishness.

Communicating Boundaries Effectively

Effectively communicating boundaries is like designating a VIP section for your personal space. To achieve this, use assertive communication to clearly convey your limits and needs. Assertive communication serves as the superhero cape when establishing boundaries, involving direct, honest, and respectful expression of your limits. There is no need for passive-aggressive notes or dramatic exits – simply engage in straightforward conversations like mature individuals. Boundaries operate on a two-way street – you establish them and honour others' boundaries.

Boundaries in Different Areas of Life

Boundaries extend across various aspects of life, serving as the fences that safeguard our emotional wellbeing from becoming chaotic. Whether in personal relationships or professional environments, knowing when to set limits sets the stage for healthy interactions.

1. Boundaries in Personal Relationships

In personal relationships, boundaries function as the secret ingredient for maintaining harmony. They assist in defining our needs, space, and values, conveying the message, "I care about you, but I also require some breathing space." Boundaries are crucial in relationships as they establish acceptable behaviours and help us maintain our sense of self. They provide a framework for healthy communication, respect, and mutual understanding.

2. Boundaries in the Workplace

In the workplace, boundaries act as invisible protective barriers to our sanity and professionalism. They facilitate navigating complex interactions with colleagues and supervisors, ensuring that work remains work and not a continuous drama series. Establishing boundaries in the professional setting is like steering your ship through turbulent waters with grace and authority.

Negotiating boundaries with colleagues and supervisors demands finesse and a touch of diplomacy. Colleagues can sometimes be overly inquisitive, encroaching on personal space and work-related interactions. Managing boundaries with them involves setting clear limits on personal space, time, and work-related engagements. It is like indicating a "Do Not Disturb" sign without explicitly displaying it.

Establishing boundaries with supervisors resembles setting the tone for a professional dance – you lead, but with mutual respect and understanding. Clear communication regarding workload, feedback, and personal time helps maintain a healthy balance between work and wellbeing.

Maintaining and Enforcing Boundaries

Establishing boundaries requires consistent attention, much like tending a garden and occasionally removing weeds. Self-care practices bolster our boundaries while addressing boundary breaches with finesse ensures the integrity of our VIP section. Although setting boundaries may occasionally lead to conflicts, it is an essential step in nurturing healthy relationships. Learning to communicate assertively and navigate conflicts constructively can ultimately strengthen our connections with others. Self-care serves as the guardian of boundaries. Practices such as mindfulness, carving out a "me time", and knowing when to say no help reinforce our limits, recharge our energy, and fortify our boundaries like a stronghold.

Dealing with Boundary Violations

Boundary violations are inevitable, much like a friend who consistently disregards our personal space. Handling these situations gracefully involves assertively addressing the issue, reaffirming our boundaries, and if necessary, renegotiating the terms. Feeling uncomfortable, resentful, or disrespected in a situation are signs that our boundaries may be disregarded. Trust your instincts and emotions as indicators that your boundaries may not be honoured.

Conclusion

Establishing and upholding boundaries is an effective method for empowering ourselves and fostering healthier relationships. By applying the strategies covered in this lesson, you can develop a more equitable and satisfying life in which your requirements are valued and respected. Keep in mind that it is never too late to start setting boundaries that promote your overall wellbeing and improve your standard of living. Embrace the influence of boundaries and observe how they positively influence all areas of your life.

CHAPTER EIGHTEEN

LIFE IS WORTH LIVING

Life, with its diverse array of experiences, presents us with a complex fabric woven with joy, sorrow, triumph, and despair. This intricate existence prompts deep questions about its essential value. Is life characterised by suffering and struggle, or does it possess a deeper significance that makes it worth living? An examination of the philosophical, psychological, and sociocultural aspects of life shows that, despite its challenges, life inherently has value, inviting us to embark on a journey of discovery, connection, and personal growth and development.

To start, recognising life's intrinsic worth involves exploring the human condition and its varied emotional landscape. Aristotle, a key figure in Western philosophy, suggested that happiness, or wellbeing, is the goal of human existence. He argued that true happiness is attained through the pursuit of virtue and the realisation of our potential, indicating that life is a quest for meaning and fulfilment. Pursuing personal or professional goals gives life purpose. By setting and accomplishing objectives, we experience autonomy and self-actualisation, reinforcing the positive aspects of existence.

Modern psychological theories, such as Viktor Frankl's logotherapy, emphasise the pursuit of meaning as a fundamental aspect of human experience. Frankl, a Holocaust survivor, asserted that even in the most challenging circumstances, life retains its value through individuals' capacity to find purpose. He suggested that suffering when approached with the right mindset, can lead to deeper self-insights and a better understanding of the world.

The resilience displayed by individuals in the face of adversity demonstrates that life, despite its trials, offers opportunities for growth and transformation. This idea aligns with numerous narratives in which individuals use their challenges to gain a deeper understanding of their existence, affirming the philosophical notion that life is indeed worth living.

The interconnected and relational aspects of human life further emphasise its worth. We are inherently social beings, and the relationships we form contribute significantly to our sense of belonging and wellbeing. The connections established with family, friends, and communities create a support system that offers comfort during difficult times and joy during moments of success. The philosopher, Martin Buber, conveyed this relational aspect of existence through his concept of "I-Thou" relationships, which underscores the importance of authentic relationships. By nurturing these relationships, individuals not only find meaning but also contribute to the wellbeing of others, fostering a collective sense of purpose that goes beyond personal struggles.

From a broader perspective, life is filled with cultural, artistic, and intellectual richness that enhances the human experience. The pursuit of knowledge, appreciation of art, and engagement with culture, demonstrate the human capacity for creativity and the desire to leave a lasting impact. Literature, music, visual arts, and scientific discoveries serve as evidence of humanity's quest for understanding, beauty, and expression. These pursuits not only enrich our lives but also elevate society, reinforcing the notion that life presents numerous opportunities for enrichment and engagement. In this context, the question of life's worth is intertwined with the impact we can have on the world around us.

Furthermore, the idea of collective progress and the potential for societal change underscores the value of life. Throughout history, individuals have tirelessly worked towards social justice, equality, and progress, often encountering significant challenges. The struggles and victories of activists, philosophers, and ordinary individuals striving to make a difference illustrate the concept that our lives, when employed for a greater purpose, can create ripple effects that shape and inspire future generations. The recognition of human rights, environmental preservation, and social fairness by various movements indicates the acknowledgement that life serves not only as a platform for personal satisfaction but also to promote the wellbeing of society and safeguard the earth for future generations.

It is important to also consider the presence of existential threats that endanger the future of humanity. The impending difficulties presented by climate change, geopolitical instability in many parts of the world, and technological progress necessitate a unified response rooted in hope and resilience. While these challenges may elicit feelings of hopelessness, they also act as drivers for collective action. The belief in the value of life motivates us to confront these challenges, create innovative solutions, and strive for a more sustainable and fairer world.

The Impact of Perspective on Life's Value

The notion that life is worth living goes beyond philosophical concepts and becomes deeply personal. The experiences, emotions, and contemplations of each person contribute to a diverse fabric of existence that, when acknowledged, unveils the beauty of life in its entirety. Acts of kindness, love, and empathy linger in memory, reinforcing the value of life. When we take the time to ponder our experiences, we often discover moments of gratitude that illuminate the significance of our journeys, even in the face of hardships.

Influence of Perspective on the Value of Life

Perspective acts as a lens through which we perceive the world around us. Altering our perspective can change the way we view the worth of our lives, helping us recognise the beauty in ordinary moments and find happiness in everyday experiences. Perspective plays a vital role in determining the value we attribute to our lives. Our perception of the world around us and the interpretation of our experiences can significantly impact our overall happiness and contentment. Adopting an optimistic outlook can lead to a greater appreciation for life's pleasures and a better ability to navigate through its challenges. A negative perspective can impede our capacity to find meaning and purpose, resulting in a sense of discontent and despondency.

The Concept of the Value of Life

What confers value upon life? Is it the pursuit of happiness, the relationships we build, or the obstacles we overcome? Exploring the complexities of this profound question can lead us to a deeper understanding of our purpose and existence. What brings us joy? Reflecting on our values and interests can unearth the essence of who we are and what truly holds significance for us. Embracing these elements can guide us towards a more meaningful existence.

Finding Purpose and Meaning

Finding purpose and meaning is another crucial element in making life meaningful. In a world brimming with endless opportunities, finding purpose and significance can anchor us during tumult and uncertainty. When we have a clear understanding of what is important to us and why, it provides direction to our lives and a sense of fulfilment.

Reflecting on our values and interests can help us identify what truly matters to us and steer us towards activities and objectives that align with those values. Whether it involves pursuing a vocation that resonates with our passions or engaging in pastimes that bring us happiness, finding purpose gives our lives a sense of meaning beyond the daily routines. Finding purpose in life involves reflecting on our values, passions, and aspirations. By identifying what truly matters to us and aligning our actions with these core beliefs, we can find a sense of meaning and direction in our life's journey.

Setting Meaningful Goals and Objectives

Our goals provide us with direction, while our objectives shape our path. Establishing meaningful goals that align with our values and objectives can infuse our lives with purpose and determination. Setting meaningful goals and objectives is a potent method for increasing the value we place on our lives. When we have something to aim for, it provides us with a sense of purpose and determination. By establishing goals that align with our values and interests, we can develop a path for personal development and satisfaction. Whether it involves obtaining a degree, starting a family, or making a positive impact in our community, having goals provides us with something to strive for and a feeling of accomplishment when we achieve them.

Cultivating Resilience in the Face of Challenges

Life is not always smooth sailing - it throws unexpected obstacles and tests our resilience. Cultivating resilience can equip us with the tools to withstand the challenges and emerge stronger on the other side. Building resilience is crucial in navigating life's trials and setbacks. Resilience is the ability to recover from adversity and maintain an optimistic perspective. It enables us to embrace change, surmount obstacles, and grow stronger in the process.

Cultivating resilience involves developing coping mechanisms, practising self-care, seeking support from others, and reframing challenging situations in a more positive manner. By building resilience, we can not only weather life's storms but also thrive in the face of adversity. Resilience acts as our internal shield, protecting us from life's adversities. Recognising its importance and nurturing it can empower us to recover from setbacks and flourish in the face of challenges.

Developing resilience requires practising self-care, cultivating a positive mindset, and seeking support from others. By cultivating coping strategies, such as mindfulness, problem-solving skills, and emotional regulation techniques, we can navigate through adversities with strength and perseverance. Building emotional resilience is like exercising a muscle - it requires practice and persistence. Discovering strategies to enhance our emotional resilience, such as practising self-care, seeking support, and fostering a growth mindset, can fortify our inner strength.

Nurturing Relationships and Connections

We are inherently social creatures, desiring connection and a sense of belonging. Nurturing meaningful relationships can not only enhance our quality of life but also deepen our appreciation for the interconnected nature of humanity. Nurturing relationships and connections with others is another pivotal aspect of a gratifying life. Human beings are social beings, and our connections with others contribute significantly to our overall wellbeing. Effective communication and connection-building skills are crucial in fostering healthy relationships and building a support system. Engaging in meaningful and authentic relationships not only provides us with a sense of belonging but also allows for personal growth and enrichment.

From shared laughter to comforting embraces, relationships play a fundamental role in enriching our lives. Examining the importance of connections and cultivating meaningful relationships can elevate our sense of purpose and fulfilment. Relationships offer us emotional support, companionship, and a sense of belonging. By nurturing meaningful relationships with others, we can experience joy, empathy, and a deeper appreciation for the shared moments that enrich our lives.

Communication and Relationship-Building

Communication is the foundation of any relationship, fostering understanding, empathy, and connection. Unveiling effective communication strategies and relationship-building techniques can pave the way for deeper, more meaningful relationships that enhance our existence.

Importance of Continuous Learning and Growth

Life is like a recipe - the secret ingredient to a fulfilling existence is continuous learning and growth. Embracing new challenges, acquiring new skills, and expanding our knowledge not only keeps our minds sharp but also enriches our lives in ways we never thought possible. Continuous learning and growth are indispensable for enhancing the quality of life. By embracing a mindset of curiosity and seeking learning opportunities, we can expand our knowledge, skills, and perspectives. The acquisition of knowledge and personal growth can be achieved through formal education, reading, participating in workshops or seminars, or immersing ourselves in new experiences. By embracing continuous learning and self-improvement, we keep our minds active, expand our perspectives, and discover fresh avenues for self-expression and fulfilment.

Practical Steps for Personal Development

Practical steps for personal development involve making gradual, consistent changes that accumulate over time, rather than expecting overnight transformations. Setting specific goals, seeking feedback, and stepping out of our comfort zones are practical actions that can propel us towards becoming the best versions of ourselves.

The Power of Gratitude

Gratitude possesses the power to transform even the most ordinary moments into sources of joy. Expressing gratitude for the people, experiences, and blessings in our lives helps in cultivating a positive mindset that can shape our perspective and overall wellbeing.

Gratitude and mindfulness are potent tools for shaping a fulfilling life. Embracing gratitude enables us to focus on the positive aspects of our lives and appreciate the small joys around us. Practising mindfulness assists us in being present in the moment, reducing stress, and enhancing our overall wellbeing. Nurturing a sense of gratitude and practising mindfulness can foster a deeper connection to ourselves, others, and the world around us, leading to a more fulfilling and meaningful life.

Practising gratitude involves acknowledging the blessings and positive aspects of our lives and nurturing a sense of contentment and appreciation. Mindfulness, on the other hand, entails being fully present in the moment, reducing stress, and enhancing overall wellbeing. Together, these practices can elevate our daily experiences and enrich our lives in no small ways.

Engaging in mindfulness enhances life's quality by allowing us to fully experience the present moment without judgment or distraction. By doing so, we can savour life's simple pleasures, reduce stress, and improve our overall quality of life.

Overcoming Obstacles and Embracing Change

Life is an unpredictable journey filled with challenges and adversities. Navigating these obstacles requires resilience, perseverance, and a healthy dose of humour. By confronting challenges head-on, we not only grow stronger but also discover our true potential. Overcoming obstacles and embracing change is an integral part of the human experience.

Challenges and adversities are inevitable, but how we navigate them determines the value we assign to our lives. Rather than viewing obstacles as roadblocks, we can choose to see them as opportunities for growth and transformation. Embracing change can act as a catalyst for personal growth and development, leading to new experiences and a renewed sense of purpose. By embracing change and overcoming obstacles, we unlock our potential and discover the resilience within us.

Embracing Change as a Catalyst for Growth

Change is the only constant thing in life, and instead of fearing it, we should embrace it as a catalyst for growth. Whether it is a career change, a relationship shift, or a personal transformation, change offers us the opportunity to reinvent ourselves, discover new passions, and evolve into the individuals we are meant to be.

Conclusion

Life is unquestionably worth living, given its intricacies and obstacles. By examining it through the perspectives of philosophy, psychology, and social interaction, we can recognise the inherent value of human existence. The pursuit of meaning, the support gained from relationships, the depth of arts and culture, the push for societal advancement, and the personal contemplations, all contribute to affirming the intrinsic worth of life. Therefore, it is crucial for us to embrace our existence, seize opportunities for growth, connection, and expression, and actively participate in shaping a life that resonates with purpose and fulfilment. Ultimately, life is an extraordinary gift that invites us to engage, reflect, and appreciate the journey we are on.

As we navigate life's complexities, let us remember that each breath we take is a reminder of the precious gift of existence. Embracing the value of life involves finding purpose, building resilience, nurturing relationships, pursuing growth, practising gratitude, and embracing change. By cherishing these principles and living each day with intention and gratitude, we can genuinely appreciate the richness and worth of the life we are fortunate to live. Let us continue to savour the moments, overcome challenges, and embrace the journey with open hearts and minds, for life is indeed worth living.

CHAPTER NINETEEN

NO ONE HAS ALL THE ANSWERS TO LIFE'S QUESTIONS

The quest for understanding life's profound questions has spanned across cultures, epochs, and civilizations, from ancient philosophical discourses to contemporary debates on existentialism, indicating its enduring relevance throughout human history. Despite numerous attempts from various disciplines to provide definitive answers, life has taught me that no single individual or discourse can claim to possess all the answers to life's numerous questions.

Life presents us with profound questions that often do not have easy answers, challenging our perspectives and understanding, from the mysteries of existence to the complexities of human relationships. This lesson delves into the nature of uncertainty, the importance of diverse viewpoints, and the transformative power of continuous learning. Embracing ambiguity and the unknown can lead us to wisdom, humility, and a deeper sense of peace amidst the unanswered questions that define our existence. This lesson also examines the multifaceted dimensions of human experience, the limitations of our knowledge, and the value of questioning which ultimately enriches our understanding of life rather than limiting it to absolute answers.

The Complexity of Life's Questions

Life often presents us with questions that seem more like riddles than straightforward inquiries, challenging us with its complexities. From pondering the meaning of existence to grappling with personal dilemmas, the range of life's questions is as vast as the universe itself, each opening a Pandora's box of complexities. It is important to recognise the diversity of life's questions, as human inquiries range from deeply philosophical to practical concerns, each demanding a different perspective and thus yielding varied answers based on context, culture, personal experiences, and belief systems. Therefore, no single source can claim to encompass the myriad pathways that constitute human understanding.

The pursuit of absolute answers also prompts reflection on the nature of knowledge itself, as the foundations upon which we build our understanding are inherently limited. As fields such as science, philosophy, and theology advance, new paradigms continuously challenge established truths, illustrating the fluidity of knowledge and the ever-expanding horizons of human inquiry. It becomes apparent that the questions we ask evolve quicker than the answers we get, suggesting that claiming exhaustive answers is presumptive and intellectually disingenuous.

Life's richness often lies in its ambiguities and uncertainties. The questions that arise from human existence rarely lead to simple answers; instead, they reflect the dynamic and ever-changing nature of life. Philosophers like Jean-Paul Sartre and Søren Kierkegaard emphasised that the search for meaning is a fundamental aspect of the human condition. Questioning encourages introspection, prompting us to evaluate our beliefs, values, and aspirations. Instead of seeing unanswered questions as a lack of clarity, they can be seen as opportunities for personal growth and a deeper understanding of ourselves and the universe.

Furthermore, the beauty of human relationships is found in the shared exploration of life's questions. Through conversations with others, we gain diverse insights that enrich our perspectives. Engaging in discussions about life's mysteries acknowledges the vulnerability and complexity of the human experience, ultimately connecting us through shared uncertainty.

The Depth and Breadth of Life's Inquiries

Delving into life's inquiries means embracing the vastness of human experience and the intricacies of our existence. These questions provide gateways to better understanding ourselves and the world around us. By exploring the depths and breadths of life's inquiries, we embark on a journey of self-discovery and enlightenment that enriches our lives in unexpected ways. Life is inherently filled with uncertainties, and not all questions come with neat and tidy answers. Embracing the ambiguity that accompanies life's inquiries is a testament to our willingness to stand in the face of the unknown and acknowledge the limitations of our understanding. Some questions may forever remain shrouded in mystery, and recognising the boundaries of our knowledge humbles us, reminding us that we are mere mortals trying to make sense of the infinite complexities of existence.

Cultivating a Lifelong Learning Mindset

From childhood to old age, life is a continuous learning experience. Cultivating a mindset of curiosity and a thirst for knowledge ensures that we approach life's questions with an open heart and a nimble mind. By remaining perpetually inquisitive, we not only find answers but also enjoy the thrill of the search itself. Curiosity is the driving force that propels us to seek answers and unravel the mysteries of life. Embracing a mindset of continuous learning allows us to adapt, grow, and evolve in our quest for knowledge and understanding.

In a world teeming with different cultures, traditions, and belief systems, seeking wisdom from diverse perspectives can illuminate our understanding of life's questions in ways we never imagined. Learning from the rich reservoir of human experiences broadens our horizons and offers fresh insights into age-old inquiries. Every culture and tradition holds a treasure trove of wisdom passed down through generations. Immersing ourselves in the teachings and practices of diverse societies gives us a broader perspective on life's questions and introduces new approaches to age-old dilemmas.

Navigating Challenges Through Humility

Life resembles a turbulent rollercoaster, with unexpected twists and turns. When confronted with life's challenges, it is common to feel overwhelmed and directionless. Embracing humility and openness may hold the key to navigating these obstacles. It is important to acknowledge that nobody has all the answers, and that is perfectly fine. By recognising our limitations and being open to new perspectives, we can face life's uncertainties with curiosity rather than fear.

Embracing Vulnerability

In our pursuit of understanding and purpose, it is crucial to welcome vulnerability. Acknowledging that we do not have all the answers can be empowering. It enables us to form deeper connections with others, share our difficulties, and seek support and guidance. Embracing vulnerability in the quest for answers can lead to profound insights and personal development, demonstrating that it is normal not to have everything figured out.

Finding Peace in Unanswered Questions

Life is filled with enigmas that may remain unsolved. Rather than becoming ensnared in the endless quest for answers, finding peace in accepting unanswered questions can provide great strength. Embracing the unknown can be liberating, granting us the opportunity to appreciate the unpredictability and complexity of life.

Embracing the Beauty of Mystery and Wonder

There is a certain enchantment in not knowing everything. Embracing the beauty of mystery and wonder can inspire feelings of awe and humility in us. It allows us to marvel at the vastness of the universe and recognise the extraordinary nature of existence. By approaching the unknown with open hearts and inquisitive minds, we can discover joy and inspiration in life's unanswered questions.

Conclusion

The fact that no one has all the answers to life's questions is not simply an expression of humility, but rather an acknowledgement of the intricate and diverse nature of human existence. The multitude of questions, the limitations of knowledge, and the acknowledgement of ambiguity compel us to embrace uncertainty as a catalyst for personal and communal growth. As we navigate the complexities of life, the act of questioning not only enriches our understanding but also encourages us to engage more deeply with ourselves and with others. In a world filled with complexities, it is this very journey of inquiry - the willingness to contemplate, explore, and ponder – that eventually enhances our shared human experience.

As we conclude this lesson, let us remember that it is through accepting uncertainty and embracing diverse perspectives that we truly develop and evolve. By remaining curious, open-minded, and humble in the face of life's mysteries, we invite a sense of wonder and peace into our lives. While no one may have all the answers to life's questions, it is in our shared journey of exploration and discovery that we find meaning, connection, and a deeper understanding of the intricacies of our existence.

CHAPTER TWENTY

NOTHING IN LIFE IS PERMANENT

Life is like a woven fabric, incorporating experiences, emotions, and changes. Nothing in it is permanent. The idea that nothing lasts forever reminds us of the fleeting nature of life. This applies to various aspects of human life, from the changing seasons to personal and societal changes. Embracing impermanence helps us to value the present and build resilience in the face of change.

From birth, we are surrounded by constant change. The physical world is dynamic; seasons change, landscapes evolve, and even celestial bodies move and transform. This applies to personal lives too. Relationships grow and fade, ambitions change, and individuals adapt to their environment and challenges. Heraclitus captured this idea by saying, "You cannot step into the same river twice," emphasizing constant transformation.

Understanding Impermanence

Life is full of changes, like a rollercoaster ride with its ups and downs. Impermanence, the concept that nothing lasts forever, has been a recurring theme in philosophy and literature throughout history. From ancient Eastern teachings to modern Western thought, impermanence has been a consistent topic.

The Impermanence of Relationships

The impermanence of life is evident in relationships. Friendships from childhood may fade as priorities change. Romantic relationships can endure or dissolve due to time and circumstances. The fleeting nature of human relationships brings both joy and sorrow. It urges us to cherish moments with loved ones, knowing that every interaction is precious and temporary.

Relationships are dynamic, evolving like a dance, with moments of harmony and occasional missteps. From friendships to romances, relationships go through transitions like changing seasons. Embracing these changes, communicating openly, and adapting together, are essential for resilient connections to withstand the highs and lows of life.

Personal Growth and Identity

Recognising impermanence is crucial for personal growth. Every individual's identity evolves through experiences, education, and introspection. This journey involves uncertainty and self-doubt, but also the realisation that past choices do not define the future. Change is inherent in the human experience, and acknowledging the temporary nature of struggles and accomplishments promotes resilience and humility.

Societal Structures and Cultural Norms

Impermanence extends to societal structures and cultural norms. Stable institutions, like governments and economic systems, change with societal values and technological advancements. History is filled with examples of once-powerful empires that fell due to stagnation, emphasising the need for adaptation. Cultures are influenced by diverse perspectives and communication technologies, leading to innovation but also resistance to change.

Acceptance and Resilience

Embracing impermanence promotes resilience in individuals and communities and fosters a philosophical mindset. Navigating the ups and downs of life requires embracing change and loss for emotional wellbeing. Instead of dwelling on the past or worrying about the future, we can develop mindfulness, which entails being fully present in, and aware of, the current moment. Mindfulness helps shift focus away from things that cannot be changed, fostering a deep connection with the unfolding of life. This acceptance enables us to welcome change as an essential part of life, leading to a more peaceful and satisfying existence.

Embracing Change and Uncertainty

Life is as unpredictable as a squirrel on a highwire, requiring us to embrace its unpredictability. Just like a chameleon adapts to its surroundings, we must also adapt to life's ever-changing landscape. Flexibility is crucial in navigating life's uncertainties.

Coping with Loss and Transition

Loss and transition can be overwhelming, like unwelcome guests barging in, unannounced. However, even in the darkest times, there is hope. Grief is a rollercoaster of emotions that can leave us feeling lost. Allowing ourselves to feel, heal, and seek support is crucial in navigating the healing process.

Finding Stability Amid Impermanence

In life's complexity, loss and change are woven into our experiences. Finding meaning in upheavals, growing from challenges, and appreciating the beauty of impermanence is important. Practising mindfulness and being fully present can ground us in the present moment, providing stability in life's flux.

Cultivating Inner Strength and Equanimity

Building inner strength and equanimity is like developing a steady anchor to weather life's uncertainties. By nurturing resilience and remaining balanced, we can navigate life's curveballs with grace. Acknowledging feelings, seeking support, and maintaining a positive mindset are key to emotional resilience.

Strategies for Enhancing Adaptability

Adaptability is a valuable trait in a world of constant change. Embracing flexibility, seeking growth opportunities, and being open to learning from challenges can help us thrive in ever-evolving circumstances. Just as a flower blooms and withers, finding joy in life's fleeting moments can enrich our experience. Embracing the impermanence of all things allows for appreciation of the beauty and wisdom that come with letting go. Life consists of a succession of cycles, each bringing its unique gifts and lessons. By recognising that everything has its appropriate time and location, we can accept and appreciate the natural ebb and flow of life.

Living Fully in the Present Moment

Fully embracing the present moment is essential in a world where nothing is permanent. The only moment that truly matters is the present one. By fully embracing the present moment, adapting to change as a natural part of life, and finding beauty in every impermanent experience, we can relish the richness of our journey with a sense of wonder and resilience. Embracing the inherent impermanence of our experiences as we navigate life's ever-changing tides can provide us with a deep sense of freedom and peace. Through cultivating resilience, mindfulness, and a willingness to let go, we can learn to live fully in the present moment and find joy in the beauty of life's constant change. May we find comfort in the realisation that nothing in life is permanent, but everything holds the potential for growth, transformation, and new beginnings.

Conclusion

The lesson that nothing in life is permanent is a timeless truth that permeates every aspect of human existence. By acknowledging the inevitability of change, we are better prepared to navigate the complexities of our relationships, personal growth, and societal dynamics. Embracing the ephemeral nature of life fosters an appreciation for each moment, allowing us to derive meaning and joy from our experiences. Ultimately, it is through this acceptance of impermanence that we can cultivate resilience, find beauty in transitions, and embark on a journey of self-discovery that honours the fleeting nature of life itself.

Embracing change is not a source of anxiety but an invitation to fully engage with the richness of our shared human experience, transforming the transient into a celebration of existence.

CHAPTER TWENTY-ONE

PEOPLE CHANGE WITH TIME

Change is an integral part of human experience, intricately linked with personal growth, societal influences, and the passage of time. People change as they progress through different stages of life, encounter diverse experiences, and adapt to evolving environments. This lesson seeks to delve into the multifaceted nature of change in individuals, exploring psychological, emotional, and social factors that drive transformation, while also considering the implications of these changes for interpersonal relationships and broader societal structures.

At the heart of human existence lies the inevitability of change. From infancy to adulthood, we undergo significant transformations that mould our identities, beliefs, and behaviours. Psychologists often emphasise the importance of developmental stages outlined by theorists such as Erik Erikson, who delineated the eight stages of psychosocial development. Each stage presents specific challenges and opportunities for change, which individuals must navigate to achieve a healthy psychological state. For example, the transition from adolescence to young adulthood is characterised by an exploration of identity and autonomy, often resulting in shifts in values and priorities. This crucial period can lead to the formation of new beliefs and a re-evaluation of self, illustrating that individuals inevitably change as they seek to understand their place in the world.

The potential for change is not confined to individual circumstances but is greatly influenced by external factors. The environment in which we are situated plays a pivotal role in shaping our experiences and perspectives. Cultural, social, and economic contexts can catalyse personal transformation. For instance, exposure to diverse cultures through travel or education frequently challenges preconceived notions and encourages us to adopt new viewpoints. This phenomenon is particularly pertinent in today's globalised society, where the exchange of ideas and lifestyles is more pronounced than ever before. The necessity of being able to adjust to new surroundings and embrace change is crucial for both survival and development, demonstrating that change is not only unavoidable but also vital for personal and collective progress.

Emotional experiences also act as potent instigators of change. Life events, whether positive or negative, can trigger introspection and result in significant shifts in behaviour and perspective. The loss of a loved one, the arrival of a child, or the conclusion of a significant relationship can elicit deep emotional reactions that urge us to reevaluate our principles and priorities. These transformative moments often serve as triggers for change, leading to a reconsideration of life decisions and an exploration of previously unexplored paths. The process of recovering from trauma or grief illustrates how we can emerge from challenging experiences with a renewed sense of purpose and comprehension. Thus, our emotional landscape plays a crucial role during our personal development.

Moreover, the influence of social relationships on individual change should not be underestimated. Interpersonal dynamics profoundly shape how we perceive ourselves and subsequently evolve. The relationships forged throughout life - whether with family, friends, colleagues, or romantic partners - serve as crucial contexts in which we negotiate our identities. For example, the influence of a mentor can motivate someone to pursue a different career path, while friendships often lead to shifts in interests and values. Social interactions provide feedback mechanisms that either reinforce or challenge existing beliefs and behaviours, creating an environment where change is both attainable and often necessary for growth.

Despite the positive aspects of change, it is important to acknowledge the difficulties it can bring. The process of transformation is not always seamless; it can be filled with uncertainty, discomfort, and resistance. Many individuals have a natural inclination towards stability and may resist change due to fear of the unknown or a reluctance to leave familiar comfort zones. This resistance can manifest in various ways, from an unwillingness to embrace new ideas to an inability to let go of past identities. Overcoming such barriers often requires courage, self-awareness, and a willingness to confront deeply held beliefs. Individuals who navigate these challenges successfully often emerge with a deeper understanding of themselves and their capacity for change, demonstrating that while transformative experiences can be challenging, they are also essential for personal growth and development.

The Certainty of Change in Life

Like the changing seasons or shifting tides, change in life is a constant. From career shifts to personal transformations, change shapes us into the resilient individuals we are meant to be. It is often said that change is the only constant in life, and this holds true when considering the catalysts behind positive transformations. Personal growth and self-improvement are common drivers of positive change. As individuals, we strive to become improved versions of ourselves, learning from our experiences and acquiring new skills. This internal drive to evolve and develop often leads to positive changes in character, behaviour, and mindset.

Personal growth thrives on change, as it pushes us out of our comfort zones and challenges us to evolve. Through change, we encounter new opportunities, learn from our mistakes, and adapt to the ever-shifting landscapes of our lives. As we journey through life, circumstances and experiences shape our perceptions and values. This can lead to personal growth, prompting us to change certain behaviours, beliefs, or habits to align with our evolving sense of self-held beliefs. Individuals who successfully navigate these challenges often emerge with a deeper understanding of themselves and their capacity for change, illustrating that transformative experiences, while difficult, are essential for personal evolution.

Life events like marriage, becoming a parent, advancing in a career, or experiencing loss can lead to significant changes in individuals. These transitions can impact their priorities, responsibilities, and perspectives, ultimately influencing their behaviour and attitudes towards others and their surroundings. The desire for self-improvement and the pursuit of new goals often drives people to change by learning new skills, pursuing higher education, or striving for career advancements, acting as a catalyst for personal growth and achievement.

Another factor contributing to positive personal transformation is the influence of role models and inspirational figures who have achieved greatness, overcome challenges, or made a positive impact in their communities. Observing their actions and attitudes can inspire us to strive for similar qualities and ultimately lead to positive changes in our lives.

People can also undergo negative transformations due to various causes, such as the influence of negative peers or environments. The people we surround ourselves with and the environments we immerse ourselves in significantly impact our thoughts and actions. Being around people who engage in harmful behaviours or being in a toxic environment can lead to a deterioration of character and negative change. Traumas and life-altering events can also contribute to negative change, as individuals may struggle to cope, leading to negative behaviours and attitudes. These experiences can deeply impact emotional wellbeing, causing a spiral of negativity and harmful actions.

When a Good Person Changes to Be Bad

When a good person changes to be bad, it can be distressing to witness. In such cases, it is important to approach the situation with empathy and understanding, recognising that people are complex, and their behaviours may reflect internal struggles or external circumstances. If you notice someone undergoing a negative transformation, it is important to communicate openly and honestly with them; express concerns, offer support without judgment, and encourage them to seek professional help or counselling.

The Effects of Change on Relationships

Embracing change in relationships can be challenging, disrupting familiar dynamics, routines, and expectations. It may take time for both partners to adapt to new circumstances, roles, or individual transformations, leading to temporary tension or conflicts. When one person undergoes significant changes, it is essential to communicate openly and honestly to avoid misinterpretation, misunderstandings, or emotional distance, ultimately affecting the relationship's stability and intimacy.

Change has the potential to either facilitate the growth of a relationship or cause divisions within it. While some couples manage to develop and progress together, others may discover that their paths are diverging due to differences in priorities, interests, or values. It is important to be aware of these changes early to determine the most suitable way forward.

Adapting to Change

Embracing change necessitates acknowledging its inevitability. Developing an open mindset is essential to understanding that both people and circumstances change. This approach will assist in adjusting to new situations and finding ways to support each other during these transitions. Maintaining open channels of communication is crucial when dealing with change. Consistently communicating with your partner, family, friends, or colleagues to voice concerns, share expectations, and discuss any changing needs or frustrations is important. During times of change, it becomes crucial to provide support and empathy to those undergoing transformations. Offering a listening ear, empathy, and encouragement can help alleviate anxieties and strengthen relationships amidst the upheaval.

The Psychological Effects of Change

Change can elicit a variety of emotions and psychological reactions, ranging from excitement and anticipation to fear and uncertainty. Understanding the psychological impact of change can help us in navigating its complexities with compassion and self-awareness. Change often triggers a rollercoaster of emotions, from euphoria to anxiety, as we navigate the uncharted territory of transformation. By acknowledging and understanding our emotional responses to change, we can cultivate self-compassion and resilience in the face of uncertainty.

Coping with Stress and Uncertainty

During periods of change, coping strategies such as self-care, seeking support from loved ones, and practising relaxation techniques can help us manage stress and uncertainty. By prioritising our mental and emotional wellbeing, we can navigate change with greater ease and grace.

Recognising Resistance to Change

Change may be as unwelcome as a flat tyre on a road trip, but acknowledging our resistance is the first step to getting back on track. Whether it is fear, comfort, or sheer stubbornness, recognising it is like using GPS to find our way to personal growth and development. Like persuading a friend to try something for the first time, helping others embrace change requires patience, understanding, and perhaps a gentle nudge in the right direction.

Self-Reflection in Personal Development

Self-reflection is like a mirror that not only reflects our image but also reveals the superhero cape hidden beneath our everyday clothing. Taking the time to contemplate our thoughts, actions, and emotions can lead to profound personal growth. Think of it as discovering a hidden treasure chest within yourself. From journaling to meditation to seeking guidance from a mentor, there are various tools available to help you uncover your true path.

Conclusion

Change is a natural part of life, and while it can pose difficulties, it also presents opportunities for personal development and stronger connections. Understanding the reasons why people change, acknowledging how change impacts relationships, and developing coping strategies can help in successfully manoeuvring through the complexities of change. Approaching change with an open mind, effective communication, and mutual support, allows us and our relationships to adjust and thrive in a constantly changing world. Keep in mind that change is constant, and our ability to handle it with grace and resilience will ultimately influence our personal growth and the resilience of our relationships.

People change for various reasons, whether positive or negative. Positive change is often spurred by personal growth, the influence of role models, and a desire for self-improvement. On the other hand, negative change may stem from negative peer influence or traumatic experiences. When a good person undergoes negative change, it is important to approach them with empathy, understanding, and support. By recognising the factors behind their change and providing the necessary support, we can potentially guide them back towards growth and positive change.

As we reflect on the complex nature of why people change, it is important to remember that change is not just a destination but an ongoing journey. Embracing the ups and downs of life's changes allows us to evolve, learn, and ultimately thrive. By cultivating resilience, nurturing meaningful relationships, and engaging in self-reflection, we empower ourselves to gracefully and authentically navigate the uncertainties of change. May this journey of change be a source of growth, wisdom, and fulfilment as we embrace the beauty and challenges that come with life's ever-evolving nature.

CHAPTER TWENTY-TWO

Our Family Has No Replacement

In the complex fabric of human existence, few connections are as deep or indispensable as those formed within the family framework. That the family has no replacement holds profound meaning, encapsulating the special ties of kinship that cultivate an enduring sense of belonging and selfhood. The family, in its diverse forms, acts as the fundamental support upon which we navigate life's intricacies. This lesson seeks to examine the inherent value of the family, the influence of familial connections on personal growth, and the consequences of familial absence.

At its essence, the family is defined not only by blood relations but also by shared experiences, values, and emotional bonds that unite us. These relationships, whether cultivated through marriage, kinship, or chosen connections, form a web that offers security, affection, and companionship. The teachings acquired within the realm of the family often leave the deepest imprint; they shape character, impact decision-making, and shape moral viewpoints. Children raised in a nurturing family structure are more likely to develop a strong sense of self-worth and resilience, which are essential qualities for navigating life's ups and downs.

The nurturing environment provided by families plays a pivotal role in psychological development. From the early stages of life, we depend on our families to fulfil our physical and emotional needs. The significance of this nurturing is evident in the field of child psychology, where research consistently shows that children raised in stable, loving, and attentive family environments tend to perform better academically and socially. On the other hand, a lack of strong familial support can lead to emotional challenges, feelings of isolation, and a tendency towards maladaptive behaviours. Thus, family serves not only as a backdrop to our lives but as the very foundation on which emotional wellbeing and stability are constructed.

The importance of the family extends beyond the individual and permeates societal structures. Families are microcosms of society, reflecting broader social, cultural, and economic realities. They act as primary agents of socialisation, instilling societal norms and values in the next generation. In various cultures across the world, families operate within different structures – nuclear, extended, single-parent, and blended – yet they share the common aim of nurturing relationships that uphold community unity. It is within these familial contexts that we learn to navigate relationships, resolve conflicts, and develop empathy which are skills crucial for fostering harmony within broader social circles.

That our family has no replacement implies a certain fragility inherent in familial relationships. The loss of a family member, whether through death, estrangement, or significant life changes, can trigger profound emotional upheaval. Grieving such losses involves more than mourning a person; it often entails the breakdown of a support system cultivated over a lifetime. Studies in bereavement psychology reveal that the death of a close family member can lead to a cascade of psychological effects, including depression, anxiety, and a diminished sense of self. The absence of the unique bond shared with family members is irreplaceable, and no substitute can fill that void. While friendships and other relationships may offer comfort, they rarely replicate the deep relationships that define familial love.

Furthermore, the concept of the family can evolve throughout our life, adapting to changing circumstances, yet this adaptability should not diminish its profound significance. Modern society often embraces non-traditional family structures, encouraging us to define our familial ties. For example, many choose to form chosen families, characterised by strong connections among friends who become like relatives. The fundamental aspects of the family, such as love, loyalty, and mutual support, remain consistent despite the various forms that families may take. This evolution highlights the similarity in the emotional and existential void experienced when the family is absent.

The Importance of The Family

The family holds significant importance in providing emotional support, a sense of belonging, and stability in our lives. They provide unconditional love, understanding, and companionship, which shape our beliefs, values, and identity. Strong family connections act as a comforting presence in a chaotic world, like a warm blanket on a cold day. Having a supportive family network is comparable to having a dedicated cheerleading squad, ready to celebrate victories and offer support during struggles. They are the true champions in our lives, and their significance cannot be underestimated.

Strengthening Family Relationships

Communication, empathy, and quality time spent together are essential in nurturing strong family bonds. Engaging in shared activities, practising active listening, and expressing gratitude for one other can contribute to strengthening relationships within the family. Effective communication within the family is crucial, as it plays a significant role in maintaining strong relationships. Understanding others' unique characteristics and perspectives fosters a sense of closeness and unity. Trust and empathy serve as the glue that binds family relationships together, providing support during challenging times and brightening even the darkest days.

Building Resilience Through Family Support

During difficult times, family support can make a substantial difference. Standing united in the face of challenges can help weather any storm. The family is not only about being there for one another during tough times but also about encouraging personal growth and development and fostering a culture of continuous improvement.

Shared Memories and Traditions

Family history and heritage serve as the foundation of our identity and sense of belonging. Celebrating the unique story of our family can instil a sense of pride and connection. Meaningful family rituals, whether weekly traditions or annual vacations, strengthen family bonds and create enduring memories that weave the family's story together. Creating lasting memories and traditions as a family can be as simple as participating in regular activities, celebrating special occasions together, and preserving shared experiences through photos or mementoes. Establishing meaningful rituals for our family can help fortify bonds and create enduring memories for future generations.

Coping with Loss and Grief as a Family

In times of loss, coming together as a family can provide comfort and strength. Supporting one another through shared grief can alleviate the burden on everyone involved. Preserving and honouring the memories of lost loved ones can be a healing process for the family, paying tribute to their impact on our lives.

Offering Support During Life's Challenges

Offering unwavering support and being a reliable source of strength for family members in times of difficulty can create a sense of security and assurance. Navigating life's challenges becomes more manageable when we work together, seeking guidance and assistance as needed. By leaning on one another for advice and support, we can overcome obstacles as a unified front.

Celebrating Achievements Together

Acknowledging and celebrating the achievements of every family member promotes a sense of pride and unity. By rejoicing in accomplishments together, we strengthen our bond and create lasting memories. Creating a culture of encouragement within the family promotes positivity and motivation. By cheering one another on during milestones and successes, we cultivate a supportive environment that uplifts everyone's spirits.

Resolving Family Conflicts

During times of conflict, it is important to approach the situation with empathy, patience, and a willingness to listen. Open communication, seeking understanding, and finding common ground are essential in resolving conflicts within the family unit.

Conclusion

That our family has no replacement serves as a poignant reminder of the unique and irreplaceable role that the family plays in our lives. Families are not just a collection of individuals; they are intricate networks of emotional support, identity, and continuity. They shape our values, influence our behaviours, and define our connections to society. The loss of the family echoes through our emotional landscape, leaving an indelible mark that no other relationship can replicate. As we recognise and cherish these bonds, we are reminded of the family's profound impact on our existence and the vital need to nurture these relationships throughout our lives. Thus, it is incumbent upon us to honour and appreciate our familial ties, understanding that they are the cornerstone of our identities, our resilience, and ultimately, of our humanity.

Family members' love and support are invaluable, providing a source of strength, joy, and companionship throughout our life's journey. Embracing the unique bonds we share with our loved ones, nurturing these relationships, and cherishing shared memories and traditions can enrich our lives in countless ways. Remember, our family has no replacement, and the connections we cultivate with them are a treasure to be cherished and nurtured. Together, may we continue to support, celebrate, and stand by one another through all the ups and downs that life may bring.

113

CHAPTER TWENTY-THREE

A Girl-Child Is Not Inferior to a Boy-Child

In contemporary society, the battle for gender equality remains an ongoing struggle, raising questions about inherent biases that have historically positioned individuals in a hierarchy based solely on their gender. One of the most profound assertions that can be made in this discourse is that a girlchild is not inferior to a boychild. This statement encapsulates the essence of gender equality, emphasising the equal potential that children of both genders possess. This lesson delves into the complex dimensions of this assertion, from social constructs and psychological implications to economic empowerment and educational access, thereby affirmatively demonstrating that gender should not serve as a determinant in assessing the capabilities and worth of any child.

To understand the roots of perceived inferiority, we must critically examine the historical and cultural contexts that have perpetuated gender biases. In many societies across the globe, patriarchal ideologies have dictated the value of individuals based on their gender since time immemorial. Girls have often been relegated to subordinate roles, considered as lesser beings compared to their male counterparts. This systemic devaluation has led to a plethora of consequences, such as limited access to education, forced early marriages, and numerous forms of discrimination and violence. However, these deeply entrenched norms do not reflect inherent capabilities but rather societal constructs that have been passed down through generations.

Research has increasingly indicated that the notion of inferiority associated with girl-children is unfounded. Many studies in developmental psychology reveal that the intellectual capabilities of girls and boys are virtually indistinguishable. For instance, standardised testing across various educational systems around the world has shown that girls can achieve academic excellence equal to or exceeding that of boys in numerous subjects, including mathematics and the sciences, traditionally considered male-dominated fields. Furthermore, girls often exhibit strengths in collaborative and communicative skills, which are invaluable in both academic and professional environments. Hence, the premise that a girlchild possesses any inherent inferiority to a boychild is contradicted by empirical evidence showing equality in potential and aptitude.

The significance of education cannot be overstated in the context of empowering girl-children. Education serves as a powerful catalyst for economic and social development, yet access to quality education remains one of the most critical challenges faced by girls globally. According to data from organisations such as UNESCO, approximately 130 million girls are out of school, a fact that not only affects individual lives but also stunts national development.

When girls are educated, they contribute dynamically to the economy, fostering innovation and leadership. Studies indicate that every additional year of schooling for girls results in an increase in their future earnings and a positive impact on their families and communities. The empowerment of girls through education, therefore, dispels any lingering notions of inferiority by validating their capacity to effect change at both micro and macro levels.

The economic dimension of gender equality highlights the fallacy of inferiority. Gender disparities in employment and pay persist, fuelled by stereotypes that suggest that certain professions are 'more suited' for men than for women. Despite these societal biases, women have demonstrated remarkable resilience and capability in the workforce. From CEOs of Fortune 500 companies to trailblazers in politics and science, women have proven that their contributions to society are not only substantial but essential.

Progressing towards gender parity in the workplace is vital, not only for the empowerment of women but also for the advancement of society. By dismantling the constructs that inhibit girls' professional growth, we can illustrate that capabilities are not determined by gender, but rather by opportunity, encouragement, and access.

Moreover, the emotional and psychological dimensions of a girl child's upbringing deserve attention. The impact of societal messaging on gender roles begins early and can have lasting effects on the self-esteem and aspirations of young girls. When girls are consistently exposed to narratives that undermine their worth or potential, they may internalise these beliefs, leading to diminished self-confidence. In contrast, by promoting messages of empowerment and worthiness, society can foster an environment where both girl-children and boy-children are encouraged to pursue their passions and develop their talents, free from the constraints of gender-based expectations.

Initiatives that focus on mentorship and role models for girls can serve as an essential force in combating inferiority complexes, enabling girls to visualise a future unbounded by archaic gender norms.

The Boychild Perspective

From a boychild's perspective, the idea that a male child is superior has been ingrained for centuries. This mindset often stems from traditional societal expectations, where boys are considered heirs to the family name, providers, and the ones who carry on the family legacy. However, it is essential to challenge these notions and recognise that gender does not determine a person's worth or capabilities. Embracing gender equality empowers boys to break free from societal pressures and explore their passions and talents fully.

The Girlchild Perspective

The girlchild perspective is equally important. Many young girls have often faced discrimination based on their gender, resulting in limited opportunities and a lack of recognition for their accomplishments. However, it is essential to highlight the incredible achievements of girls throughout history, ranging from scientific breakthroughs to leading social and political movements. Girls should be given equal opportunities and support, allowing them to pursue their aspirations, dreams, and potential.

Why Parents Want Boychildren

Historically, parents may have preferred boy-children due to cultural or societal norms, such as the belief that sons would support them in old age or continue the family lineage. However, these ideas are outdated and rob girls of the chance to showcase their unique abilities. Parents should realise that the value of a child is not predicated on their gender but rather on their talents, strengths, and potential to create positive change in the world.

Advantages of Having a Girl-child

Raising a girl-child can bring numerous advantages to a family. Girls often possess qualities such as empathy, emotional intelligence, and communication skills that can foster stronger relationships within the family unit. Additionally, studies have shown that societies with higher gender equality tend to be more prosperous and have better overall wellbeing. By empowering girls, we promote a healthier society based on fairness, respect, and collaboration.

What Girl-children Can Achieve

Girls can achieve greatness in any field they choose to pursue. In all disciplines, including science, technology, engineering, mathematics, arts, and humanities, girls have broken barriers and continue to make significant contributions. From renowned scientists like Marie Curie to trailblazers like Malala Yousafzai, we witness the immense potential that girls possess. By providing equal opportunities and encouraging their passions, we unleash their boundless potential.

The Role of a Girl-child in the Family

Girl-children play a vital role in every family. Just like boy-children, they bring unique perspectives, strengths, and talents. Girls often excel in nurturing and caregiving roles, creating a nurturing environment not just for immediate family members but for the community. Their resilience and determination inspire and create a positive impact on their siblings, parents, and subsequent generations.

Why Parents Should Value Their Girlchildren

Parents should value their girl-children because they are valuable in every sense. The love, care, support, and opportunities provided to girls will empower them to lead fulfilling lives, fostering personal growth and positive societal change. By creating an atmosphere of equality and acceptance, parents lay the foundation for a just and inclusive society.

Conclusion

The assertion that a girl-child is not inferior to a boy-child is more than a mere phrase; it is a profound declaration of the need for societal change. Through addressing the cultural constructs of gender, promoting equitable education, leveraging economic empowerment, and fostering a supportive psychological framework, we can forge a future where the potential of every child is celebrated and nurtured equally, irrespective of gender. By advocating for these principles and dismantling biases, society can fully recognise and harness the inherent worth and potential of all children.

The true progress of humanity hinges upon acknowledging and promoting equality among genders, ensuring that every child, regardless of their gender, is allowed to thrive and contribute to a better world. It is high time we realise that a girl-child is not inferior to a boy-child. Both genders possess remarkable potential. By embracing gender equality, we can challenge outdated beliefs and empower girls to embrace their passions and excel in any field they choose. Parents play a critical role in nurturing and supporting their girl-children, thereby creating a brighter and more equitable future for all. Let us break the chains of gender bias and embrace the power of gender equality.

CHAPTER TWENTY-FOUR

THE OLDER WE ARE, THE LESS THE PEOPLE IN OUR LIVES

Life has taught me that as we journey through the various stages of life, a notable and often unsettling phenomenon occurs: the gradual reduction of the number of people with whom we maintain close relationships. This process, which can be observed across cultures and contexts, raises important questions about the nature of human relationships, the evolution of social dynamics, and the implications of an increasingly isolated existence as one progresses through life. This lesson explores the manifold reasons behind this trend, while also reflecting on the emotional and psychological ramifications that accompany a diminishing social circle.

From the outset, it is crucial to acknowledge that the nature of human relationships is inherently fluid. During childhood and adolescence, we are commonly surrounded by a plethora of peers, family members, and educational figures. These formative years are characterised by frequent social interactions, which lay the foundation for interpersonal skills and emotional intelligence. However, upon entering adulthood, many people find their social environments shifting dramatically. The responsibilities and demands associated with careers, marriage, and parenthood often consume substantial portions of our time, leading to a gradual prioritisation of certain relationships over others. Thus, where there existed a vast number of friends and acquaintances before, only a handful of significant relationships will remain as we navigate the complexities of adult life.

As we progress further into middle age and then into later years, the trends of relationship reduction become more pronounced. Factors such as retirement, the empty nest syndrome - the phenomenon where children leave home - and the natural course of mortality contribute significantly to the shrinking of social circles. The transition into retirement, while often heralded as a time for newfound freedom, can also lead to social stagnation. With colleagues no longer present to engage in daily interactions, we may find ourselves isolated, struggling to cultivate new relationships in a context where social opportunities become increasingly limited. For many, the social networks built within the workplace are crucial to maintaining a sense of community and belonging; once severed, this connection creates a void that can be challenging to fill.

The dynamics of familial relationships often shift as individuals approach older age. The responsibilities associated with raising children begin to fade as they seek their own paths, leaving parents to grapple with the complexities of their evolving identities. Empty nesters may experience a profound sense of loss, not only of the physical presence of their children but also of the daily interactions that build familial bonds. Simultaneously, relatives may become more dispersed geographically, with adult children often moving to different cities or even countries in pursuit of opportunities. This phenomenon of geographical separation further aggravates feelings of isolation, as traditional familial gatherings become sparse.

The inevitability of mortality also has a substantial impact on the reduction of social circles as we age. The loss of friends, peers, and family members can lead to heightened feelings of grief and loneliness. Each loss not only diminishes the number of people we interact with regularly but also imposes an emotional burden that can make establishing new relationships a daunting task. For those in their later years, the prospect of forming new relationships often feels less appealing in the light of the experiences of loss that have shaped their recent history. Thus, the natural progression towards fewer relationships becomes connected with a reluctance to seek out new ones.

Despite the challenges posed by an ever-reducing social circle, it is essential to recognise that the quality of relationships often prevails over quantity. As people age, they may find themselves focusing on deeper, more meaningful relationships. While their social networks may diminish, the relationships that remain often reflect a profound emotional investment cultivated through shared experiences and mutual understanding. The friendships and familial bonds that endure through hardship and change become paramount, often offering substantial emotional support and companionship.

The purposeful cultivation of relationships in later life can significantly enhance an individual's overall wellbeing. Societal perceptions increasingly acknowledge the importance of social networks for emotional health, especially among ageing populations. Engaging in community-based activities, volunteering, joining clubs, or participating in group hobbies can facilitate the formation of new relationships and mitigate feelings of isolation.

Technology has emerged as a powerful tool in combating loneliness, offering avenues for individuals to maintain and strengthen relationships through virtual platforms. Video calls, social media, and online communities enable ageing individuals to connect with distant friends and relatives, thus fostering a sense of connectedness despite geographical barriers.

The Importance of Social Connections

Social connections are like the sprinkles on the cupcake of life – they add flavour, sweetness, and a little extra something special. As we age, these connections become even more crucial for our wellbeing and quality of life. Just like a fine wine, our social networks tend to change and mature with age. Friendships might dwindle in quantity, but they often gain in quality. It is like going from a crowded nightclub to a cozy dinner party – fewer people, but more meaningful conversations.

Factors Affecting Social Networks in Older Age

Several factors contribute to the decreasing size of social networks as people age. Firstly, as individuals transition into retirement, they may lose the social connections they had at work, resulting in a significant reduction in daily interactions. Geographical mobility and health-related issues can limit the opportunities for seniors to engage in social activities and meet new people. The loss of friends and family members through natural causes may also contribute to a shrinking social circle.

1. Health and Mobility Limitations

As the years go by, our bodies might not be as active as they once were. Health issues and mobility limitations can make it harder to maintain a wide circle of friends. Suddenly, coffee dates turn into conference calls from the couch.

2. Changes in Family Dynamics

Family dynamics can also shift as we age. Children grow up, move away, or become busy with their own lives. This can impact the closeness of family relationships and alter the support system we have relied on for years.

3. Retirement and Work Transitions

Retirement can be a game-changer when it comes to social connections. The water cooler chats and office happy hours that once filled our social calendar are replaced by a quieter, more introspective pace of life. Suddenly, you have all the time in the world – but fewer workmates to share it with.

Changes in Social Circles as We Grow Older

1. Navigating Loss and Grief

As we age, loss becomes a more frequent visitor in our lives. Friends and loved ones pass away, leaving holes in our social circles. Navigating this grief while trying to maintain other relationships can be like walking a tightrope on roller skates – challenging and a little shaky.

2. Shifting Priorities and Interests

Our interests and priorities often change as we grow older. Suddenly, watching the television takes precedence over going to club. These shifts can lead us to seek out different social circles that align more closely with our current passions and values.

Challenges of Maintaining Relationships in Later Life

Senior citizens encounter various challenges in maintaining relationships as they age. One significant challenge is a decrease in physical capabilities, making it harder to attend social gatherings or engage in activities they once enjoyed. Chronic health conditions and mobility issues can hinder seniors' ability to participate in social events. Furthermore, the loss of a spouse or close friends can greatly impact their social support system, leaving them feeling more isolated.

1. Geographical Distance and Relocation

In the game of life, sometimes the board gets flipped, and we find ourselves scattered across the map from our nearest and dearest. Geographical distance and relocation can put a strain on relationships, making it harder to grab a cup of coffee or share a spontaneous laugh.

2. Communication Barriers and Technological Adaptation

Keeping up with the latest technology trends can feel like trying to learn a new dance move – awkward and slightly confusing. Communication barriers, whether due to technological challenges or simply feeling out of touch with the digital age, can hinder the maintenance of relationships in later life.

3. Changing Social Norms and Expectations

Just when you think you have got this whole socialising thing down, the rules change. As we age, social norms and expectations can shift, leaving us feeling a bit like a grandparent trying to navigate a social media platform. Adapting to these changes while staying true to ourselves can be a balancing act worthy of a circus performer.

Cultivating Meaningful Relationships in Later Life

1. Engagement in Community Activities

As we age, it is crucial to stay connected with others to combat feelings of isolation. Engaging in community activities and groups can provide a sense of belonging and purpose. Whether it is joining a book club, volunteering at a local charity, or participating in a fitness class, these activities offer opportunities to meet new people and foster meaningful relationships.

2. Building Intergenerational Relationships

Building relationships with individuals of different age groups can be incredibly rewarding. Interacting with younger generations can bring fresh perspectives, energy, and joy into our lives while sharing our wisdom and experience can enrich the lives of others. Whether it is mentoring a young person, spending time with grandchildren, or participating in intergenerational programmes, these relationships can help us stay connected and engaged in a diverse community.

3. Seeking Out Social Activities

Seniors can actively cultivate relationships by seeking out social activities, such as joining clubs, volunteer work, or hobby groups. These activities provide opportunities to meet new people with similar interests and establish meaningful connections.

4. Keeping In Touch with Loved Ones

Regular communication with family and friends is crucial. Phone calls, video chats, or sending letters are all effective ways to stay connected and maintain relationships despite physical distance.

5. Engaging In Intergenerational Activities

Participating in intergenerational programmes or volunteering with younger generations can foster meaningful connections and provide a sense of purpose for seniors.

6. Focusing On Quality, Not Quantity

Instead of trying to expand the social network, seniors should focus on deepening relationships with existing connections. Taking the time to nurture and invest in a few close friendships can bring immense satisfaction and support.

The Role of Technology in Social Connections

Technology has become an essential tool for staying connected in today's digital age, even for seniors. From video calls with loved ones to social media platforms that provide a virtual social network, technology offers various ways for seniors to maintain relationships and engage with others. Embracing technology can bridge the gap between physical distance and help seniors stay connected with friends and family members far and near.

Technology plays a crucial role in bridging the social gap for seniors. Communication platforms such as video calls, social media, and messaging apps enable seniors to connect with loved ones regardless of geographic distance. Online communities and forums provide opportunities for seniors to meet like-minded individuals and build new relationships based on shared interests.

Quality vs Quantity in Social Relationships

As we grow older, the focus shifts from having a large social circle to nurturing quality relationships that bring genuine connection and support. Quality over quantity means investing time and energy in relationships that are meaningful, supportive, and fulfilling. These relationships provide a sense of belonging, emotional support, and companionship, enhancing overall wellbeing and happiness in our later years. Remember, it is not about the number of friends we have, but the depth of connection we share that truly matters.

Conclusion

The reduction of people in one's life as they age is a complex phenomenon shaped by various social, emotional, and psychological factors. While the diminishing number of relationships can provoke feelings of isolation and sadness, it is important to recognise that the nature and quality of these relationships often carry more significance than their sheer number. As we navigate the later stages of life, a renewed focus on cultivating deeper connections, engaging in community activities, and utilising technology can provide opportunities to counterbalance the inevitable reductions in social circles. Understanding the dynamics of ageing and relationships fosters a more profound appreciation for the bonds we share, reminding us that love, companionship, and emotional support transcend the mere quantity of friends and acquaintances, marking the essence of human experience.

That the older we are, the less the number of people in our lives captures a profound truth about the shifting landscape of social connections as people age. While the number of relationships may decrease, the depth and significance of those who endure can bring immense joy, companionship, and support in later life. By understanding the complexities of ageing and social networks, we can work towards fostering meaningful relationships that enrich our lives and contribute to a fulfilling journey through the golden years.

Although social networks tend to diminish as people grow older, it is important to recognise the value of maintaining relationships in ageing. By understanding the challenges seniors face and leveraging technology to sustain social connections, older individuals can combat loneliness and maintain a fulfilling social life. Through active engagement in activities, communication with loved ones, intergenerational interaction, and prioritising quality relationships, seniors can cultivate meaningful relationships that enhance their wellbeing and overall quality of life.

CHAPTER TWENTY-FIVE

WE NEED OTHER PEOPLE IN OUR LIVES

In an increasingly digital world, where technological advancements have reshaped the landscape of interpersonal interactions, life has taught me that we need other people in our lives, and this will remain so throughout life. Have you ever thought about how much you rely on other people in your day-to-day life? Even if you consider yourself to be self-sufficient and independent, the truth is that you will need other people in your life. From emotional support to practical help, human relationships are vital to our overall wellbeing and success.

In an era characterised by rapid technological advancements and an increasing emphasis on self-sufficiency, it is easy to romanticise the notion of independence. Individuals often aspire to be self-reliant, equating autonomy with strength and success. However, a critical examination of human social structures reveals that, regardless of how self-sufficient one may appear, the fundamental truth remains that people are an essential component of a well-rounded life. In this increasingly interconnected world, the value of human relationship cannot be overstated. Regardless of how self-sufficient we may strive to be, the reality remains that we all need other people in our lives.

This lesson explores the multidimensional nature of human interdependence, illustrating how our relationship with others enriches our experiences, facilitates personal growth, and bolsters resilience through life's many challenges. It also explores the profound importance of human interaction, delving into the biological and psychological foundations of social connection, the numerous benefits it offers, and the detrimental effects of isolation on mental health. From building support networks to striking a healthy balance between independence and interdependence, the following paragraphs shed light on the essential role that relationships play in our overall wellbeing.

Psychological Importance of Human Relationship

Human beings are inherently social creatures; the need for relationship is woven into the fabric of our biology and psychology. From infancy, the presence of caregivers provides the essential emotional support necessary for healthy psychological development. Renowned psychologist, John Bowlby's attachment theory highlights how strong emotional bonds formed in early childhood set a precedent for future relationships and influence mental health throughout life. Research supports this notion, indicating that individuals with robust social ties exhibit lower levels of anxiety and depression, report higher life satisfaction, and show resilience in the face of adversity.

The absence of meaningful relationships can lead to numerous psychological afflictions, including loneliness, a condition that has reached epidemic proportions, particularly in contemporary societies. Loneliness not only affects mental wellbeing but also manifests physically. Studies have shown that chronic loneliness can be as detrimental to health as smoking fifteen cigarettes a day, elevating risks of heart disease, stroke, and cognitive decline.

The Social Fabric and Community Cohesion

Beyond the individual psychological benefits, human relationships are the cornerstone of social structures and community cohesion. Social capital, a term popularised by sociologist, Robert Putnam, refers to the networks of relationships among people in a society that enable people to function effectively. Strong ties within communities foster trust, facilitate cooperation, and promote social cohesion, which are essential for addressing collective challenges ranging from public health crises to environmental sustainability.

In many societies, multicultural interactions can further enrich human relationships, bridging the gaps between different backgrounds and fostering understanding and empathy. Civic engagement, volunteerism, and social activism - often the result of strong community ties - exemplify how human relationships galvanise collective action for social good. The power of connection, therefore, extends beyond the individual and contributes to the broader societal framework, suggesting that a society strong in interpersonal ties is better equipped to tackle adversity and foster innovation.

Economic Implications of Social Networks

The economic benefits of human connection are equally compelling. Networks of trust and familiarity can facilitate trade, entrepreneurship, and innovation. Businesses thrive on relationships; the ability to forge connections can lead to meaningful collaborations, partnerships, and networking opportunities that drive economic growth. The role of mentorship, for instance, illustrates how human connection can positively impact professional journeys and economic mobility.

Moreover, companies increasingly recognise the value of cultivating a workplace culture that emphasises teamwork and collaboration among employees. Organisations that prioritise strong inter-team relationships not only enhance employee satisfaction but also improve productivity and job performance. The modern workforce, particularly among younger generations, increasingly demands environments that foster inclusivity and connection, where individuals feel valued and engaged.

Navigating Technology and Maintaining Human Bonds

The advent of digital communication tools has transformed how we connect with others. While technological innovations such as social media platforms, messaging applications, and video conferencing can facilitate connections over distances, they may also dilute the depth of interpersonal relationships. Studies suggest that digital interactions, while convenient, often lack the emotional richness of face-to-face encounters. Consequently, there is a pressing need to navigate the complexities posed by technology and ensure it complements rather than replaces human connection.

To mitigate the potentially detrimental effects of technology-mediated interaction, individuals and organisations must be intentional about fostering genuine connections. This involves prioritising in-person interactions whenever possible, practising active listening, and cultivating empathy in both personal and professional settings. Community initiatives - such as local gatherings, support groups, and collaborative projects - can serve as vital platforms for fostering authentic human connections in a digital age.

Why We Need People in Our Lives

1. Collaboration and Teamwork

No matter how skilled or knowledgeable we may be, there are always areas where we can benefit from working with others. Collaboration and teamwork are essential in both personal and professional settings. By pooling together different talents and strengths, we can achieve more significant results than we would on our own. When we collaborate with others, we can also learn from their experiences and expertise. This can help us grow personally and professionally, expanding our knowledge and skills in ways that would not be possible in isolation.

2. Building Relationships and Networks

Another critical aspect of why we need other people, no matter how self-sufficient we are, is the ability to build relationships and networks. Whether it is for personal friendships or professional connections, having a strong network of people around us can open numerous opportunities and possibilities. Networking is essential for career advancement, job opportunities, and personal growth. By forming genuine connections with others, we can create a network of people who can support us, provide guidance, and offer valuable advice when needed.

Building and nurturing relationships requires effort and intention. Whether through regular check-ins, shared activities, or open communication, investing time and energy into meaningful connections can create a strong support system that enriches our lives and helps us navigate challenges with a sense of belonging and resilience.

Support networks come in various forms, including family, friends, colleagues, and community groups. Each plays a unique role in providing different types of support, from emotional to practical assistance, ensuring a well-rounded network that meets diverse needs.

3. Recognising Interdependence

Recognising the interdependence between individuals is crucial. While self-sufficiency is admirable, the reality is that we are all interconnected in various ways. Whether it is through emotional support, collaboration, or networking, people play a fundamental role in our lives. So, the next time you find yourself believing that you do not need anyone's help or support, take a moment to reflect on the importance of human connections. Remember that no one is an island, and we all need people in our lives to thrive and succeed.

The Importance of Human Connection

Human connections are essential for various reasons. Firstly, a strong support system can provide us with emotional support during difficult times. When we have people in our lives who care about us and are there to listen to us, it can help reduce stress and improve our mental health. Human connections can also provide us with different perspectives and ideas. By surrounding ourselves with a diverse group of people, we can gain valuable insights that we may not have considered on our own. This can be especially beneficial when facing challenges or making important decisions.

It is imperative to recognise that self-sufficiency is often a myth perpetuated by societal norms that value individualism. While it is commendable to cultivate skills that promote personal autonomy, such as financial literacy, problem-solving capabilities, and emotional intelligence, such attributes are often bolstered through collective experiences. For instance, many of the achievements that individuals celebrate as products of their self-reliance are, in fact, the result of collaborative efforts involving mentors, peers, and communities. The shared pooling of knowledge, skills, and resources serves to amplify individual capacities, enabling people to reach heights they could not attain in isolation.

The complexities of contemporary life necessitate a collaborative approach to problem-solving. In our increasingly sophisticated world, challenges often transcend individual capabilities, demanding a confluence of perspectives and expertise. The COVID-19 pandemic served as a poignant illustration of this reality, as societies relied on collective action and cooperation to combat the global health crisis. The development of vaccines, the establishment of public health guidelines, and the coordination of emergency responses were all results of collaborative efforts among scientists, healthcare professionals, and policymakers. These examples underscore that self-sufficiency is not only impractical in many circumstances but also at odds with the collaborative nature of problem resolution.

It is also important to acknowledge that the strength of our connections with others enhances our capacity for empathy and philanthropy. Engaging with diverse perspectives and experiences fosters a deeper understanding of the human condition, encouraging individuals to cultivate a sense of responsibility towards others. This interconnectedness can inspire acts of kindness and solidarity, propelling communities towards collective wellbeing. In establishing support networks, we can contribute to a culture of reciprocity, wherein acts of generosity and compassion pave the way for mutual growth.

Despite the apparent value of human connection, the modern world frequently amplifies the allure of isolation. Digital technology, while providing avenues for communication, may paradoxically contribute to feelings of disconnection. Social media platforms can create an illusion of interaction while at the same time engendering a sense of loneliness, as online engagements often lack the depth and intimacy of face-to-face encounters. It is crucial, therefore, to consciously cultivate authentic relationships that transcend mere online interactions, as these bonds nourish our emotional and psychological health.

Biological Basis of Social Connection

In a world where we have evolved from relying on one another for survival, the need for social connection remains deeply ingrained in our biology. Research shows that social interaction triggers the release of oxytocin, the 'love hormone,' promoting feelings of trust and bonding.

Psychological Benefits of Human Interaction

At the heart of human existence lies the inherent need for social interaction. From an early age, humans are imbued with an intrinsic desire to connect with others, as evidenced by the importance placed on familial bonds, friendships, and community ties. Renowned psychologist, Abraham Maslow, articulated a hierarchy of needs that emphasises the significance of belonging and love as foundational elements for achieving self-actualisation. Regardless of how adept we are at managing solitude or navigating challenges independently, the absence of meaningful relationships can lead to a profound sense of isolation, detracting from our overall wellbeing.

Human interaction is like a workout for our brains, stimulating areas associated with empathy, problem-solving, and emotional regulation. It provides a sense of belonging, reduces stress, and enhances overall wellbeing by fostering a supportive environment for personal growth and resilience.

Benefits of Social Interaction

In addition to enriching our lives through shared experiences and collective problem-solving, human connections provide a robust support system that is crucial for emotional resilience. Life is fraught with uncertainties, ranging from personal challenges such as illness and loss to broader societal crises. During such tumultuous times, the presence of empathetic support from friends, family, and colleagues can make a profound difference in our ability to cope. Studies have consistently shown that social support is correlated with better mental health outcomes, as relationships help mitigate stress and foster a sense of belonging. The infusion of compassion, understanding, and encouragement from others can fortify our resolve, enabling us to confront adversity with renewed strength.

Engaging with others can boost our mood, increase feelings of happiness, and provide a sense of purpose. Sharing experiences, laughter, and even tears with someone can validate our emotions and make us feel understood and cared for. Socialising challenges our minds, from deciphering social cues to engaging in meaningful conversations. These mental exercises help sharpen our cognitive abilities, enhance memory retention, and reduce the risk of cognitive decline, leading to better overall brain health.

The Impact of Isolation on Mental Health

Isolation can take a toll on our mental health, leading to feelings of loneliness, depression, and anxiety. Prolonged isolation may also weaken our immune system, increase inflammation, and contribute to various health issues due to a lack of social support. Loneliness is not just a fleeting emotion but a significant risk factor for mental health disorders. Studies have shown a strong correlation between persistent loneliness and conditions like depression, substance abuse, and even cognitive decline in older adults, emphasising the detrimental impact of social isolation.

Conclusion

Human connection is indispensable, resonating throughout the domains of psychology, social structures, and economics. As the bedrock of individual wellbeing and societal progress, these connections provide solace and support during personal trials and contribute to the fabric of community life and economic stability. While technology has undoubtedly transformed the dynamics of our relationships, we must remain vigilant in nurturing the deep, meaningful relationships that sustain us. To thrive in both personal and collective spheres, we must commit to cultivating relationships grounded in authenticity, empathy, and mutual respect, recognising that it is through these connections that we can truly flourish as individuals and as a society.

It is evident that no matter how self-sufficient we may perceive ourselves to be, our intrinsic need for human connection is undeniable. From fostering emotional wellbeing to enhancing cognitive function, the benefits of social interaction are vast and impactful. By recognising the importance of building support networks and embracing both independence and interdependence, we can cultivate a fulfilling and enriched life that thrives on the power of human relationships.

While self-sufficiency is a commendable pursuit, it is essential to recognise that the fabric of human existence is woven from complex interdependencies. Our connections with others play a critical role in enhancing our lives, facilitating personal and communal growth, and providing vital emotional support in times of need. As we navigate the intricacies of modern life, it is incumbent upon us to foster and prioritise these relationships, acknowledging that our strength is often amplified when we embrace the inherent interconnectivity of human experience. Ultimately, recognising the indispensable role of people in our lives is a testament to our shared humanity, advocating for a society that values cooperation, empathy, and the bonds that unite us all.

CHAPTER TWENTY-SIX

SUCCESS IS A JOURNEY, NOT A DESTINATION

Success is a multifaceted concept that has been the subject of exploration, debate, and introspection for centuries. While many people often perceive success as a destination or an endpoint characterised by wealth, accolades, or recognition, a more profound understanding reveals that success is, in fact, a journey - a continuous and evolving process shaped by experiences, growth, and personal development.

Success is like that elusive bar of soap in the shower – everyone is trying to grab hold of it, but it is slippery and keeps sliding away. But what exactly is success? Is it all about money, fame, or power? This lesson seeks to explore the notion that success is a journey rather than a destination, examining the intricate dynamics of personal goals, the significance of resilience, and the importance of lifelong learning in the pursuit of success.

To begin with, the initial misconception that success can be captured within a singular achievement often limits our potential. People often establish narrow definitions of success based on societal standards, which usually emphasise tangible accomplishments. For instance, common markers of success include high-paying jobs, prestigious titles, or material wealth. However, such definitions are inherently reductive, as they overlook the broader spectrum of personal aspirations and the numerous factors contributing to an individual's sense of fulfilment. The pursuit of success should encompass a variety of personal and professional ambitions, which can evolve and change over time.

Consider the journey of a young graduate entering the workforce. This individual may visualise success as landing a specific high-paying job. However, upon entering the workforce, they may discover that personal satisfaction, work-life balance, the development of valuable skills, and the cultivation of meaningful relationships are equally important components of their success. The journey of self-discovery, professional development, and emotional intelligence gained through various experiences ultimately contributes to a deeper understanding of what success means to them. This evolving landscape reveals that equating success with a singular destination is a misguided approach; it is instead a continuous process defined by growth and self-awareness.

Moreover, the nature of success as a journey emphasises the importance of resilience in overcoming challenges and setbacks. The road to success is often fraught with hurdles such as failures, rejections, and disappointments. These obstacles can be disheartening, yet they serve as crucial learning experiences that shape character, foster determination, and build resilience.

Take, for instance, the life of Thomas Edison, whose path to inventing the light bulb was marked by thousands of failed attempts. Rather than viewing these failures as insurmountable setbacks, Edison embraced them as integral parts of his journey, famously stating, "I have not failed. I've just found 10,000 ways that won't work." The perspective that each setback is a learning opportunity empowers us to persevere and adjust our strategies, ultimately leading to greater resilience and ingenuity.

The journey of success fosters the cultivation of lifelong learning. The cultivation of knowledge and skills is an iterative process that never truly ends. In today's fast-paced and ever-changing world, the ability to adapt, learn, and grow is paramount. Successful individuals understand that a commitment to continuous learning - whether through formal education, professional development, or personal exploration - is fundamental to ongoing growth and achievement. This sentiment resonates in various fields, from technology to the arts, where innovation and creativity flourish through a sustained engagement with new ideas and practices.

Furthermore, the appreciation for success as a journey encroaches upon the aspect of enjoying each step along the way. Oftentimes, the continual chase for an endpoint can overshadow the beauty and significance of the processes and experiences that comprise that journey. The milestones, the relationships formed along the way, and the personal evolution that occurs during this pursuit hold intrinsic value. Celebrating these moments fosters a sense of gratitude and fulfilment, reinforcing the notion that success transcends mere accomplishments. It is about the lessons learnt, the connections made, and the person we become throughout the process.

Viewing success as a journey rather than a destination encourages a mindset that embraces rather than fears change. People who recognise that success is an ongoing process are more inclined to seek new opportunities and experiences, stepping outside their comfort zones to explore the unfamiliar. This adaptability not only enriches personal and professional lives but also fosters a greater sense of purpose and adventure in the pursuit of their goals. In this light, success becomes synonymous with exploration, experimentation, and the courage to evolve in alignment with one's values and aspirations.

Overcoming Challenges and Setbacks

Success, a concept often romanticised in contemporary society, is seldom a straightforward journey. It is characterised by a series of challenges and setbacks that test our resolve and determination. To truly understand success, we must recognise that it is not merely defined by the attainment of goals, but by the resilience demonstrated in overcoming obstacles encountered along the way.

Life's challenges can manifest in various forms - personal struggles, professional setbacks, or external circumstances beyond our control. Each setback presents a unique set of hurdles that can provoke self-doubt and frustration. However, it is precisely during these trying times that we are afforded the opportunity for growth and self-discovery. The ability to navigate through adversities is not merely an adjunct to success; rather, it is an integral component of it.

History is replete with examples of individuals who have faced significant obstacles yet have triumphed against the odds. To illustrate, one might consider the life of Thomas Edison, who famously encountered thousands of failed experiments before successfully inventing the light bulb. Edison's tenacity and unwavering spirit in the face of repeated failure highlight a critical lesson: setbacks are not definitive roadblocks but rather steppingstones towards achievement. Each failure provided Edison with invaluable insights that ultimately propelled him towards success.

Overcoming challenges fosters the development of crucial life skills such as problem-solving, adaptability, and resilience. Each challenge faced presents an opportunity to cultivate these skills, which are indispensable in both personal and professional contexts. For instance, an entrepreneur who faces a significant business failure must learn to assess what went wrong, adjust their strategies, and emerge from the experience with a renewed perspective. This capacity to adapt and evolve is what often distinguishes successful individuals from those who relinquish their aspirations in the face of adversity.

Moreover, setbacks can serve as a catalyst for motivation and inspiration. When confronted with a challenge, we may discover an inner strength we were previously unaware of, igniting a passionate drive to pursue our goals with renewed vigour. This is particularly evident in stories of those who have overcome personal hardships, such as athletes who rise from injuries or individuals who recover from significant life challenges. Their journeys resonate with many, serving as powerful reminders that resilience can lead to extraordinary outcomes.

The path to success is not a linear trajectory but rather a complex and often tumultuous journey marked by challenges and setbacks. The capacity to confront and overcome these difficulties is crucial in shaping our character and fostering personal growth. By embracing adversity as an inherent component of the success narrative, we can cultivate resilience, adaptability, and unwavering determination. Ultimately, it is through the trials of life that we learn to appreciate the sweet rewards of success.

Finding Meaning and Fulfilment in the Journey

In our contemporary society, the concept of success is often distilled into a narrow narrative dominated by wealth, prestige, and social standing. However, this restrictive interpretation overlooks the manifold nature of fulfilment and meaning inherent in the journey towards achievement. It is imperative to recognise that the pursuit of success comprises not only the attainment of specific goals but also the experiences, values, and lessons learnt along the way.

The journey to success is a combination of challenges, personal growth, and resilience. Each obstacle encountered serves as a lesson, providing opportunities for self-discovery and development. For example, many prominent figures have transformed their failures into steppingstones to success. J. K. Rowling, author of the *Harry Potter* series, faced numerous rejections before achieving international acclaim. Her experiences during these trying times were not merely setbacks; they fostered a profound understanding of perseverance and humility. This illustrates that fulfilment is often derived from the process of overcoming adversity, emphasising that the journey itself is laden with invaluable insights.

The relationships created during the pursuit of success play a crucial role in enhancing the significance of our journey. Collaborative efforts and networking serve to establish bonds that can provide emotional support, mentorship, and inspiration. For instance, entrepreneurs often build communities that encourage innovation and creativity. These relationships not only facilitate the exchange of ideas but also nurture a sense of belonging and shared purpose. Engaging with others fosters a collaborative spirit, prompting us to reflect on our aspirations and align our values with those of our peers. Consequently, the journey becomes a shared experience, amplifying its fulfilment through mutual motivation and encouragement.

The journey to success necessitates continuous self-reflection and realignment of our goals and values. As we navigate our paths, we often encounter shifting priorities and newly discovered passions. This dynamic process encourages adaptability and introspection, allowing us to reassess what true success means to us personally. For example, a corporation's pursuit of profit may lead its leaders to overlook the importance of ethical practices and social responsibility. However, through self-reflection prompted by public sentiment and personal values, they may redefine success to encompass a broader range of societal contributions, ultimately achieving both professional fulfilment and lasting impact.

Finding meaning in the journey to success often involves a deepening of our purpose. When we tie our ambitions to a higher cause or vision, we cultivate a profound sense of fulfilment that transcends mere material gains. People engaged in socially responsible endeavours, such as environmental conservation or community service, frequently report heightened satisfaction and clarity in their pursuits. The labour invested in fulfilling a purpose fosters resilience during trying times, as we are buoyed by a motivating mission. Thus, the pursuit of success becomes intertwined with the quest for contributing positively to society, creating a virtuous cycle of fulfilment.

Celebrating Milestones and Achievements

Success is a complex concept characterised by the attainment of goals and the realisation of aspirations. It is often perceived as the destination of a long and strenuous journey; however, the significance of milestones and achievements during this journey cannot be overstated. Celebrating these milestones serves not only as a means of acknowledging progress but also as a motivational tool that reinforces commitment and resilience.

Milestones, often defined as significant points of progress in the pursuit of a larger goal, act as markers that delineate the journey towards success. They provide us with an opportunity to pause and reflect on the various stages we have navigated, thereby facilitating a deeper understanding of the path taken. Reflecting on achievements - whether they are small or large - gives us a sense of accomplishment that underscores our efforts and dedication. This acknowledgement of progress is essential; it helps to cultivate an appreciation for the hard work invested and the skills developed along the way.

When we celebrate our milestones, we reinforce the narrative of our achievements, which can be instrumental in building self-efficacy and confidence. Moreover, celebrating achievements acts as a potent motivational tool. The journey to success is often fraught with challenges and setbacks, which can lead to feelings of discouragement or self-doubt. Recognising and celebrating milestones serves as a reminder of the progress made, reigniting the intrinsic motivation needed to persevere.

Psychologically, the act of celebration triggers positive emotions, reinforcing our determination to continue striving for our ultimate goals. Whether through personal reflections, shared celebrations with colleagues or friends, or the simple act of treating ourselves, these moments of recognition help sustain momentum. They transform the pursuit of success from a daunting task into a series of rewarding experiences, creating a positive feedback loop that encourages ongoing effort and commitment.

Acknowledging milestones can significantly enhance wellbeing, creating a sense of balance and fulfilment in the journey towards success. In a culture that often prioritises outcomes over processes, it is imperative to cultivate an appreciation for the journey itself. Celebration provides us with an opportunity to relish our experiences, connect with others, and celebrate not just the outcome, but the road travelled. This practice contributes to a holistic sense of achievement, promoting mental health and emotional resilience. By consciously recognising our successes, we can mitigate stress and anxiety, fostering a more positive outlook on our professional and personal lives.

The act of celebrating milestones and achievements along the path to success serves as a vital component of your journey. These celebrations enhance motivation, reinforce self-efficacy, and promote a sense of wellbeing, ultimately contributing to the sustained pursuit of our goals. As we strive for success, it is important to remember that each step of the journey deserves recognition. By valuing these moments, we acknowledge the hard work that has been invested and lay the groundwork for continued growth and achievement. Thus, celebrating milestones is not merely an act of recognition; it is, in fact, an essential strategy for ensuring success both in the present and in future endeavours.

Embracing the Journey Towards Success

Success is often regarded as a destination, a target to be achieved after overcoming various obstacles and challenges. However, a more insightful perspective reveals that success is not merely an endpoint; it is a journey replete with experiences that shape our character and define our aspirations. Embracing this journey entails recognising the importance of growth, the value of resilience, and the pursuit of lifelong learning.

The journey towards success fundamentally involves personal growth and self-discovery. It is through the process of striving towards our goals that we uncover our strengths and weaknesses. Each setback provides an opportunity for introspection, allowing us to analyse our reactions and adapt our strategies. The development of emotional intelligence, coupled with the understanding of our capabilities, emerges as a fundamental part of this process. As we navigate through challenges, we become more attuned to our passions and interests, thereby fostering a deeper understanding of what success truly means to us as individuals.

Moreover, resilience emerges as a core tenet of the journey towards success. The road is often fraught with uncertainty and adversity; setbacks and failures are inevitable. However, it is our ability to persevere in the face of such difficulties that ultimately defines our character. Resilience encourages us not merely to endure hardships but to learn from them, transforming obstacles into steppingstones. This proactive approach cultivates a growth mindset, enabling us to view failures as valuable lessons rather than insurmountable barriers. In this context, success becomes less about avoiding failure and more about developing the courage to rise again after a fall.

The journey towards success is intricately linked to the commitment to lifelong learning. In our ever-changing world, the knowledge and skills that once ensured success can quickly become outdated. Therefore, embracing the journey means cultivating a mindset that values continuous improvement and adaptation. This involves seeking new experiences, embracing challenges, and functioning in environments that encourage innovation and creativity. The willingness to learn - whether from mentors, peers, or even competitors - enriches our understanding and equips us with the tools necessary to navigate future obstacles. In essence, lifelong learning transforms the pursuit of success into a continuous cycle of development rather than a finite goal.

Embracing the journey towards success is a complex endeavour that encompasses personal growth, resilience, and lifelong learning. Recognising that success is not only about the achievement of specific goals but about the transformation one undergoes on the path towards those goals, alters our approach and attitude. By valuing the experiences gained along the way, we not only enrich our lives but also pave the way for sustained success and fulfilment. In a world that often emphasises results, it is essential to remember that the journey itself - filled with lessons, challenges, and growth - is what truly defines success.

Conclusion

The conception of success as a journey and not merely a destination provides a holistic perspective that encourages us to appreciate the ongoing process of achievement and personal growth. By redefining success in this way, we open ourselves to the many experiences that enrich our lives, cultivate resilience in the face of setbacks, embrace lifelong learning, and celebrate each milestone along the way. Success is not confined to a singular point in time but rather unfolds as a complex concept woven from the entirety of our experiences, aspirations, and growth. Adopting this perspective not only enhances our understanding of success but also empowers us to embark on our unique pathways with intention, curiosity, and enduring passion.

The journey to success is a rich tapestry woven from experiences, relationships, self-discovery, and purpose. By embracing this journey holistically, we can derive a profound sense of fulfilment and meaning that extends beyond conventional metrics of achievement. The resilience cultivated through challenges, the connections formed with others, and the alignment of your goals with a greater purpose collectively enrich the experience of pursuing success. Therefore, it is essential to approach the quest for success not merely as a destination but as a journey that merits recognition and appreciation.

CHAPTER TWENTY-SEVEN

THE ROAD TO SUCCESS IS NOT ALWAYS SMOOTH

Success is universally acknowledged as an objective sought by individuals across various domains - be it in careers, academics, or personal endeavours. However, life has taught me that the path to achieving success is often fraught with challenges, obstacles, and setbacks. Navigating the road to success is a journey filled with twists, turns, and unexpected obstacles. The path to achieving our goals is rarely straightforward, often presenting challenges that test our resolve and determination

This lesson explores the notion that the road to success is not always smooth by examining the inherent difficulties faced by individuals, the significance of resilience and perseverance, and the role of failure as a steppingstone towards eventual success. We will also explore the complexities of success and delve into the strategies and mindsets that can help individuals overcome hurdles along the way. By embracing failure as a steppingstone, cultivating resilience, seeking support, and celebrating small wins, we can learn to navigate the ups and downs of the journey towards our desired outcomes.

To understand the difficult journey towards success, it is imperative first to define what success means. Success is typically perceived as the accomplishment of an aim or purpose, and it can manifest in various forms, depending on individual aspirations. For some, success may be the attainment of a prestigious job or financial stability, while for others, it may involve personal growth, fulfilment, or making a meaningful contribution to society. Regardless of the definition, the challenges that aspiring individuals encounter on their quests are often remarkable and multifaceted.

One primary factor contributing to the difficulty of the journey to success is the presence of external obstacles. These obstacles can arise in the form of economic downturns, social inequalities, and institutional barriers. For instance, individuals from marginalised backgrounds may face systemic disadvantages that hinder their access to quality education and employment opportunities. In this context, societal structures can create a landscape that is particularly challenging to navigate, thus complicating the pursuit of success. Moreover, competition in various fields has escalated dramatically in the 21st century, with job markets becoming increasingly saturated. This heightened competition often forces individuals to work harder and smarter, thereby raising the stakes and intensifying the stress associated with the pursuit of success.

Another layer of complexity arises from internal struggles that we must confront on our paths. Psychological factors such as self-doubt, anxiety, and fear of failure, often plague those who are striving for success. The pressure to meet certain expectations - whether self-imposed or societal - can lead to mental health challenges that further complicate our trajectory towards achieving our goals. For example, students pursuing higher education may grapple with imposter syndrome, feeling unworthy of their achievements and questioning their capabilities. Such mental barriers can hinder progress, making the journey to success feel even more formidable.

In the face of these challenges, resilience and perseverance emerge as essential qualities for overcoming adversity. Resilience is the capacity to recover quickly from difficulties, while perseverance refers to the persistence in doing something despite facing obstacles. Individuals equipped with these traits are often better positioned to navigate the rough road to success. Historical figures such as Thomas Edison and J. K. Rowling serve as salient examples of how resilience can yield ultimate success. Edison's many failures in inventing the light bulb and Rowling's rejection by multiple publishers did not thwart their determination. Instead, their unwavering resolve in the face of setbacks ultimately led to groundbreaking achievements that changed the world.

Additionally, it is crucial to recognise that failure itself plays a key role in the journey towards success. Failure is often viewed negatively in contemporary culture, equated with inadequacy or defeat. However, it is important to re-contextualise failure as an integral part of the learning process. Each failure provides invaluable lessons and insights that contribute to personal growth, equipping us with the knowledge and experience necessary to pursue our goals more effectively. For instance, many entrepreneurs have faced multiple failures before achieving success with their ventures. These experiences often foster creativity, adaptability, and innovative problem-solving skills, which are essential attributes in an ever-evolving landscape.

The acknowledgement of failure as a steppingstone to success can foster a culture of growth and learning. In educational settings, promoting a growth mindset - where failures are seen as opportunities for improvement rather than setbacks - can empower students to embrace challenges and pursue their aspirations with greater confidence. Similarly, in workplaces, organisations that cultivate a culture of learning from failures can inspire employees to take risks and innovate without the fear of punitive consequences.

Overcoming Obstacles to Success

Success, often defined as the achievement of desired goals, is rarely an unobstructed journey. The path is typically fraught with obstacles that can hinder progress and test the resolve of individuals striving to reach their aspirations. However, overcoming these challenges is not merely a necessity; it is a vital component of the journey towards success.

Obstacles can manifest in various forms, including personal limitations, societal pressures, and unforeseen circumstances. For instance, an individual may face financial constraints that prevent access to education or professional development. Additionally, deeply embedded societal norms may discourage unconventional pursuits, fostering an environment where fear of failure stifles ambition. Furthermore, unforeseen events, such as economic downturns or health crises, can abruptly alter an individual's trajectory, intensifying feelings of uncertainty and discouragement. The ability to confront and surmount these obstacles distinguishes successful individuals from their less resilient counterparts.

Cultivating a mindset oriented towards growth is paramount. This approach encourages us to view challenges as opportunities for learning and development rather than insurmountable barriers. Embracing resilience and adaptability fosters an environment where we can experiment, fail, and ultimately forge a path towards success.

Building a support network is crucial in navigating obstacles. Encouragement from mentors, peers, or family can provide invaluable perspectives and motivation during challenging times. This communal aspect of success reinforces the notion that while the journey may be personal, the support and shared experiences of others can significantly facilitate overcoming hurdles.

The path to success is inevitably fraught with challenges, yet it is the manner these obstacles are addressed that ultimately defines our journey. By fostering a growth mindset and seeking support, we can transform potential setbacks into steppingstones, paving the way for achievement and fulfilment. The narrative of success is not only about the destination but rather the resilience demonstrated in overcoming the barriers encountered along the way.

Navigating the Challenges of Success

Success, often perceived as the pinnacle of achievement, brings with it a unique set of challenges that can complicate the very triumphs it celebrates. While the allure of success captivates many, it is imperative to understand that the journey does not end with our accomplishments; rather, it evolves into an intricate navigation of new obstacles and responsibilities.

The first challenge that people often encounter post-success is the pressure of expectations. With achievements come heightened scrutiny from peers, family, and society at large. This phenomenon, often termed the "success paradox," can lead to increased anxiety and a fear of failure. We may feel compelled to maintain or exceed our prior performance, resulting in a relentless pursuit of perfection that can overshadow the original joy of our achievements.

Success can strain personal relationships. As we ascend to greater heights, we may inadvertently alienate friends and family who perceive our success as a sign of change. This shift can create feelings of jealousy and resentment, complicating previously close bonds. Therefore, successful individuals need to remain grounded and cultivate empathy, ensuring that personal relationships are not sacrificed on the altar of accomplishment.

The landscape of success is often marred by the threat of complacency. After reaching a significant milestone, we may find comfort in the status quo, impeding further growth. The challenge lies in recognising that success is not a destination but a continuous process that demands resilience and adaptability. Successful individuals must strive to set new goals and embrace ongoing learning, fostering an innovative mindset that propels them beyond their current achievements.

While success is undoubtedly a commendable pursuit, it is accompanied by a host of challenges that necessitate careful navigation. By addressing the pressures of expectations, nurturing personal relationships, and cultivating a mindset geared towards continuous growth, we can transform these challenges into opportunities for further development. Ultimately, the true measure of success lies not only in the attainment of goals but in the ability to navigate the complexities that follow.

Failure as a Steppingstone to Success

In the pursuit of success, failure often occupies a paradoxical role, characterised by both stigma and potential. Society has long heralded success as the hallmark of achievement, yet it is essential to recognise that the path to success is often paved with setbacks and disappointments. Embracing failure is not merely an act of acceptance; it is a critical component of personal and professional development. Embracing failure nurtures resilience. Resilience refers to the capacity to withstand adversity and bounce back from setbacks. When we encounter failure, we are presented with an opportunity to reassess our goals, strategies, and motivations. This process of reflection can lead to a deeper understanding of our strengths and weaknesses, ultimately fortifying our ability to persevere in the face of future challenges.

Failure is a profound teacher, offering lessons that can only be learnt through experience. The process of navigating failure encourages critical thinking and problem-solving. We must analyse what went wrong, explore alternative solutions, and adjust our approaches accordingly. This learning capacity can be pivotal, as it fosters a mindset geared towards continuous improvement. Consider the story of J. K. Rowling whose initial manuscript of "Harry Potter" was rejected by multiple publishers. Rather than succumbing to defeat, she utilised the feedback from those "failures" to refine her work, ultimately leading to one of the most successful literary franchises in history. Such examples underscore the notion that failure, if embraced, can be transformed into a powerful catalyst for learning and growth.

Furthermore, failure can stimulate innovative thinking and creativity. In an environment where failure is stigmatised, people may become risk-averse, stifling creativity and the exploration of new ideas. Conversely, when failure is perceived as a normal part of the process, individuals are more likely to take calculated risks and experiment with unconventional solutions. The technology industry exemplifies this dynamic, where companies are often encouraged to adopt a "fail fast" mentality. This approach champions rapid prototyping and iterative development, allowing teams to innovate and improve based on real-world feedback. The willingness to embrace failure not only enhances creativity but also fosters a culture of collaboration and open-mindedness.

Embracing failure is an essential precursor to success. Through the cultivation of resilience, the acquisition of valuable lessons, and the encouragement of innovative thinking, failure becomes a transformative experience rather than a deterrent. As individuals and organisations strive towards their goals, it is imperative to recognise that setbacks are not the end of the road but rather steppingstones leading to greater achievements. By reconfiguring our perception of failure, we can harness its potential, thereby enriching our journey towards success. Embracing failure is not merely a strategy; it is a mindset that empowers and inspires progression in all facets of life.

The Power of Resilience and Persistence

In the pursuit of success, the road is often fraught with challenges, obstacles, and setbacks that can dissuade even the most determined individual. However, amidst these trials, two fundamental qualities - resilience and persistence - emerge as paramount in determining our ability to achieve our goals. These characteristics not only fortify us against adversity but also cultivate a mindset conducive to continuous growth and accomplishment.

Resilience, defined as the capacity to recover quickly from difficulties, embodies a mental toughness that allows individuals to navigate the unpredictable tides of life. Those who exhibit resilience are often characterised by their ability to maintain a positive outlook despite failures or setbacks. For instance, the story of Thomas Edison, who famously stated, "I have not failed. I've just found 10,000 ways that won't work," exemplifies resilience. Edison's pursuit of inventing the electric light bulb was marked by numerous challenges; however, his ability to rebound from failures and view them as learning experiences ultimately led to his monumental success. This capacity to adapt and thrive in the face of adversity is a hallmark of resilient individuals, enhancing not only their chances of achieving their goals but also shaping a robust character.

Complementing resilience is the quality of persistence, often described as the steadfast adherence to an objective despite encountering difficulties. It is the unwavering commitment to push forward, regardless of the potential for failure. The iconic figure of J. K. Rowling illustrates this aspect poignantly. Before the success of the *Harry Potter* series, Rowling faced a series of rejections from publishers and endured significant personal hardships. Yet, her persistence in refining her manuscript and her dedication to her craft eventually culminated in one of the best-selling book series in history. Rowling's journey underscores that success is often a function of enduring effort coupled with tenacity, illustrating that persistent effort can bridge the gap between aspiration and achievement.

The interplay between resilience and persistence forms a robust foundation for achieving success. Resilience provides us with the psychological tools to cope with and recover from setbacks, while persistence fuels the continuous effort required to pursue long-term objectives. Together, these qualities bring about a powerful synergy that empowers us to transform challenges into opportunities for growth. It is important to note that the cultivation of these traits is not an inherent trait but can be developed through intentional practice and reflection.

The broader implications of resilience and persistence extend beyond individual success. In a world increasingly marked by volatility and change, fostering these qualities within communities and organisations can lead to collective advancement and innovation. Organisations that nurture a culture of resilience and encourage persistent pursuit of their mission often outperform their counterparts, adapting swiftly to market changes and overcoming obstacles through cohesive teamwork and unwavering commitment.

The power of resilience and persistence in achieving success cannot be overstated. These qualities enable us to face challenges head-on and maintain our momentum despite the inevitable difficulties encountered along the journey. By embracing resilience and persistence, we not only enhance our prospects for success but also contribute to a collective ethos of perseverance and progress, paving the way for a future where the pursuit of excellence is indelibly marked by determination and unwavering resolve.

Learning from Setbacks and Adversity

Life is inherently fraught with challenges, and it is often through encountering setbacks and adversities that we develop resilience and gain profound insights. While the experience of facing difficulties can be painful and disheartening, it also presents invaluable opportunities for personal and professional growth. Embracing the lessons derived from these obstacles nurtures a robust character, fosters critical life skills, and ultimately paves the way for future success.

One of the most significant lessons learnt from adversity is the cultivation of resilience. Resilience is the ability to bounce back from setbacks, and it plays a crucial role in our capacity to cope with stress and navigate life's uncertainties. Research indicates that people who experience and overcome challenges tend to develop a stronger sense of self-efficacy and emotional stability. For example, athletes who endure injuries often emerge with a renewed sense of determination and an enhanced capacity to handle pressure. Through the process of rehabilitation, they not only strengthen their physical capabilities but also fortify their mental resilience, learning to overcome not just physical limitations but also psychological barriers.

Setbacks often serve as a catalyst for self-reflection and personal growth. When confronted with failure, we are compelled to examine our motivations, goals, and strategies. This introspective process can lead to a deeper understanding of our strengths and weaknesses, prompting us to refine our skills and improve our approaches. For instance, a student who performs poorly on an examination may discover faulty study habits or a lack of engagement with the material. This realisation can trigger a transformative journey towards adopting more effective learning strategies and fostering a growth mindsct - an essential attribute in both academic and professional environments.

Moreover, facing adversity tends to foster empathy and compassion. Individuals who have successfully navigated their turbulent experiences often develop a heightened sensitivity to the struggles of others. This empathetic understanding is crucial in cultivating meaningful relationships and contributes positively to community dynamics. For example, professionals who have experienced significant challenges are often more inclined to support their colleagues through difficult times, fostering an atmosphere of solidarity and collaboration in the workplace. This interconnectedness reinforces the notion that shared experiences of adversity can create stronger bonds and a more supportive environment.

In the broader context, societal progress commonly emerges from adversity. Historically, many social movements have been ignited by challenges faced by marginalised groups, leading to transformative change. The civil rights movement in the United States, for example, arose from the profound injustices and setbacks faced by African-Americans. The collective response to adversity galvanised individuals to come together, advocate for equality, and ultimately inspire legislative reforms. Such instances underscore that adversity can serve as a powerful motivator for action, catalysing change on both individual and collective levels.

Setbacks and adversity, while often painful and unwelcome, are integral to the human experience. The lessons derived from these challenges - resilience, self-reflection, empathy, and societal progress - are essential components of personal and communal growth. By embracing and learning from these experiences, we not only develop the tools necessary for overcoming future obstacles but also contribute to a richer and more compassionate society. Ultimately, it is through adversity that we uncover our true potential and capacity for profound change, both within ourselves and in the world around us.

Celebrating Small Wins and Milestones

In the relentless pursuit of goals and aspirations, we often overlook the significance of small victories and milestones. The relentless focus on large-scale achievements can obscure the recognition of incremental progress, which is, in fact, a vital component of personal and professional development. Celebrating small wins fosters a sense of achievement, cultivates motivation, and contributes to long-term success. It is imperative to understand the psychological and practical benefits of acknowledging these seemingly trivial milestones within any endeavour.

Recognition of small wins plays an essential role in maintaining motivation and momentum. In the context of long-term projects or challenging undertakings, the road to success can appear daunting and overwhelming. Frequent acknowledgement of small accomplishments creates a series of motivational boosts that encourage us to persevere. For instance, in a professional setting, an employee might accomplish a small project task that is a step towards a larger objective. By celebrating this achievement - whether through a simple acknowledgement from a manager or a self-reflective moment of pride - the individual is likely to experience renewed vigour and commitment to the overarching goal. This process reinforces a growth mindset, wherein individuals begin to see learning and progress as a continuous journey rather than a destination, thus empowering them to tackle further challenges.

Celebrating small milestones fosters a positive emotional environment. We are social beings, and recognition from peers and superiors can significantly impact our emotional wellbeing. Celebrating achievements, regardless of their size, can strengthen bonds within teams and promote a cooperative atmosphere. For example, organisations that engage in team celebrations for reaching small project milestones cultivate a culture of appreciation and acknowledgement, which can lead to elevated employee satisfaction and allegiance. These emotional rewards not only enhance individual morale but also contribute to collaborative synergy, ultimately paving the way for greater collective achievements.

Celebrating small wins can improve resilience in the face of adversity. In any pursuit, setbacks and obstacles are inevitable. Acknowledging and celebrating incremental victories provides a buffer against discouragement. When we embrace our progress, no matter how small, we develop a more robust emotional framework to deal with challenges. This positive reinforcement encourages us to approach difficulties with a proactive mindset, viewing them as opportunities for learning rather than insurmountable barriers.

The act of celebrating small wins and milestones is a cornerstone of personal and professional growth. By recognising and appreciating incremental achievements, we cultivate motivation and resilience, enhance emotional wellbeing, and contribute to a supportive atmosphere within teams and organisations. As we navigate our personal and professional journeys, it is critical to pause and acknowledge the steps taken along the way. In doing so, we not only honour our progress but also ignite the passion and determination that propel us towards our larger aspirations. Therefore, let us embrace the practice of celebrating small wins, for it is in these moments that we find the strength to continue striving for our goals.

Conclusion

The road to success is not always smooth, but it is the twists, turns, setbacks, and triumphs that shape us into the individuals we are meant to become. Embrace the challenges, seek support, learn from adversity, and celebrate every step forward. Success is not just a destination; it is a journey to be savoured and celebrated along the way.

As we reflect on the journey towards success, it becomes clear that it is not always smooth sailing. Embracing the inevitable setbacks and challenges, learning from failures, and persisting with determination are all integral parts of the process. By adopting a resilient mindset and seeking support when needed, we can navigate the road to success with confidence and determination. Remember, success is not just about reaching the destination, but also about embracing the growth and learning that comes from the journey itself.

CHAPTER TWENTY-EIGHT

Some People Don't Want You to Succeed

In the complexities of human relationships and societal interactions, the phenomenon of envy and resistance towards the success of others is a prevalent issue that has been observed across various cultures and communities. Life has taught me that the journey towards personal or professional achievement often unveils not only the support of allies but also the hindrances posed by those who, for a multitude of reasons, may not wish for someone to thrive. It is an unfortunate reality that some individuals harbour an intrinsic resistance to the success of others, motivated by envy, fear, or hatred. Understanding the underlying motives of these detractors is crucial for us to strive and achieve our goals, as it allows us to navigate our paths with resilience and clarity.

At the heart of this phenomenon lies the concept of envy. The human condition is marked by comparative analysis; individuals often evaluate their self-worth and achievements against those of their peers. This comparison can be both motivating and destructive, depending on one's mindset. For some, the success of others serves as an inspiration, propelling them towards their own aspirations. For others, witnessing a peer's accomplishments can evoke feelings of inadequacy and resentment. Such feelings can manifest in various ways, from passive-aggressive remarks to active sabotage. This reaction is rooted in a belief that one's success is diminished by the successes of others, a zero-sum mentality that fosters a toxic environment.

Fear plays a significant role in the dynamics of competition and the reluctance to see others succeed. This fear can stem from a variety of sources, including but not limited to, job insecurity, societal pressure, or the instinctual drive to maintain a social hierarchy. In professional settings, for example, an employee may feel threatened by a colleague who displays exceptional talent or ambition, fearing that their position may be jeopardised. This sense of vulnerability can prompt individuals to undermine their competitors subtly, either through gossip or through withholding support. Such behaviours are often masqueraded under the guise of self-preservation, highlighting a collective anxiety about the fragility of one's status in this competitive world.

Perception plays a key role in shaping the attitudes of those who prefer others to remain stagnant in their pursuits. While one person may view success as a collective advancement for a group, another may interpret it as a personal threat. In some circles, the prevailing attitude suggests that success is a limited resource, an immutable pie from which only a few can benefit. This scarcity mentality can breed hostility, causing individuals to resist the success of others even if such success does not detract from their potential achievements. Thus, for those who are inclined to see the world as zero-sum, success becomes a double-edged sword – a triumph for one that may be perceived as a loss for another. The implications of this resistance to success are profound, not only for the individuals targeted by detractors but also for the broader community and society at large.

When people are dissuaded from pursuing their ambitions due to the negative influences of others, the collective progress of society is stunted. Innovations go unexplored, talents remain dormant, and potential becomes wasted. This is particularly evident within workplace environments, educational institutions, and social networks where collaboration and mutual support are essential for growth. When the spectre of envy overshadows encouragement and teamwork, the foundational elements of a progressive society are jeopardised. In response to this reality, we need to cultivate resilience and a strong sense of self-worth.

Understanding that some individuals may not wish for our success is not only liberating but also empowering. This acknowledgement allows us to fortify ourselves against external negativity and focus on our journey. By surrounding ourselves with supportive and uplifting individuals, we can create an environment that fosters growth and collaboration, effectively countering the influences of detractors. Building a robust network of mentors, peers, and allies can encourage us to overcome obstacles and realise our goals.

Furthermore, fostering an inclusive mindset that celebrates the success of others can create a ripple effect, encouraging a culture of mutual upliftment. By actively promoting the successes and achievements of others, we can shift the narrative from that of competition to collaboration. This paradigm shift not only benefits the individual but also enhances the collective strength of a community or organisation, creating a positive environment where innovation and success thrive.

Understanding the Roots of Envy

Have you ever felt like someone is giving you the side-eye for your achievements? Envy might be lurking in the shadows. It stems from a mix of admiration and discontent. So, when your success shines brighter than theirs, envy can rear its ugly head. Sabotage is not just for spy movies. In real life, it can come from a place of insecurity or fear. When others feel threatened by your success, they may try to trip you up. It is like their way of saying, "I can't handle you doing better than I."

Ever had someone downplay your wins or give backhanded compliments? Those subtle digs could be signs of envy. Watch out for passive-aggressive behaviour and unsolicited criticisms – they are like red flags for hidden envy. Sabotage is not always blatant. It can sneak up in small ways, like "forgetting" to include you in important meetings or spreading rumours behind your back. Stay sharp for these sneaky tactics that aim to trip you up.

Building Resilience Against Criticism

When naysayers rain on your parade, build an umbrella of resilience. Remember, their negativity often stems from their insecurities. So let their words slide off you like water off a duck's back. Arm yourself with positivity armour. Focus on your strengths and achievements, and do not let anyone's negativity dull your shine. Keep your eyes on the prize, and let your success speak louder than their doubts.

Shielding Yourself from Detractors

When negativity knocks on your door, do not invite it in for breakfast. Set boundaries with toxic people who bring you down. Surround yourself with supportive people who lift you up instead of dragging you down. In a world full of critics, be your own biggest cheerleader. Practise self-care, celebrate your wins (no matter how small), and remind yourself of your worth. Your self-validation is a shield against the arrows of naysayers.

Conclusion

In an environment where success can breed jealousy and competition, it is crucial to remain steadfast in your pursuits and resilient in the face of detractors. By understanding the motivations behind negativity, recognising the signs of sabotage, and surrounding yourself with a supportive network, you can not only overcome the obstacles on your path but also emerge stronger and more determined than ever. Remember, the opinions of others should never define your worth or limit your potential. Stay focused, stay true to yourself, and let your success speak louder than any naysayer ever could.

CHAPTER TWENTY-NINE

INSIDE EVERY PROBLEM LIES AN OPPORTUNITY

In the complex and often tumultuous journey of life, we encounter many challenges, dilemmas, and adversities that can seem overwhelming and insurmountable. Problems, by their very nature, elicit frustration, disappointment, and a pervasive sense of helplessness. However, within the very fabric of these problems lie opportunities for growth, innovation, and transformation. Life has taught me that in a world filled with challenges and obstacles, it is easy to perceive problems as roadblocks to success. However, hidden within every difficulty lies a unique opportunity waiting to be unearthed. By shifting our perspective and embracing a growth mindset, we can transform seemingly insurmountable challenges into steppingstones for growth and success.

This lesson explores the philosophical and practical dimensions of the assertion that inside every problem lies an opportunity, emphasising the importance of perspective, resilience, and creativity in addressing the challenges we face in life. To understand the relationship between problems and opportunities, it is important first to recognise the subjective nature of problems themselves. A situation that one individual perceives as a problem may be viewed by another as a challenge, a chance for advancement, or an impetus for change. This divergence in perception underscores the importance of mindset in navigating life's obstacles.

Carol Dweck, a psychologist known for her work on the concept of a growth mindset, posits that individuals who embrace challenges as learning opportunities are more likely to achieve success and fulfilment. Thus, a fundamental tenet in transforming problems into opportunities is the cultivation of a mindset that encourages exploration, curiosity, and adaptability.

Historically, some of the most revolutionary advancements in human society have emerged in response to significant problems. Take, for instance, the global public health threat posed by infectious diseases. The emergence of the COVID-19 pandemic served as a catalyst for unparalleled scientific collaboration and innovation. Researchers and healthcare professionals across the globe united to develop vaccines in record time, an endeavour that would have seemed unfeasible before the crisis. The urgency created by the pandemic not only resulted in medical breakthroughs but also highlighted systemic challenges within healthcare systems, prompting calls for reform and greater investment in public health infrastructure. In this instance, what began as a devastating global crisis evolved into a profound opportunity for scientific advancement and societal reflection.

The concept of opportunity arising from adversity is not limited to grand-scale scenarios; it also resonates within the individual experience. Personal hardships, be they financial difficulties, health issues, or relationship crises, often serve as crucibles for personal growth and transformation. For example, an individual facing job loss may initially experience anxiety and insecurity; however, this situation could also present the impetus to pursue a long-held passion, engage in further education, or embark on entrepreneurial endeavours. Such transitions, while often uncomfortable, can lead to greater self-awareness, resilience, and an expanded skill set. The famous author, J. K. Rowling, for instance, wrote the first *Harry Potter* novel while experiencing significant personal difficulties, illustrating how challenges can lead to creative expression and success.

The ability to view challenges as opportunities also plays a crucial role in business and organisational contexts. In an ever-evolving economic landscape, companies often face disruptions - technological advancements, shifts in consumer behaviour, and unforeseen global events can all pose significant risks. However, astute leaders recognise that these disruptions can also usher in opportunities for innovation and competitive advantage. The rise in ecommerce is a prime example. Traditional brick-and-mortar retailers that were initially unscathed by digital transformation faced daunting threats, yet those who embraced technology and adapted their business models thrived. This adaptation often necessitates a willingness to take calculated risks, invest in new technologies, and consistently seek consumer feedback - strategies that stem from a proactive and opportunity-oriented approach.

In educational settings, the recognition of problems as opportunities can foster a culture of inquiry and experimentation. Students are more likely to engage deeply with their learning experiences when they are encouraged to approach challenges with a sense of curiosity and a willingness to fail. This mindset not only enhances critical thinking and problem-solving skills but also cultivates character traits such as perseverance and resilience. Educators who frame learning objectives in terms of overcoming challenges and solving real-world problems instil in their students the understanding that difficulties can lead to mastery and personal growth.

Nevertheless, it is essential to acknowledge that the transition from problem to opportunity is not always simple and may require significant effort, reflection, and support. Individuals and organisations may need to invest time and resources to navigate the complexities of their challenges effectively. Additionally, not every problem will yield immediate opportunities, nor will the paths to those opportunities always be clear or straight. Therefore, cultivating emotional intelligence, seeking mentorship, and fostering supportive networks become crucial components in the journey of transforming problems into opportunities.

Recognising Problems as Opportunities

In an ever-evolving world, challenges are an inherent aspect of the human experience. The conventional perception surrounding problems often tilts towards negativity, leading individuals and organisations to view them solely as obstacles to overcome. However, this narrow-minded view overlooks a fundamental truth: problems can serve as fertile ground for innovation and growth. Recognising problems as opportunities is not merely a philosophical stance; it is a pragmatic approach that can bring about change and foster resilience.

Problems often illuminate areas in need of improvement. When confronted with an issue, there exists the impetus to analyse the underlying causes and devise solutions. For instance, companies facing declining sales may reevaluate their marketing strategies, ultimately leading to enhanced customer engagement and product development. Thus, what initially presents as a setback can be transformed into a launching pad for strategic innovation.

The recognition of problems as opportunities cultivates a mindset geared towards adaptability. In times of crisis, those who can reframe their perspective are better equipped to explore alternative pathways. This adaptability is crucial in a landscape characterised by rapid technological advancements and shifting consumer behaviours. Organisations that embrace challenges as opportunities tend to foster a culture of creativity and collaboration, wherein diverse ideas can flourish.

The ability to view problems through a lens of opportunity not only encourages problem-solving but also builds resilience. Individuals and teams that engage with challenges constructively develop a robust skill set that encompasses critical thinking, collaboration, and perseverance. Such resilience is instrumental in navigating future adversities, as those equipped with the mindset to seize opportunities often emerge stronger and more competent.

Turning Problems into Possibilities

The ability to transform problems into possibilities has become essential for personal and societal advancement. This transformative approach fosters resilience and cultivates innovation. Embracing challenges as opportunities for growth can lead to remarkable outcomes in various spheres of life, including education, business, and individual development.

The educational sector exemplifies the potential for problem-solving to inspire creativity. Students often encounter academic challenges that may initially seem insurmountable. However, when educators frame these challenges as learning opportunities, students are encouraged to develop critical thinking skills and adaptive strategies. This shift in perspective allows learners to explore alternative solutions, ultimately enhancing their intellectual capabilities and preparing them for future uncertainties.

On a personal level, individuals are confronted with numerous challenges throughout their lives. The ability to reframe difficulties as opportunities for personal development can lead to increased resilience and self-efficacy. Those who adopt a growth mindset are more inclined to embrace adversity, viewing it as a chance to learn and evolve. Such an attitude enhances individual wellbeing and fosters a supportive community that values collaboration and collective problem-solving.

In the world of business, organisations often face obstacles that threaten their viability. Successful enterprises harness the power of problem-solving by viewing setbacks as steppingstones to survival and success. For instance, companies that analyse market demands and customer feedback can change their strategies to meet evolving needs. This dynamic approach mitigates risks and leads to the creation of new products and services, thereby driving economic growth.

The process of turning problems into possibilities is a vital skill that holds the potential to transform lives and organisations alike. By embracing challenges as opportunities for growth, society can foster a culture that prioritises resilience, innovation, and collaboration. As we navigate the complexities of the modern world, we must cultivate this mindset, ultimately paving the way for a brighter and more prosperous future.

Identifying Opportunities within Problems

In the realm of problem-solving, the ability to discern opportunities embedded within problems is a critical skill that can lead to innovative solutions and competitive advantages. Identifying these opportunities requires a strategic approach that encompasses analytical thinking, creativity, and a proactive mindset. Reframing the problem is a fundamental strategy that enables individuals to view problems from alternative perspectives.

By shifting the focus from the obstacles presented by a problem to the potential benefits that could arise, we can uncover fresh insights and solutions. For instance, when confronted with a market downturn, rather than perceiving it merely as a setback, businesses can consider it an opportunity to reassess their offerings, enhance customer engagement, or explore untapped markets.

Engaging in collaborative brainstorming can significantly enhance the identification of opportunities. Diverse teams bring varied experiences and viewpoints, fostering an environment where conventional thinking can be challenged. Group discussions can stimulate creativity and lead to innovative solutions that solitary reasoning might overlook. Such collaboration often results in a more comprehensive understanding of the problem and opens pathways to potential opportunities.

Employing a systematic approach to data analysis can illuminate trends and patterns that might indicate areas ripe for exploitation. By scrutinising customer feedback, market research, and competitive analyses, organisations can pinpoint gaps in the market or identify shifts in consumer behaviour that signal emerging opportunities. This data-driven methodology allows for informed decision-making that can strategically align an organisation's resources with market demands.

Maintaining a positive mindset is essential in the pursuit of opportunities within problems. A resilience-oriented approach enables individuals and organisations to remain agile and adaptive in the face of adversity. Embracing a culture of experimentation, where failure is viewed as a learning opportunity, can inspire innovation and empower teams to pursue unconventional solutions.

The identification of opportunities within problems is a multifaceted endeavour that combines reframing, collaboration, data analysis, and a positive mindset. By adopting these strategies, individuals and organisations can transform obstacles into avenues for growth and success, ultimately fostering a culture of innovation and resilience in an ever-evolving landscape.

Conclusion

The assertion that inside every problem lies an opportunity encapsulates a profound truth about human experience. Challenges, whether personal or collective, not only test our limits but also offer avenues for self-discovery, innovation, and growth. By adopting a proactive and open mindset, individuals and organisations can harness the potential embedded within problems, leading to transformative outcomes that enrich lives and advance society.

As we navigate the complexities of our world, it is essential to embrace the notion that adversity does not solely signify struggle; rather, it serves as a powerful impetus for exploration, progress, and ultimately, the realisation of new possibilities. In the words of the renowned physicist, Albert Einstein, "In the middle of every difficulty lies opportunity." Let us strive to embrace this perspective as we confront the multifaceted challenges that life presents.

CHAPTER THIRTY

You Are Not a Failure Until You Give Up

In the proverbial tapestry of life, the threads of success and failure are intricately woven together, creating a complex pattern that defines our human experience. It is a common belief that failure is an endpoint, a definitive moment that marks the conclusion of one's efforts or aspirations. However, this perception is fundamentally flawed. Life has taught me that you are not a failure unless you give up. This invites us to reconsider the nature of failure, resilience, and the indomitable human spirit. By examining the philosophical foundations of this statement, we can cultivate a deeper understanding of success and the importance of perseverance in our personal and collective journeys.

At the heart of this assertion lies the idea that failure is not an intrinsic condition or state of being; rather, it is a temporary setback on the path to achieving our goals. Failure, when viewed through a constructive lens, becomes a vital component of growth and learning. The most successful individuals in history - be they in the realms of science, art, politics, or sports - have often encountered failures that tested their resolve and commitment to their pursuits.

Embracing the notion that you are not a failure until you give up fosters resilience, which is an essential attribute in a world rife with challenges and uncertainties. Resilience is the ability to bounce back from adversity, to adapt to change, and to persist in the face of difficulty. This quality is critical for personal development and societal progress. When we refuse to concede defeat, we contribute to a culture of innovation and continuous improvement that benefits entire communities. For example, in the field of medicine, researchers regularly encounter setbacks in clinical trials and studies. However, it is their tenacity in pursuing answers that ultimately leads to groundbreaking treatments and cures. The collective human effort to overcome adversity is what drives society forwards, and in this context, the mindset that you are not a failure until you give up becomes a powerful motivator for collective and individual action.

The psychological dimensions of this statement warrant exploration. The fear of failure often paralyses individuals, leading to inaction and stagnation. This fear can be so overwhelming that it fuels a cycle of avoidance behaviour, where the prospect of failure outweighs the potential for success. However, when we redefine failure not as an outcome but as a part of the learning process, the psychological barrier dissolves. This reframing allows us to take calculated risks, explore new opportunities, and engage in endeavours that we might otherwise shy away from. By fostering an environment where failure is seen as a natural and acceptable aspect of growth, we can unleash our creativity and potential. It is in this space of courage and exploration that true innovation and achievement are born.

On a broader scale, the societal implications of the belief that you are not a failure until you give up are profound. In cultures that stigmatise failure, you may feel ostracised or humiliated when you do not achieve immediate success. This stigma can deter you from taking risks, pursuing your dreams, and contributing to the community, ultimately hindering societal advancement.

A culture that celebrates perseverance and resilience cultivates an atmosphere of encouragement and support. When you witness others overcoming difficulties and setbacks, you are inspired to adopt the same mindset. This communal approach to success and failure helps in the development of a resilient society where collaboration and support mechanisms thrive, empowering individuals to strive for their goals without the fear of being labelled as failures.

In the journey towards success, setbacks and failures are inevitable companions. However, it is not the missteps themselves that define our paths but rather how they are navigated and leveraged. In life, we are bound to face obstacles, setbacks, and failures that can make us question our abilities and worth. It is essential to understand that facing adversity is not a sign of failure, but rather an opportunity for growth and self-discovery.

By embracing challenges with a positive mindset and cultivating resilience, we can navigate through tough times and emerge stronger than before. Embracing failure as a steppingstone to success is a mindset shift that can lead to profound personal and professional growth. By understanding the psychology of learning from mistakes, cultivating resilience, and embracing a growth mindset, we can transform setbacks into opportunities for growth.

The Importance of Persistence and Resilience

Persistence and resilience are not just buzzwords but essential traits that can make all the difference in overcoming obstacles. Understanding the power of perseverance allows us to navigate tough times with determination and grit. Cultivating resilience in the face of failure helps us bounce back stronger and wiser than before. Resilience is like the superpower that helps us bounce back from failure with grace and determination. It is the ability to face adversity head-on, learn from our mistakes, and come back stronger than ever. By cultivating resilience, we can weather any storm that comes our way and emerge victorious on the other side.

Overcoming Setbacks and Challenges

Setting realistic goals and expectations lays the foundation for a successful journey towards overcoming setbacks. Developing problem-solving skills equips us with the tools needed to tackle obstacles head-on. By approaching challenges strategically, we can turn stumbling blocks into steppingstones towards progress. Reflecting on mistakes is like mining for gold in the rough terrain of failure. It is about taking a step back, analysing what went wrong, and extracting valuable lessons that can guide us towards future success. By being honest with ourselves and willing to learn from our missteps, we can turn setbacks into invaluable opportunities for growth.

Turning setbacks into opportunities is not just about wishful thinking – it is about rolling up our sleeves and getting down to business. By creating concrete action plans for improvement, we can turn our newfound knowledge and insights into tangible steps towards success. Whether it is setting specific goals, seeking out mentorship, or honing our skills, taking action is key to transforming failure into accomplishment.

Practical strategies for turning setbacks into opportunities include reflecting on the mistakes made, extracting key learnings, and creating action plans for improvement. Embracing challenges, celebrating small wins, and seeking feedback for continuous improvement are also effective tactics. By approaching setbacks with a solution-oriented mindset, we can transform obstacles into steppingstones for success.

Building Confidence through Trial and Error

We have all been there - the dreaded moment when a mistake rears its head, making us question our abilities and choices. Embracing challenges and taking calculated risks is the secret recipe to turning those stumbling blocks into steppingstones towards success. By facing obstacles head-on, we not only learn valuable lessons but also prove to ourselves that we have what it takes to navigate the ups and downs of our life's journey.

Cultivating a Growth Mindset for Success

A growth mindset is like a secret weapon in our arsenal for success. Embracing a positive and open attitude paves the way for endless possibilities and growth. Believing in our potential for personal development empowers us to seize opportunities, learn from failures, and continuously evolve into the best version of ourselves. Having a positive and adaptive mindset is like having a secret weapon in our arsenal against failure. It is all about staying open to new possibilities, adapting to change, and maintaining a sunny outlook even when things do not go as planned. By nurturing this mindset, we can turn setbacks into opportunities and keep moving forwards on our path to success.

Learning from mistakes is like studying for the ultimate life examination. It is not just about memorising the answers but truly understanding why things went wrong and how we can do better next time. By digging deep into our mistakes, we can uncover valuable insights that pave the way for future success. In the game of life, having a growth mindset is like having a cheat code for success. It is all about believing that our abilities can be developed through dedication and hard work, even in the face of setbacks. By embracing challenges and viewing failure as a temporary setback, we can keep our eyes on the prize and continue to grow and excel.

Learning from Failure and Building Resilience

When life gives you lemons, make lemonade – but do not forget to add some sugar and ice. Mistakes and missteps can be the ultimate teachers if we are willing to pay attention. Take a step back, analyse what went wrong, and extract the valuable lessons hidden in the mess. It is like finding a diamond in the rough, except the rough is your epic failure. Embrace the opportunity to learn and grow from your blunders because it is all part of the journey.

Failure is not the end of the road; it is more like a pothole you can fill with determination and resilience. Think of your failures as steppingstones that lead you closer to success – each stumble getting you one step closer to your goals. Embrace the idea that failure is not fatal; in fact, it is essential for growth. So, put on your hard hat, grab your tools, and start building your success story, one failure at a time.

Building a Support Network of Individuals

Life's journey is a little less rough when you have a team of cheerleaders in your corner. Surround yourself with people who lift you up, encourage you to keep going when the going gets tough, and most importantly, pass you the tissues when you need a good cry. Building a support network is like having your own personal pit crew, ready to fix your flat tyre of self-doubt and refuel your engine of motivation.

Utilising Professional Guidance and Resources

Sometimes, we need a little extra help to navigate the winding roads of personal growth. Seeking professional guidance and utilising available resources is like having a GPS for our soul – guiding us towards our destination with expert advice and support. Whether it is therapy, workshops, or self-help books, do not be afraid to tap into the wealth of resources available to help you become the best version of yourself.

Celebrating Progress and Small Wins

In a world that often focuses on the big wins, do not underestimate the power of celebrating the small victories along the way. Every step forwards, no matter how small, deserves a high-five or a victory dance. Acknowledge your achievements, pat yourself on the back, and bask in the glory of your progress. Remember, Rome was not built in a day, but each brick laid was cause for celebration. In the pursuit of success, it is easy to get caught up in the big picture and overlook the small victories along the way. By celebrating each milestone and progress made, no matter how insignificant it may seem, you acknowledge your hard work and dedication. These small wins pave the way for more significant achievements, boosting morale and keeping you motivated to keep pushing forwards. Remember, every step counts on the journey to success.

Embracing Failure as a Pathway to Success

Nobody gets excited about failing. By changing how we view failure, we can turn it from a dreaded foe to a trusted ally in our journey to greatness. Failure is like the tough love coach of personal growth. It pushes us out of our comfort zones, challenges us to do better, and ultimately helps us become stronger and more resilient individuals. Embracing failure means embracing the opportunity to learn, grow, and evolve into our best selves.

Embracing Challenges and Taking Risks

Stepping out of our comfort zones can be terrifying, but it is where the magic happens. Embracing challenges, whether big or small, prepares us to tackle the unexpected with grace and resilience. By taking calculated risks, we set ourselves up for growth and innovation, pushing boundaries and discovering new solutions. So go ahead, face that fear head-on, and watch as you emerge stronger and more confident on the other side.

Overcoming Fear of Failure and Taking Risks

The fear of failure can be paralysing, holding us back from pursuing our dreams and taking risks. But what if we flipped the script and saw failure as a valuable teacher rather than a cruel foe? By identifying and addressing our fear of failure, we can break free from its grip and embrace uncertainty with open arms. Stepping out of our comfort zones becomes not a daunting task but an exciting opportunity for growth and self-discovery.

Identifying and Addressing Fear of Failure

The fear of failure often stems from a deep-seated belief that making mistakes is a sign of weakness or incompetence. By recognising and challenging this mindset, we can reframe failure as a natural part of the learning process. Understanding that missteps are essential for growth allows us to face challenges with courage and resilience, paving the way for new opportunities and successes.

Overcoming the fear of failure involves reframing our perspective on mistakes and setbacks. By viewing failure as a natural part of the learning process and an opportunity for growth, we can diminish the fear associated with it. Adopting a growth mindset, focusing on lessons learnt rather than perceived shortcomings, and taking calculated risks can help in overcoming this fear.

Embracing Uncertainty

"Life begins at the end of our comfort zone" is a cliche, but undeniably true. Embracing uncertainty and venturing into the unknown not only expands our horizons but also strengthens our resilience in the face of adversity. By taking risks and stepping out of familiar territory, we open ourselves up to a world of possibilities and experiences, each one shaping us into a more confident and capable individual.

Leveraging Feedback for Improvement

Feedback is like a compass, guiding us towards improvement and growth. By receiving and processing constructive criticism with an open mind, we unlock valuable insights that help us hone our skills and performance. Implementing feedback is not just about making changes for the sake of it;

it is about actively seeking ways to enhance our capabilities and reach new heights of success through continuous improvement.

Feedback can be a powerful tool for continuous improvement when utilised effectively. To leverage feedback, it is important to be open to receiving constructive criticism, actively listen to feedback, and implement actionable suggestions for enhancement. By incorporating feedback into our development process and using it as a catalyst for growth, we can continuously refine our skills and performance.

Feedback without action is like a book left unread - it holds potential but remains untapped. By implementing feedback and incorporating suggestions into our practices, we actively work towards improving our performance and capabilities. Whether it is tweaking a strategy, refining a skill, or adjusting our approach, every bit of feedback we act upon brings us one step closer to achieving our goals and reaching new levels of success.

Receiving and Processing Constructive Criticism

Criticism can be tough to swallow, but when delivered constructively, it becomes a powerful tool for growth. By receiving feedback with an open mind and a willingness to learn, we can identify areas for improvement and make meaningful changes. Processing criticism with grace and humility allows us to see our blind spots and take actionable steps towards becoming the best version of ourselves.

Conclusion

The notion that you are not a failure until you give up encapsulates a powerful philosophy that underscores the importance of perseverance in the human experience. By reframing our understanding of failure as a temporary setback rather than a definitive end, we unlock the potential for growth, innovation, and success.

In a world characterised by challenges, we must foster an environment where obstacles are viewed as opportunities for learning rather than deterrents. Embracing this philosophy not only enhances our lives but also contributes to a more vibrant and dynamic society, primed for continuous advancement and infinite possibilities. Thus, as we navigate the complexities of life, let us remember that our true failures lie not in our setbacks but in our willingness to surrender.

The ability to learn from failures and setbacks is a crucial skill on the road to success. By reframing failures as valuable learning experiences, cultivating resilience, and embracing a growth mindset, we can not only bounce back stronger but also propel ourselves towards our goals.

Remember, it is not about avoiding failure but rather about how we choose to respond to it. By integrating the strategies discussed in this lesson and viewing failures as steppingstones, we can harness the power of mistakes to continuously progress and thrive in our endeavours.

Remember that you are not a failure until you give up. Every setback and challenge you face is an opportunity for learning and growth. By embracing a growth mindset, persisting in the face of adversity, and seeking support when needed, you can overcome any obstacle that comes your way. Celebrate your progress, no matter how small, and keep moving forwards with determination and resilience. With the right attitude and perseverance, success is always within reach.

CHAPTER THIRTY-ONE

MONEY DOES NOT SOLVE REAL PROBLEMS

The age-old adage that "money cannot buy happiness" serves as a fundamental truth that reflects the limitations of financial wealth in addressing the complexities of our existence. While monetary resources can undoubtedly facilitate access to various necessities and luxuries, it is essential to recognise that they do not fundamentally solve many of the underlying issues that challenge individuals and societies. In examining the multifaceted relationship between money and the resolution of real problems, we can discern that financial resources alone are insufficient to remedy issues related to emotional wellbeing, social justice, mental health, and environmental sustainability.

At the core of this lesson lies the distinction between superficial solutions and those that are meaningful and sustainable. Money can provide immediate relief or gratification – such as purchasing a new car, acquiring a larger home, or indulging in lavish vacations. However, these purchases often serve as mere distractions from deeper, more significant problems. For instance, an affluent individual may turn to material possessions to fill an emotional void, seeking validation or happiness in the consumption of goods. Yet, such attempts often yield ephemeral satisfaction, leading to a cycle of craving and dissatisfaction. The transient nature of material wealth underscores the fact that emotional and psychological issues cannot be rectified through financial means alone; instead, they require introspection, human connection, and often professional support.

The notion that money can address societal issues such as inequality, healthcare accessibility, and education is fraught with complexities. While financial investment is undoubtedly a critical component of systemic change, it alone cannot eradicate the root causes of these problems. For example, in societies marked by economic disparity, throwing money at issues such as public education or healthcare does not guarantee equitable access or outcomes. Investments must be paired with thoughtful policy reform, community engagement, and strategic planning to ensure that funds are utilised effectively, prioritising the urgency of social justice and the dismantling of systemic barriers. A blind injection of capital may temporarily alleviate symptoms of inequality but will fail to address the core structural problems that perpetuate discrimination and disenfranchisement.

Furthermore, mental health, increasingly recognised as a critical facet of overall wellbeing, exemplifies the limitations of monetary solutions. With rising awareness regarding mental health issues, a significant gap exists between the financial resources available for treatment and the actual efficacy of these resources in promoting holistic wellbeing. Just as money cannot buy happiness, it cannot provide a guaranteed solution for mental health conditions.

Accessing mental healthcare may be contingent on financial means, yet the therapeutic process itself is rooted in relationship-building, empathy, and understanding - elements that cannot be purchased. Individuals often find themselves grappling with feelings of loneliness or isolation that financial wealth cannot alleviate. Emotional support from family and friends, along with community networks, plays an essential role in fostering resilience and healing, demonstrating that interpersonal connections are key in addressing mental health challenges.

Seeking to address environmental crises through financial investments also reveals the inadequacies of money as a universal solution. Global environmental challenges, such as climate change and resource depletion, require more than capital; they demand systemic changes to habits, policies, and lifestyles. While substantial funding for renewable energy projects and conservation efforts is necessary, these investments must coincide with widespread societal commitment and action to transform consumer behaviours and governmental priorities.

When money is viewed as the sole remedy for environmental issues, the danger lies in the potential for 'greenwashing' - the practice of misleading consumers regarding the environmental benefits of a product or service. Substantively addressing ecological crises necessitates a cultural shift and collaborative action that transcends financial transactions.

That money does not solve real problems is substantiated through an exploration of emotional wellbeing, social justice, mental health, and environmental sustainability. The superficial allure of financial wealth can often blind individuals and societies to the deeper, systemic issues at play. While money can play a role in facilitating solutions and alleviating immediate hardships, it cannot replace the intricate, nuanced human experiences that contribute to the resolution of real problems.

Recognising and addressing the complexities of these challenges requires a holistic approach that values collaboration, compassion, and critical thinking over mere monetary transactions. Ultimately, sustainable improvement in individual and systemic health depends on our ability to forge meaningful relationships and engage deeply with the pressing issues at hand. In our collective pursuit of a better world, we must embrace this truth: that real problems demand more than money – they require meaning, compassion, and action rooted in shared values.

The Illusion of Money as a Solution

Money, with its shiny promises of fixing everything, often appears as a quick remedy to life's woes. The allure of financial solutions can be intoxicating, luring us into believing that more money equals fewer problems. However, beneath the surface, real problems are intricate webs of emotions, beliefs, and circumstances that money alone cannot untangle. From relationship dynamics to mental health challenges, the complexities of real problems run deep, requiring more than just a financial band-aid.

Unpacking the Layers of Personal Struggles

Personal challenges are like onions – they have layers. Peeling back these layers reveals a mix of past experiences, societal influences, and internal narratives that shape our struggles. To truly address personal challenges, we must delve beyond the surface and confront the root causes. External factors like financial instability or societal expectations often interact with internal beliefs and mindsets to create personal challenges. Understanding this interplay is key to navigating the complexities of our struggles and finding lasting solutions that go beyond just throwing money at the issue.

The Temporary Nature of Monetary Fixes

Money can offer temporary relief, but it rarely provides long-term solutions to deep-seated problems. The fleeting nature of monetary fixes highlights the importance of addressing root causes and building resilience that does not crumble at the first sign of financial strain. Societal pressures to equate success and happiness with financial wealth can warp our beliefs about money's ability to solve all problems. By recognising and challenging these ingrained beliefs, we can free ourselves from the illusion that money is the ultimate solution to our struggles. Our mindset shapes how we perceive and tackle challenges. Cultivating a growth mindset that embraces learning, and resilience can empower us to navigate complex problems with creativity and perseverance, regardless of our financial resources.

Developing Emotional Intelligence for Wellbeing

Emotional intelligence, which is the ability to understand and manage emotions effectively, is crucial for holistic wellbeing. By nurturing our emotional wellbeing, we can build inner strength, resilience, and problem-solving skills that transcend the limitations of monetary solutions.

Building Resilience and Coping Strategies

Life is a rollercoaster of ups and downs, and building resilience is like having a sturdy seatbelt. It is about bouncing back from setbacks, finding strength in adversity, and facing challenges head-on. Money cannot buy happiness but exploring non-monetary coping mechanisms can. Whether it is meditation, hobbies, exercise, or connecting with nature, finding what truly soothes our soul can be more valuable than any material possession.

Cultivating Meaningful Relationships

In the stormy seas of life, meaningful relationships act as anchors. They provide comfort, guidance, and a safe space to weather the toughest of times. Investing in relationships is a treasure trove of emotional wealth that can outshine any bank balance. In a world obsessed with status and superficial connections, nurturing authentic relationships is like watering a garden of emotional wellbeing. It is about quality over quantity, depth over shallowness, and genuine connections that light up our lives. Meaningful relationships provide crucial emotional support and connection during difficult times. Building strong bonds with others fosters a sense of belonging and community, contributing to our overall wellbeing and capacity to cope with adversity.

From Money to Holistic Wellbeing

Practical steps for shifting focus from money to holistic wellbeing include practising gratitude, developing emotional intelligence, engaging in self-care routines, and seeking personal growth opportunities. By prioritising these aspects, we can gradually shift our focus from monetary solutions to a more balanced and fulfilling approach to life's challenges.

Self-Discovery Beyond Financial Status

True wealth lies not in bank accounts but in the depths of self-discovery. It is about exploring who we are beyond material possessions, unravelling our passions, values, and dreams, and embracing the journey of personal growth with open arms. Just like a plant needs sunlight and water to thrive, personal growth requires dedication and nourishment. It is a lifelong journey of learning, evolving, and becoming the best version of ourselves, leading to a fulfilment that money can never buy.

Redefining Success Beyond Material Wealth

Success is not just a number in our bank balance or the car we drive. It is about the impact we make, the lives we touch, and the legacy we leave behind. Redefine success as a journey of growth, contribution, and making a difference in the world. Happiness is not a destination reached by a certain income level. It is a holistic blend of inner peace, meaningful relationships, personal growth, and living in alignment with our values. Embrace the journey of wellbeing, where true happiness transcends monetary measures.

Can Money Truly Solve All Our Problems?

While money can alleviate certain challenges, it often falls short of addressing the root causes of our struggles. True solutions require a deeper understanding of our emotional wellbeing, resilience, and relationships. Our mindset shapes how we perceive and approach challenges. By cultivating a positive and growth-oriented mindset, we can enhance our problem-solving abilities and navigate obstacles with resilience and clarity.

Conclusion

It is evident that while money may provide temporary relief, true solutions to our real problems lie in introspection, resilience, and meaningful relationships. By redefining our perspectives on success and happiness, and embracing personal growth beyond monetary measures, we can cultivate a life rich in fulfilment and authenticity. Always remember that money, though powerful, will never be the sole answer to our deepest challenges - it is our inner strength and emotional wealth that truly shape our journey towards a more meaningful and rewarding existence.

CHAPTER THIRTY-TWO

WORLDLY POSSESSIONS ARE WORTHLESS

In the complexity of human existence, the pursuit of material wealth has been a constant thread interwoven into the cultural, social, and economic fabrics of societies across the globe. The allure of worldly possessions is a powerful force that can shape individual identities, dictate social hierarchies, and even influence collective values. Nevertheless, an examination of the essence of these possessions reveals a stark reality: they are transient, ephemeral, and ultimately, hollow. The notion that worldly possessions are mere vanities is not merely a philosophical musing; it reflects a profound understanding of human nature, the limitations of material wealth, and the enduring significance of spiritual and emotional fulfilment.

Defining Worldly Possessions

Worldly possessions are the tangible goods and material wealth that we accumulate throughout our lives. Material possessions are simply the tangible things we own – from the clothes in our wardrobes to the car in our driveway. While they can bring comfort and convenience, they also play a significant role in shaping our identity and how we are perceived by others. But are they worth all the hype? In a world where social media likes and fancy cars reign supreme, material possessions have become the currency of social status. From designer handbags to the latest technology gadgets, it is easy to get caught up in the allure of owning shiny, new things.

At the heart of the argument against the value of worldly possessions lies the understanding of their inherent impermanence. Material goods can provide comfort and pleasure, yet this satisfaction is normally fleeting. The latest technological gadget, the most luxurious automobile, or the grandest mansion can quickly lose their lustre. Advertisements and societal pressures relentlessly promote the idea that happiness can be achieved through the acquisition of more possessions, creating an insatiable cycle of desire. As each new item is purchased, the fervour of satisfaction diminishes, leading individuals to seek the next acquisition in a never-ending quest. This cycle of consumption reminds us that worldly possessions, despite their immediate allure, ultimately fail to deliver lasting joy or contentment.

The attachment to material possessions often breeds a profound sense of insecurity. In our modern world, where success is often measured by one's possessions rather than character, individuals may find themselves trapped in a chronic state of comparison. The prevalence of social media aggravates this phenomenon, encouraging individuals to showcase their material wealth, leading to feelings of inadequacy among those who may not possess as much. This societal construction of value fosters an environment where self-worth is intrinsically linked to material possessions, resulting in a fragile foundation for personal identity. The irony is that the more one seeks validation through worldly possessions, the more one may feel empty and unfulfilled.

The obsession with material wealth can distract individuals from pursuits that offer genuine fulfilment. The time and energy devoted to accumulating goods could be redirected towards fostering relationships, engaging in meaningful work, or pursuing spiritual growth. The philosopher, Socrates, posited that a life examined is a life worth living, suggesting that introspection and personal development should be prioritised over the relentless pursuit of wealth. Indeed, many individuals who have experienced significant wealth ultimately express regret for the relationships lost and the personal growth stifled in their quest for material success. The stories of reformed billionaires, who have turned away from their previous lives of excess, serve as poignant reminders of the limitations of worldly possessions.

On a broader societal level, the relentless pursuit of material wealth has significant implications for the environment and global inequalities. The manufacturing and disposal of consumer goods contribute to environmental degradation, while the wealth gap between those who have and those who have not continues to widen. This disparity is, in part, a consequence of a cultural value system that prioritises consumption over sustainability and ethical considerations. The late environmentalist and author, Arne Naess, emphasised the significance of deep ecology, arguing for a shift in perspective that prioritises ecological wellbeing over material gain. Recognising the vanities of worldly possessions can be a critical step towards fostering a more equitable and sustainable world, one in which individuals value material wealth.

It is important to acknowledge that not all material possessions are inherently vanity. Some objects may carry significant sentimental value, serving as reminders of personal achievements or cherished memories. In this sense, it is not the possession itself that holds value but rather the emotional significance attached to it. Understanding this distinction can allow you to cultivate a healthier relationship with material goods, viewing them as tools for enriching life rather than sources of self-worth.

Chasing External Validation

Many people chase material wealth in the hopes that it will bring them validation and admiration from others. However, relying on external approval to feel good about ourselves can lead to a never-ending quest for more.

The Temporary Nature of Material Wealth

Worldly possessions are often deemed as vanity because they are temporary and do not provide lasting satisfaction or fulfilment. The pursuit of material goods can lead to a never-ending cycle of desire and consumption, ultimately leaving individuals feeling empty and disillusioned.

While it is easy to get swept up in the allure of material wealth, it is crucial to remember that possessions are fleeting and can disappear in an instant. Balancing the desire for material goods with the understanding of their transient nature involves practising mindful consumption, prioritising quality over quantity, and being intentional with purchases. Cultivating a sense of gratitude for what we already have and focusing on experiences and relationships can also help maintain a healthy perspective on the fleeting nature of possessions. Material wealth is subject to all sorts of risks – from market crashes to natural disasters. What we have today can easily be lost tomorrow, highlighting the impermanence of material possessions.

Impact of Economic Fluctuations

Economic fluctuations can have a significant impact on our material wealth. A booming economy might make us feel invincible, while a recession can quickly strip away our sense of security and abundance. Marketing and advertising play a huge role in promoting consumer culture and convincing us that we need more things to be happy. From influencer endorsements to flashy commercials, we are constantly bombarded with messages that urge us to buy, buy, and buy.

Social Comparison and Status Anxiety

Consumer culture breeds a sense of social comparison and status anxiety, where we measure our worth based on what we own compared to others. This constant comparison can lead to feelings of inadequacy and insecurity, perpetuating a cycle of consumption driven by the need to keep up appearances.

The True Value of Non-Material Wealth

In a world obsessed with material possessions, it is easy to overlook the true treasures in life - relationships and experiences. The joy of sharing moments with loved ones and creating memories that last a lifetime far outweighs the temporary happiness derived from material goods. Investing in personal growth and wellbeing is a valuable non-material wealth that can bring lasting fulfilment. Whether it is learning a new skill, cultivating a hobby, or focusing on self-care, these endeavours enrich our lives in ways possessions never can.

Cultivating Inner Contentment and Gratitude

Finding contentment and gratitude within ourselves can lead to a profound sense of fulfilment. By practising mindfulness and being present in the moment, we can appreciate the beauty of life's simple pleasures and cultivate a deeper sense of inner peace. Embracing minimalism and simplifying our lives can free us from the burden of excess possessions. By decluttering both our physical and mental space, we create room for what truly matters, allowing us to focus on experiences and relationships that bring genuine happiness.

Detaching From Worldly Possessions

It is easy to fall into the trap of equating our self-worth with the things we own. By letting go of this attachment to worldly possessions, we can begin to define ourselves by our values, actions, and relationships, leading to a more authentic sense of identity. Breaking free from the attachment to material goods involves a shift in mindset towards embracing minimalism, simplifying our lifestyle, and focusing on experiences rather than possessions. Practising gratitude, mindfulness, and self-reflection can also help us detach from the superficial allure of consumerism.

Practising generosity and philanthropy can provide a deeper sense of fulfilment than any material possession ever could. By sharing our resources with others in need, we not only contribute to the wellbeing of society but also cultivate a sense of purpose and interconnectedness beyond ourselves. As we navigate the complexities of a society driven by consumerism and the pursuit of material wealth, it is essential to remember that true fulfilment lies beyond the realm of possessions. By embracing gratitude, fostering meaningful relationships, and prioritising personal growth, we can discover a more profound and lasting sense of contentment. Let us strive to detach ourselves from the temporary allure of worldly possessions and instead focus on cultivating inner richness and genuine happiness that transcends material wealth.

Between Personal Growth and Inner Peace

As we shed the weight of material expectations, we create space for personal growth and inner peace to flourish. By shifting our focus from what we own to who we are, we unlock a sense of fulfilment that no amount of material possessions can match. It is time to redefine success and find joy in the simple things life has to offer.

The Cycle of Attachment and Discontentment

We have all been there - longing for the newest gadget or the trendiest fashion item, only to feel a fleeting sense of satisfaction before the next desire takes hold. This vicious cycle of attachment to material goods can lead to a constant feeling of discontentment, as we chase after possessions to fill a void that can never truly be satisfied by external means.

Breaking Free from the Clutches of Materialism

So, how do we break free from the clutches of materialism that keep us trapped in this cycle of craving and dissatisfaction? It starts with recognising that true fulfilment cannot be found in the accumulation of worldly wealth. By shifting our focus from external possessions to internal values and experiences, we can begin to loosen the grip that material goods have on our lives. It is completely possible to find happiness without relying on worldly possessions. True happiness stems from within, from cultivating meaningful relationships, pursuing personal growth, and living in alignment with our values and purpose. By seeking fulfilment beyond material wealth, we can discover a deeper sense of contentment and joy.

Embracing Minimalism and Simplicity

Minimalism is not just about decluttering our physical space; it is a philosophy that challenges the notion that more is always better. By embracing the idea that less can lead to more freedom, clarity, and contentment, we can learn to appreciate the beauty in simplicity and prioritise what truly matters in life. Ready to simplify your life and embrace a more minimalist mindset? Start by decluttering your space, focusing on quality over quantity when making purchases, and practising gratitude for what you already have. By consciously choosing to live with less, you can create space for what brings you true joy and fulfilment.

Finding Meaning Beyond Material Wealth

While material wealth can provide temporary comfort and convenience, true meaning and purpose come from cultivating inner wealth and spiritual growth. By connecting with our values, passions, and beliefs, we can find a deeper sense of fulfilment that transcends the fleeting satisfaction of material possessions. Embarking on the journey towards spiritual enrichment involves introspection, self-discovery, and a willingness to look beyond the surface level of life. By exploring practices such as meditation, mindfulness, and acts of kindness, we can nourish our souls and deepen our connection to something greater than we.

In a world that often equates success and happiness with external wealth and possessions, it is important to remember that true meaning and purpose lie beyond the realm of vanity. By breaking free from the cycle of attachment to material goods, embracing simplicity and minimalism, and cultivating inner wealth and spiritual growth, we can find a deeper and more enduring sense of fulfilment that transcends the temporary allure of worldly possessions. So, let us dare to prioritise what truly matters and seek meaning that lasts beyond the fleeting allure of vanity.

Conclusion

The lesson that worldly possessions are vanities presents a powerful critique of contemporary society's preoccupation with material wealth. As we navigate a world steeped in consumerism, it is essential to recognise the passing and ultimately unfulfilling nature of material acquisitions. The quest for happiness and meaning should be directed towards internal growth, relationships, and contributions to the greater good, rather than the relentless accumulation of goods. By transcending the allure of worldly possessions, we can forge a path towards a more fulfilling existence characterised by spiritual depth and genuine contentment. The challenge lies not merely in relinquishing material desires but in embracing a broader and more profound understanding of what it means to live a meaningful life.

The journey towards understanding the vanity of worldly possessions leads us to a profound realisation that true fulfilment and lasting happiness lie not in material wealth but in the richness of our inner selves and the depth of our relationship with God, our Maker, and fellow humans. By embracing minimalism, seeking spiritual growth, and detaching ourselves from the trappings of consumerism, we can find genuine meaning and purpose that transcends the superficial allure of possessions. Let us strive to cultivate a life guided by values that enrich our souls and contribute positively to the world around us, moving beyond the momentary illusions of vanity towards a more authentic and fulfilling existence.

CHAPTER THIRTY-THREE

OUR COMFORT ZONE IS OUR ENEMY

In an era where rapid technological advancements and an expanding global economy dictate the pace of personal and professional development, the concept of the "comfort zone" serves as a double-edged sword. On the one hand, the comfort zone represents a space of familiarity, safety, and stability, a psychological harbour that offers respite from the stormy seas of uncertainty and challenge. On the other hand, it can also be a deceptive chalice, luring individuals into a false sense of security that ultimately stifles growth and innovation. This lesson explores the multifaceted nature of the comfort zone, why it constitutes an enemy to personal and professional advancement and provides insight into the ways we can navigate beyond this seemingly benign threshold to achieve our fullest potential.

Introduction to Comfort Zones

We all have our safe spaces, the cosy corners of familiarity where life feels predictable and comfortable. But what happens when these zones of comfort start acting as barriers to our growth and potential? Comfort zones are like a well-worn pair of slippers – cosy, familiar, and inviting. They are the mental and emotional boundaries within which we feel safe, secure, and at ease. Stepping out of this zone can trigger feelings of discomfort, anxiety, and uncertainty.

To begin, it is essential to define what constitutes a comfort zone. In psychological terms, a comfort zone is a behavioural space where an individual feels at ease and in control. This zone is characterised by routines, predictable outcomes, and limited exposure to stress or discomfort. While the comfort zone can provide psychological safety and reinforce self-esteem, it is vitally important to recognise that the very elements that create comfort also serve to foster complacency. When we confine ourselves to our comfort zones, we forego the essential experiences that cultivate resilience, adaptability, and growth.

The first lesson to learn about the comfort zone is that it can inhibit personal growth. Growth, both personal and professional, often occurs outside the domain of comfort. Engaging in new experiences fosters learning; it challenges our existing paradigms and pushes us towards self-discovery. For instance, consider the educational journey of students - the most valuable lessons are learnt through challenges and failures rather than through passive participation. Students who embrace learning opportunities, even when uncomfortable, develop critical thinking and problem-solving skills that pave the way for future opportunities. Those who remain in their comfort zones may find themselves ill-prepared for real-world challenges, lacking the adaptability needed to thrive in new environments.

The professional landscape further exemplifies how a comfort zone can become a hindrance. In today's competitive job market, adaptability, and innovation are paramount. Organisations are continuously evolving, driven by technological innovations and shifts in consumer preferences. Professionals who resist stepping outside their comfort zones may soon find themselves obsolete, as their skills become outdated and their perspectives too narrow. A typical case can be seen in the technology sector, where employees are often required to master new software, platforms, or even entirely new skills to remain relevant. Those who embrace continuous learning and seek challenges are the ones who position themselves as leaders, whereas those who cling to their comfort zones risk stagnation and, ultimately, professional decline.

Beyond personal and professional growth, comfort zones can also have detrimental effects on interpersonal relationships and social skills. Social dynamics thrive on engagement, spontaneity, and genuine interactions. Individuals who confine themselves to familiar social circles may limit their ability to connect with diverse perspectives and ideas. For instance, forming relationships with people from different backgrounds can lead to enriching experiences and insights, broadening one's worldview. In contrast, an unwillingness to engage with unfamiliar people or environments often results in a narrowed viewpoint, inhibiting empathy and understanding - a necessity in our increasingly globalised society. Thus, the comfort zone can inadvertently foster isolation and intolerance, undermining interpersonal skills and limiting social resilience.

The question then arises: How can one effectively step beyond the comfort zone without succumbing to the anxiety that often accompanies change? The answer lies in a mindful approach to discomfort. Gradual exposure to new experiences, while setting tangible goals, can facilitate growth in manageable increments. Taking small, consistent steps towards unfamiliar territory - be it learning a new language, joining a public speaking group, or simply striking up conversations with new acquaintances - can significantly bolster confidence and resilience. Additionally, fostering a growth mindset, as advocated by psychologist, Carol Dweck, encourages individuals to view challenges and failures as opportunities for development rather than insurmountable obstacles. This transformative perspective allows for exploration and experimentation, essential components for breaking free from the confines of a comfort zone.

Furthermore, seeking mentors and forming accountability partnerships can provide the support necessary to navigate the discomfort associated with growth. Having a mentor can offer encouragement, provide insight, and serve as a sounding board for new ideas and ambitions. As individuals pursue their goals, the presence of another who supports their journey can make the process less daunting and more rewarding. Accountability partners can lend motivation and ensure commitment to stepping outside of familiar boundaries.

The Psychological Impact of Comfort Zones

Comfort zones can lull us into a false sense of security, preventing us from taking risks and exploring new possibilities. They can lead to complacency, fear of failure, and a reluctance to embrace change. Ultimately, comfort zones can hinder personal growth and keep us stuck in a state of stagnation. Comfort is soothing, but too much of it can turn into a trap, stifling our potential and limiting our horizons. When we stay within our comfort zone, we resist new challenges and experiences, leading to a lack of personal and professional growth. We become stagnant, like a pond without fresh water flowing in. Comfort zones act as invisible walls that confine us within a narrow range of possibilities. By staying within these boundaries, we miss out on valuable opportunities for learning, exploration, and self-discovery.

Benefits of Stepping Out of Our Comfort Zone

While stepping out of our comfort zones may feel daunting, the rewards that come with embracing discomfort are worth the leap of faith. Stepping out of our comfort zone challenges us to push our limits, face our fears, and embrace new experiences. This journey of self-discovery fosters personal growth, resilience, and a deeper understanding of our capabilities.

By expanding our comfort zone, we build resilience in the face of adversity and uncertainty. Each step taken outside our familiar territory boosts our confidence, empowering us to tackle challenges with courage and determination. Stepping out of our comfort zone is important because it allows us to grow, learn, and adapt to new situations. By pushing ourselves beyond familiar boundaries, we can discover new strengths, build resilience, and achieve personal development.

Breaking Out of Your Comfort Zone

Ready to break free from the clutches of your comfort zone? Here are some strategies to help you embrace discomfort and unlock your full potential. Start small by setting achievable goals that push you slightly outside your comfort zone. Whether it is learning a new skill, speaking in public, or trying a new hobby, gradual exposure to challenges can help you build confidence and resilience. Take small, incremental steps towards expanding your comfort zone. Engage in activities that make you slightly uncomfortable, and gradually increase the level of challenge as you grow more confident. Remember, progress is about embracing the discomfort, not avoiding it.

Overcoming Fear and Resistance

Fear can be a powerful force that holds us back from reaching our full potential. It often stems from a primal instinct to protect ourselves from perceived threats. By understanding the root of our fears, we can begin to challenge and overcome them. Overcoming the fear of stepping out of our comfort zone requires self-awareness, mindfulness, and gradual exposure to new experiences. By setting realistic goals, practising self-compassion, and embracing a growth mindset, we can gradually reduce fear and resistance to change.

Practising Mindfulness and Self-Compassion

Mindfulness allows us to observe our thoughts and emotions without judgment, helping us navigate discomfort with more clarity and compassion. Self-compassion reminds us that it is normal to feel fear and resistance and helps us approach challenges with kindness and understanding. A growth mindset thrives on challenges and sees failures as opportunities for growth. By embracing challenges and believing in our ability to learn and improve, we can push past our comfort zones and achieve personal growth.

Focusing on Learning and Adaptability

Embracing growth means prioritising learning and adapting to new situations. When we open ourselves up to new experiences and perspectives, we expand our comfort zones and become more resilient in the face of change.

Many successful individuals have credited their achievements to stepping outside their comfort zones. Whether it is taking on a new job, starting a business, or pursuing a passion, transformative experiences often come from embracing discomfort and uncertainty. Stepping beyond our comfort zone teaches us valuable lessons about resilience, courage, and personal growth. These experiences challenge us to push our boundaries, confront our fears, and discover our true potential.

Conclusion

The comfort zone, while enticing in its promise of safety and stability, ultimately serves as an enemy to both personal and professional growth and advancement. By inhibiting essential learning experiences, dulling adaptability, and stifling social interactions, we risk stagnation and a limited understanding of the world around us. However, through mindful engagement with discomfort and intentional efforts to expand our horizons, it is possible to transcend the limitations of the comfort zone. Embracing challenges, developing a growth mindset, and seeking supportive relationships are all vital steps in fostering a life marked by continuous growth, resilience, and fulfilment. Therefore, it is crucial to recognise that while comfort may be inviting, it is through discomfort and challenge that we transcend our limitations and discover the boundless potential that lies within us.

Stepping out of our comfort zone may feel daunting, but the rewards that come with embracing change and growth are immeasurable. By challenging ourselves, overcoming fear, and venturing into the unknown, we open up a world of possibilities and opportunities for self-discovery and transformation. Remember, our comfort zone may be familiar, but it is also where our greatest potential lies waiting to be unleashed. Embrace the discomfort, face your fears, and watch as you evolve into the best version of yourself.

Practical strategies for breaking out of your comfort zone include setting achievable goals, seeking support from friends or mentors, and focusing on the long-term benefits of growth and change. Taking small steps outside your comfort zone regularly can help you build confidence and expand your comfort zone over time.

CHAPTER THIRTY-FOUR

FORGIVENESS SETS THE OFFENDED FREE

Forgiveness is a complex concept that permeates various aspects of human life, deeply ingrained in personal relationships, societal norms, and even religious teachings. At its core, forgiveness is the conscious, deliberate decision to release feelings of resentment or vengeance towards a person or group that has offended us, regardless of whether they deserve forgiveness. While the act of forgiving is often perceived as an altruistic gesture directed towards the offender, numerous studies and philosophical discourses illustrate that it is the offended party who ultimately reaps the most substantial benefits. Thus, forgiveness can indeed be understood as a mechanism that liberates the offended by alleviating the burdens of anger, resentment, and emotional suffering.

The emotional toll of harbouring resentment cannot be overstated. When we are wronged, the natural inclination is to seek justice or revenge. Such feelings are often accompanied by a profound sense of hurt, betrayal, or injustice. However, nursing these emotions typically results in a cycle of negativity that not only hurts the perpetrator but significantly affects the victim's mental and physical wellbeing. Research from the field of psychology firmly establishes a link between the inability to forgive and various adverse health outcomes, such as heightened stress levels, anxiety, and depression. The burden of unforgiveness manifests in physiological reactions, which can lead to chronic conditions, further entrenching the cycle of suffering. In this light, choosing to forgive emerges not merely as a moral or ethical obligation but as a vital component of self-care.

The philosophical underpinnings of forgiveness suggest that it plays a fundamental role in promoting emotional resilience. When we choose to forgive, we often engage in a process of reflection and empathy, allowing ourselves to understand the context and potential motivations behind the offender's actions. This shift towards empathic understanding can be transformative, as it reframes the narrative of victimhood into one of personal agency and empowerment. By processing our grievances through the lens of forgiveness, we open the door to healing, enabling us to reclaim our emotional autonomy. This act of letting go may not signify a dismissal of the offence; rather, it denotes an acceptance and a conscious choice to refrain from allowing the past to dictate our future emotional state.

The act of forgiveness can foster healthier relationships. In interpersonal dynamics, grudges and unresolved conflicts often serve as barriers that inhibit open communication and intimacy. The willingness to forgive paves the way for dialogue, understanding, and deeper connections. When we extend forgiveness, it can create a ripple effect, encouraging the offender to also engage in reparative actions or seek forgiveness in return. This mutual exchange promotes a culture of understanding, compassion, and growth, transforming negative experiences into opportunities for relationship enhancement. The very act of forgiving can lay the foundation for rebuilding trust and refocusing emotional investments in more positive and constructive ways.

Culturally and religiously, many traditions emphasise the value of forgiveness as a pathway to peace. For instance, in Christianity, forgiveness is not just encouraged but is central to the teachings of Jesus Christ, who admonished His followers to forgive those who trespass against them. Such doctrine underscores the belief that forgiving others is essential for spiritual growth and personal salvation. Similarly, in many Eastern philosophies, the concept of releasing negative emotions aligns with achieving inner peace and enlightenment. These cultural paradigms collectively illustrate that forgiveness is not merely an individualistic endeavour; rather, it serves a larger communal purpose, contributing to societal harmony and emotional wellbeing.

Despite the innumerable benefits associated with forgiveness, it remains a complex endeavour. Many individuals grapple with the misconception that forgiving someone implies condoning their actions or absolving them of accountability. Forgiveness and accountability are not mutually exclusive. Forgiveness does not negate the severity of the wrongdoing; rather, it establishes a process wherein the offended party can move forwards without being perpetually tied to their pain. Recognising that forgiveness is a personal journey allows us to navigate our emotional landscape while safeguarding our wellbeing.

The Power of Forgiveness

Forgiveness is not just a gesture of kindness; it is a key to unlocking inner peace. By letting go of grudges and bitterness, we free ourselves from the emotional burdens that could weigh us down. Choosing forgiveness leads us on a journey towards tranquility and liberation from negativity. It allows us to release the past and embrace a brighter future. Forgiveness is not a sign of weakness but a courageous act of self-love and growth. It involves letting go of the need for revenge and choosing compassion instead.

Forgiveness is about releasing the emotional attachment to past hurts, not about excusing the behaviour that caused them. It is a decision to prioritise our peace over pain. Forgiveness impacts our mental and emotional wellbeing by reducing stress, improving mood, and fostering resilience. It is a transformative process that empowers us to heal from within.

Breaking Free from Resentment and Anger

Anger and hurt are not only bad for the people close to us but also for ourselves. We will never find true joy, inner peace, or happiness if we keep carrying and spreading hurt and anger. Let go of the toxic emotions and you will start to enjoy your life to the fullest. Forgive people for your sake. Harbouring resentment and anger only poisons our wellbeing. Forgiveness liberates us from these toxic emotions, granting us the freedom to move forwards with a lighter heart.

Benefits of Forgiveness

By embracing forgiveness, we not only lighten our emotional load but also pave the way for healthier relationships and a more fulfilling life. Forgiveness is a gift we give ourselves and not the offender. It leads to reduced anxiety, increased self-esteem, and a greater sense of inner peace, enhancing our overall mental health.

Forgiveness fosters empathy, understanding, and trust in our relationships. It allows us to break down walls of resentment and build bridges of connection with others. While forgiveness is a powerful tool for growth, it is not always easy. It requires facing difficult emotions and navigating the complexities of reconciliation, where necessary.

Dealing with Pain and Betrayal

Forgiving someone who has hurt us deeply can be daunting. It involves acknowledging our pain, processing our emotions, and choosing to let go, for our wellbeing. Reconciliation is a separate journey from forgiveness, requiring open communication, mutual understanding, and a willingness to rebuild trust. It is a delicate process that takes time, patience, and empathy.

Practising Self-Forgiveness

Forgiving ourselves can be tough, but it starts with showing ourselves some kindness. Treat yourself like you would treat a friend - with empathy and understanding. Remember, everyone makes mistakes, and you deserve forgiveness too. Let go of the heavy burden of guilt and shame. Holding onto these feelings only weighs you down. Acknowledge what you have done, learn from it, and then allow yourself to move forwards without carrying the weight of the past.

Cultivating a Forgiving Mindset

Empathy is key to forgiveness - put yourself in the other person's shoes. Understanding their perspective can help you see things in a new light and pave the way for forgiveness. Revenge and justice may feel satisfying for the moment, but true liberation comes from letting go of the desire for them. Focus on your healing and growth rather than seeking retribution.

Healing Through Forgiveness

Forgiveness is a powerful tool for inner peace. By letting go of resentment and anger, we create space for healing and tranquillity within ourselves. Through forgiveness, we can turn pain into an opportunity for growth and resilience. Embrace the lessons learnt from difficult experiences and use them to become stronger and more resilient.

Conclusion

Forgiveness is not just a gesture of kindness towards others, but a profound act of self-liberation and empowerment. By embracing forgiveness, we release ourselves from the chains of resentment and open the door to healing, compassion, and deeper connections with those around us. Letting go of past grievances allows us to step into a brighter future filled with peace, understanding, and a renewed sense of self. Embracing forgiveness truly sets us free to live more fully and authentically, enriching our lives in ways that extend far beyond the act itself.

The act of forgiveness emerges as a powerful tool for personal liberation and emotional resilience. While the ramifications of being offended can lead to a corrosive cycle of bitterness and despair, choosing to forgive offers a pathway to emotional health, deeper relationships, and a sense of peace. In both personal and collective contexts, forgiveness transcends the act of excusing wrongdoing, becoming instead a transformative process that champions healing, empathy, and personal agency. Ultimately, it is not only the offender who benefits from forgiveness, but more importantly, it is the offended who finds liberation in letting go.

The wisdom in the notion that forgiveness sets the offended free resonates profoundly, affirming that in forgiving others, we often set ourselves free.

CHAPTER THIRTY-FIVE

ATTITUDE IS EVERYTHING

In our complex human experience, the significance of attitude is a recurrent theme that resonates across various spheres of life. From personal relationships and professional endeavours to education and health, attitude serves as the foundational element that shapes our perceptions, interactions, and ultimately, our pathways to success. Our attitude can profoundly influence not only our quality of life but also the lives of those around us. It is often said that "attitude is everything," a phrase that summarises the essence of an optimistic outlook and the power of positive thinking. This lesson delves into the importance of attitude, exploring its profound impact on personal development, interpersonal relations, and professional achievement.

Defining Attitude

So, what exactly is attitude? Attitude can be defined as a person's predisposition or mental outlook towards something or someone. It reflects our beliefs, values, and perceptions. Attitude is not fixed; it can be changed and influenced by our experiences, environment, and personal choices. Ever had a bad day become worse because of a bad attitude? Attitude is not just a mindset; it is the highway our thoughts and emotions cruise on.

To begin, we must recognise that attitude fundamentally shapes our perceptions and thoughts. Psychologically, attitude can be defined as a mental and emotional entity that inheres in, or characterises a person; it embodies our beliefs, feelings, and behavioural tendencies towards a particular idea, object, or person. A positive attitude fosters resilience and adaptability. For instance, consider a student facing challenges in academic performance. A positive attitude enables them to view setbacks not as insurmountable obstacles but as opportunities for growth and learning. By cultivating a mindset that embraces challenges and persists despite difficulties, students are more likely to enhance their problem-solving skills and ultimately achieve academic success. A negative attitude can lead to a defeatist mindset, where individuals may feel overwhelmed by obstacles, leading to a cycle of failure and disengagement.

The influence of attitude extends into the realm of physical and mental health. Numerous studies have demonstrated a correlation between a positive attitude and improved health outcomes. People who cultivate an optimistic outlook tend to engage in healthier behaviours, such as regular exercise, balanced nutrition, and effective stress management. These behaviours contribute to not only enhanced physical wellbeing but also a more positive mental state. In stark contrast, those who harbour a negative attitude may succumb to stress-related health issues, contributing to chronic diseases such as hypertension and depression. The mind-body connection is irrefutable; a positive attitude can indeed serve as a catalyst for healthier living, demonstrating once again that attitude is a powerful force in determining our overall quality of life.

Interpersonal relationships are another field where attitude plays a crucial role. How we perceive ourselves and others influences our interactions, shaping relationships in both personal and professional contexts. An individual with a positive attitude is likely to exude warmth, encouragement, and support, thereby attracting similarly positive individuals into their lives. This creates a reinforcing cycle of positivity that enhances social connections and fosters a sense of community. In professional settings, a positive attitude can significantly impact teamwork and collaboration. Leaders who embody an optimistic outlook inspire their teams, fostering an environment of innovation and trust. This, in turn, enhances collective motivation and productivity, as employees feel valued and empowered to contribute their ideas. On the contrary, a negative attitude can create toxicity in relationships, leading to misunderstandings, conflicts, and a breakdown of communication.

Furthermore, attitude profoundly influences professional achievement and career advancement. Employers consistently seek individuals who demonstrate a positive, proactive approach to challenges. Such individuals are not only more likely to take initiative but also more capable of overcoming setbacks and contributing to a constructive workplace culture. Job seekers with a can-do attitude often stand out during interviews, as their enthusiasm and motivation resonate with prospective employers. A positive attitude enables professionals to navigate the complexities of workplace dynamics with grace and resilience. They tend to maintain a solution-oriented mindset, emphasising opportunities rather than limitations, which can position them favourably within their organisations.

It is important to acknowledge that cultivating a positive attitude is not merely a simplistic or superficial endeavour. It involves conscious effort and a commitment to self-reflection and personal growth. To foster a better attitude, we can engage in practices such as gratitude, journaling, mindfulness, and positive affirmations. These practices encourage us to recognise and appreciate the good in our lives while also challenging negative thought patterns that can hinder personal development. It takes discipline and determination to maintain a positive perspective, particularly in times of adversity, yet the rewards are plentiful.

Impact of Attitude on Behaviour

Our attitude is like a magic wand that can shape our actions. A positive attitude can turn mountains into molehills, while a negative one can turn a picnic into a storm. The impact of attitude on behaviour is profound. Our attitude shapes how we approach and respond to different situations. A positive attitude can lead to positive actions, while a negative attitude can hinder progress and sabotage our efforts. Understanding this impact can empower us to consciously choose the attitude we want to adopt in any given situation.

Emotional and Mental Wellbeing

Our attitude is the captain of our emotional ship. A sunny disposition can bring calm seas, while a stormy outlook can lead to choppy waters. Moreover, attitude plays a crucial role in our emotional and mental wellbeing. A positive attitude can enhance our overall mood, increase resilience, and reduce stress. On the other hand, a negative attitude can contribute to feelings of frustration, anger, and anxiety. By cultivating a positive attitude, we can improve our mental health and create a more balanced and fulfilling life.

Relationships and Interactions

Attitude is the secret sauce in our social recipes. A positive one can make friendships flourish, while a negative one can sour even the sweetest interactions. Attitude also significantly influences our relationships and interactions with others. A positive attitude can attract people, foster meaningful connections, and create a supportive environment. A negative attitude can repel others and lead to conflicts and misunderstandings. Developing a positive attitude can improve our interpersonal skills, empathy, and communication, enhancing the quality of our relationships.

Cultivating a Positive Attitude

Cultivating a positive attitude requires conscious effort and practice. One effective way is through gratitude and mindfulness. Taking time each day to appreciate the things we are grateful for and being present in the moment can shift our focus towards the positive aspects of life. This practice can change how we perceive situations and contribute to a more positive attitude.

Setting Positive Intentions and Affirmations

Think of positive intentions and affirmations as the GPS for your attitude. They can guide you towards a brighter outlook, even when you are stuck in traffic. Setting positive intentions and affirmations is another technique to cultivate a positive attitude. By stating positive beliefs and goals, we can train our minds to think positively and focus on our strengths. Affirmations help reprogramme our subconscious mind, replacing negative thoughts and beliefs with positive ones, leading to a more positive attitude.

Overcoming Negative Attitudes

Overcoming negative attitudes requires identifying and challenging negative thoughts. By becoming aware of our negative thinking patterns, we can question their validity and replace them with more positive and constructive thoughts. This cognitive restructuring can transform our attitude and lead to more positive outcomes. Negative thoughts are like weeds in our attitude garden. By recognising and uprooting them, we can make room for positivity to bloom. When life gives you lemons, make lemonade or perhaps a lemon-scented bubble bath. Shifting our perspective can turn a sour attitude into a sweet one.

Attitude in Personal and Professional Growth

Attitude can make or break our journey to personal and professional growth. Whether we are tackling a new project at work or facing a challenging situation in our personal life, having a positive attitude can make all the difference. Embracing a can-do attitude and staying resilient in the face of obstacles can propel us towards success. Attitude also plays a crucial role in personal and professional growth. It affects how we approach challenges, setbacks, and growth opportunities. By adapting our attitude in different contexts, we can optimise our performance and make the most of any situation. Using attitude as a tool for progress allows us to develop a growth mindset, embrace learning, and seek continuous improvement.

Adapting Attitude in Different Contexts

Just like a chameleon changes colours to blend into its surroundings, adapting our attitude to different contexts is key to thriving in diverse situations. Being able to switch between a determined mindset for work projects and a supportive attitude in personal relationships showcases our versatility and emotional intelligence.

Using Attitude as a Tool for Progress

Our attitude is like a *Swiss Army knife* in our personal and professional toolkit. By harnessing a positive attitude, we can navigate challenges with grace, inspire the people around us, and pave the way for progress. Viewing setbacks as opportunities for growth and maintaining a can-do spirit can turn obstacles into steppingstones towards success.

Shifting Perspectives and Mindsets

In the game of personal and professional development, shifting perspectives and mindsets can be our secret weapons. Embracing a growth mindset means seeing failures as opportunities to learn and grow; while cultivating resilience through attitude helps us bounce back stronger from setbacks. Embracing a growth mindset opens doors to endless possibilities. Instead of viewing our abilities as fixed traits, we see them as areas ripe for improvement. By believing in our capacity to learn and grow, we set ourselves up for continuous growth and success.

Cultivating Resilience through Attitude

Life throws curveballs, but our attitude determines how we swing at them. Cultivating resilience through attitude means bouncing back from challenges with grace and determination. By reframing setbacks as temporary roadblocks and maintaining a positive outlook, we can emerge stronger and more resilient than ever. Cultivating resilience through attitude is another powerful strategy for personal and professional growth. A positive attitude enables us to bounce back from setbacks, adapt to change, and persevere in the face of challenges. By maintaining a resilient attitude, we can overcome obstacles and achieve success in our endeavours.

Harnessing Attitude for Success

Attitude is not just a passenger on the road to success – it is the driver. By harnessing a positive, success-oriented attitude, we can steer our journey towards achievement and fulfilment. Developing a mindset focused on success paves the way for reaching our goals and turning our dreams into reality. Harnessing an attitude towards success involves developing a success-oriented attitude. By believing in our abilities, setting clear goals, and adopting a proactive approach, we can increase our chances of achieving our desired outcomes. Attitude acts as a driving force, fuelling our motivation, and propelling us towards success.

Attitude as a Driver of Achievement

Our attitude shapes our actions, and our actions drive our achievements. By cultivating a mindset that believes in your capabilities and stays focused on success, you set yourself up to reach new heights. Let your attitude steer you towards greatness and watch your accomplishments soar. Success is not just about what we do – it is about how we approach it. Developing a success-oriented attitude means setting clear goals, staying motivated in the face of challenges, and believing in our ability to triumph. By aligning our mindset with success, we create a roadmap towards achieving our aspirations with confidence and determination.

Conclusion

That attitude is everything underscores a profound truth about human experience. Our attitudes shape our perceptions, influence our behaviours, and ultimately determine the trajectory of our lives. With a positive attitude, we can cultivate resilience, sustain healthy relationships, and achieve our professional goals. The journey towards a more positive mindset is not without its challenges, but the potential for growth and transformation is vast.

In a world that often presents obstacles and adversities, embracing a positive attitude becomes an empowering tool that not only enhances our lives but also contributes to the wellbeing of those around us. By recognising the power that attitude holds, we can consciously choose to foster positivity, enriching our lives and the lives of others in the process. It is indeed true that attitude is everything – the cornerstone of personal success, professional achievement, and harmonious relationships.

Attitude truly is everything. By harnessing the power of a positive mindset, we can overcome obstacles, foster meaningful relationships, and pave the way for personal and professional growth. It is within our control to shape our attitude and embrace a mindset that propels us towards success and fulfilment. Remember that our attitude not only determines our actions but also shapes our reality, making it a vital ingredient in the recipe for a thriving and joyful life.

Attitude is a key determinant of human behaviour, emotions, and relationships. By cultivating a positive attitude, practising gratitude and mindfulness, overcoming negative attitudes, and harnessing attitudes for success, we can shape our lives in a meaningful and fulfilling way. With the right attitude, the possibilities are limitless, and success becomes within reach. So, choose your attitude wisely and watch as it transforms your life.

CHAPTER THIRTY-SIX

SAVING MONEY DOES NOT CREATE WEALTH, INVESTING MONEY DOES

In present-day discourse surrounding personal finance, the concepts of saving and investing are often intertwined, yet they represent fundamentally distinct approaches to financial management. While saving money is undeniably important, it is the act of investing that serves as a vehicle for wealth creation. This lesson will explain the intrinsic differences between saving and investing, explore how investments can appreciate over time, and delineate the risks and rewards associated with each approach. Ultimately, it will become apparent that while saving is a necessary precursor to financial stability, investing is the cornerstone of wealth accumulation.

To commence the discussion, it is essential to define what constitutes saving and investing. Saving typically refers to the act of setting aside a portion of one's income for future use, often held in conventional bank accounts or safes. This practice is primarily oriented towards immediate accessibility and serves as a safety net for unforeseen expenses or emergencies. The act of saving is characterised by its relatively low-risk nature, and individuals often seek to build an emergency fund or a cushion for major purchases. In contrast, investing involves the allocation of capital into vehicles such as stocks, bonds, real estate, or mutual funds to generate returns over time. Investors assume a higher level of risk, with the potential for substantial rewards, as the value of investments can appreciate significantly beyond the initial capital.

It is crucial to acknowledge the limited role saving plays in wealth generation. While having a savings account is vital for financial security and liquidity, the actual rate of return on savings accounts – typically modest and often just above or below inflation – does not provide a meaningful avenue for wealth accumulation. For instance, traditional savings accounts may offer interest rates that scarcely keep pace with inflation, effectively leading to a decrease in purchasing power over time. Consequently, funds preserved in a savings account may yield a certain level of financial safety, but they fall short of creating wealth in any substantial sense.

In stark contrast, investing presents the possibility of significant financial growth through the power of compound interest, capital appreciation, and dividend income. The principle of compound interest demonstrates how returns on investments can exponentially increase wealth over time. When individuals invest in assets such as stocks or mutual funds, they not only gain returns on their capital but also earn returns on their previously accumulated returns, leading to a virtuous cycle of growth. Historical data affirms that, over prolonged periods, the stock market can yield average substantial returns for investors.

Investing enables us to diversify our financial portfolios, thereby mitigating risk and optimising returns. By allocating funds across various asset classes, such as equities, fixed-income securities, and real estate, we can cushion ourselves against market volatility and economic downturns. This aspect of investing not only enhances the likelihood of positive returns but also provides a more robust mechanism for wealth accumulation. The diversification of investments is a strategy underscored by financial advisors globally, reflecting a widespread recognition of the advantages associated with taking calculated risks.

It is imperative to recognise that inherent risks accompany the pursuit of investment opportunities. Markets are by nature volatile, and investments can yield varying levels of returns based on economic conditions, industry performance, and investor sentiment. An excessive focus on immediate gains without a long-term strategy can lead to significant financial losses. Thus, while investing offers remarkable potential for wealth generation, it necessitates a degree of financial acumen, strategic planning, and a thorough understanding of our risk tolerance. As an investor, you must perform diligent research and consider your financial goals to construct a well-balanced portfolio that aligns with your circumstances.

It is essential to recognise that successful investing extends beyond mere stock purchases; rather, it encompasses an informed approach to various forms of investment vehicles. Real estate, for instance, can serve as a lucrative long-term investment, potentially yielding rental income and appreciation in property value. Alternative investments such as peer-to-peer lending or investing in startups can also offer attractive returns, albeit with higher risk profiles. Each of these avenues can significantly enhance your potential for wealth accumulation when approached judiciously.

When it comes to building wealth, the traditional advice has always been to save money diligently. We are often taught from an early age to save every penny and watch our expenses, with the hope that we will accumulate enough wealth over time. But is saving money enough to build long-term wealth? The answer is no. Life has taught me that saving money alone will not make anyone rich. It is investing money that has the power to generate wealth and financial freedom.

Challenging Traditional Views on Saving

While saving money is an important financial habit, it is essential to understand its limitations. Saving money may help us accumulate a safety net or achieve short-term financial goals, but it falls short of building real wealth. Money sitting in a savings account does not grow significantly over time, especially considering the impact of inflation.

Impact of Inflation on Savings

Ever feel like you are stuck in a loop of earning, saving, and barely making a dent in your financial goals? That is the savings trap. Your savings account might seem like a cosy nest egg, but inflation can slowly eat away at its purchasing power. One of the biggest limitations of saving money is the eroding effects of inflation. Inflation steadily erodes the purchasing power of your savings, meaning that the money you save today will not be worth the same in the future. Saving money, while important for short-term financial goals and emergencies, often falls short in terms of generating significant wealth due to factors such as inflation and low interest rates. Investing allows your money to grow over time and potentially outpace inflation, leading to long-term wealth accumulation.

Investing your money has the potential to generate significant returns and build wealth over time. By placing your money in various investments, you can create passive income streams that work for you. Whether it is through stocks, real estate, or other investment vehicles, investing allows your money to grow exponentially, outpacing inflation and building long-term wealth.

Building Wealth through Investments

When it comes to investing, there are numerous options to consider. One popular investment vehicle is the stock market. By investing in stocks, you become a shareholder in a company and can benefit from its growth and profitability. Real estate is another attractive investment option. By purchasing property and renting it out, you can generate a steady stream of rental income while also benefiting from property appreciation over time. Starting early and consistently contributing to your investment portfolio can have a significant impact on long-term wealth accumulation

Diversification in Investment Portfolio

While investing is crucial for building wealth, it is important to adopt strategies that maximise your returns while minimising risk. Diversification is a widely recommended strategy, which involves spreading your investments across different asset classes and sectors. This helps to mitigate risk and ensures that your investment portfolio is not overly reliant on a single investment. When it comes to investing, do not put all your eggs in one basket. By spreading your investments across different asset classes like stocks, bonds, and real estate, you reduce risk and increase your chances of success.

Setting Clear Financial Goals

Imagine going on a road trip without a destination in mind – you would just be driving aimlessly. The same goes for investing without clear financial goals. Whether it is saving for a dream vacation, buying a home, or retiring comfortably, knowing what you are investing for helps you make informed decisions and stay motivated.

Overcoming Barriers to Investing

Common barriers to investing include fear of risk, lack of financial knowledge, and misconceptions about the complexity of investment options. Overcoming these barriers through education, strategic planning, and seeking professional advice can help you navigate the world of investing more confidently. One of the barriers to investing is a lack of clear financial goals. It is important to set specific financial goals that align with your long-term aspirations. By having a clear vision of what you want to achieve, it becomes easier to dedicate resources to investing and building wealth.

Many individuals are hesitant to invest because of the perceived risk involved. However, with proper knowledge and understanding, you can make informed investment decisions that align with your risk tolerance and financial goals.

The Role of Education in Wealth Building

Investing can feel like deciphering a secret code, especially if financial jargon makes your head spin. Educating yourself on basic financial concepts like compound interest, inflation, and investment options can empower you to make wise financial decisions.

Financial literacy plays a crucial role in shifting mindsets from saving to investing. By educating yourself about investment options, understanding the power of compounding, and learning from successful investors, you can gain the confidence needed to start investing and take control of your financial future. Financial literacy programmes are essential in equipping individuals with the necessary skills and knowledge to make informed investment decisions.

Investing in Personal Development

Investing is not just about money – it is about investing in yourself too. Taking the time to enhance your skills, expand your knowledge, and develop a growth mindset can pave the way for financial growth and success. Remember, the greatest investment you can make is in yourself. It is important to invest in your personal development to enhance your financial growth. This includes not only financial education but also developing skills that can increase your earning potential and create more opportunities for investments. By continuously learning and improving yourself, you increase your chances of building long-term wealth.

Shifting Mindsets from Saving to Investing

In the game of wealth-building, saving money is like warming up on the sidelines – it is necessary, but it will not win you the game. Investing money, on the other hand, is like stepping onto the field and making strategic moves to score big. By shifting your mindset from saving to investing, you open up a world of opportunities to grow your wealth, achieve your financial goals, and secure a brighter future.

Conclusion

While saving money serves as an important foundation for financial stability and security, it is the act of investing that propels us towards wealth creation. The positive effects of compound interest, capital appreciation, and diversification collectively highlight the superior potential of investments over traditional savings accounts. Despite the inherent risks associated with investing, the rewards can be substantial, particularly for those who take a calculated and informed approach. In a rapidly evolving financial landscape, you must embrace investment as a critical component of your financial strategy. Ultimately, in the pursuit of lasting wealth, it is not saving that defines financial prosperity, but rather the prudent and strategic act of investing.

As we conclude this exploration of the dynamics between saving and investing, it is clear that the path to true wealth lies in embracing the transformative potential of investing. By understanding the limitations of saving money and harnessing the power of strategic investments, you can pave the way towards financial abundance and security. Embark on this journey of shifting mindsets, embracing financial education, and taking proactive steps towards a future where investing money, not just saving it, becomes the catalyst for realising your financial goals and building lasting prosperity.

While saving money is important for managing expenses and achieving short-term financial goals, it is investing money that holds the key to building long-term wealth. By understanding the limitations of saving, overcoming barriers to investing, and adopting strategies that align with your financial goals, you can start investing even with limited funds and pave the way towards financial freedom and prosperity.

CHAPTER THIRTY-SEVEN

WE CANNOT RISE ABOVE OUR CIRCLE OF INFLUENCE

In the complex fabric of human interactions and aspirations, the concept of a circle of influence emerges as a critical determinant of personal and professional development. Coined and popularised by Stephen R. Covey in his seminal work, *The 7 Habits of Highly Effective People*, the circle of influence refers to the area of concern and control a person exerts over their life and environment. This lesson explains the significance of this concept, that our potential for growth and success is intrinsically linked to the quality and nature of our circle of influence.

At its core, the circle of influence encompasses the people, ideas, and institutions that directly affect our lives. This circle may include family, friends, colleagues, mentors, and, perhaps, broader social networks. The relationships within this sphere are not merely superficial acquaintances; they represent interactions that shape opinions, beliefs, behaviours, and, ultimately, the trajectory of our personal and professional journey. Those who inhabit this circle can uplift, inspire, and motivate, or conversely, detract from and inhibit individual potential.

The notion that we cannot rise above our circle of influence stems from the psychological and sociocultural frameworks that govern human behaviour. Human beings are inherently social creatures, and the influences of others play a critical role in shaping our aspirations and achievements. For instance, individuals who surround themselves with ambitious and success-oriented people are likely to internalise aspirations that mirror those around them. This phenomenon can be explained through the lens of social learning theory, posited by Albert Bandura, which suggests that individuals learn behaviours, norms, and values through observations of others, especially those they regard as role models.

Our circle of influence can set implicit boundaries on what we can achieve. When we associate primarily with individuals with limited ambitions or who express scepticism about change and growth, envisioning or striving for greater accomplishments becomes increasingly challenging. Engaging with a circle rich in diverse perspectives, competencies, and achievements fosters an environment where aspirations can expand, and ideas can flourish. In this regard, it is essential to recognise the importance of cultivating a supportive and growth-oriented network that challenges us to transcend limitations.

The dynamics of influence extend beyond the mere identification of positive versus negative influences. A healthy circle of influence can be characterised by reciprocity, authenticity, and constructive feedback. It is within these environments that we not only receive inspiration but are also encouraged to reciprocate by contributing our insights and support. Therefore, proactive engagement in nurturing our circle is imperative to break free from limiting beliefs and engage in a constant process of personal development.

In the context of professional advancement, the circle of influence can significantly impact career trajectories. Networking within professional settings often elevates opportunities for career growth. The adage, "It's not what you know but who you know," captures the importance of professional relationships and connections. Individuals who actively seek to expand their professional circles by attending industry conferences, engaging in think tanks, or joining professional organisations inherently position themselves for new opportunities. Thus, the development of a robust professional circle becomes a strategic advantage in an increasingly competitive job market.

To attain a deeper understanding of our circle of influence, reflective practices such as self-assessment and feedback mechanisms can be beneficial. We should evaluate the impact of our current relationships on our aspirations and values. Such analyses can help identify which aspects of our circle may be fostering growth and which may be sowing seeds of stagnation. By actively seeking diversity in thought, experience, and expertise, we can effectively recalibrate our circles and, consequently, enhance our potential for success.

Nevertheless, the journey towards expanding one's circle of influence is not devoid of challenges. Social fears, such as fear of rejection or the discomfort of stepping into unfamiliar social territories, often deter individuals from seeking broader engagements. However, personal and professional growth requires a willingness to embrace discomfort, challenge the status quo, and overcome fears. The intentional act of seeking new relationships and connections enriches our perspective, ultimately leading to remarkable growth.

Impact of Surroundings on Personal Growth

Our surroundings play a crucial role in shaping our thoughts, beliefs, and actions. Research has shown that we are highly influenced by our social environment, as we tend to conform to the norms and behaviours of those around us. If our surroundings are limiting, it becomes difficult to break through self-imposed barriers and achieve personal growth. Our surroundings, including the people we surround ourselves with, play a crucial role in shaping who we are and who we become. Our circle of influence can either lift us up and propel us towards growth or hold us back and keep us stagnant. Understanding this impact is the first step towards taking control of our growth journey.

Recognising the Impact of Our Inner Circle

Our inner circle, consisting of family, close friends, and mentors, has a profound impact on our mindset and personal growth. These are the people who provide emotional support, challenge our limiting beliefs, and push us to step out of our comfort zone. It is essential to evaluate the quality of relationships within our inner circle and ensure they are nurturing, encouraging, and aligned with our goals.

Evaluating Your Current Circle of Influence

To improve your circle of influence, start by evaluating your current network. Take stock of the people you interact with regularly and consider how they contribute to your personal growth. Do they provide valuable insights, opportunities, and support? Or are they holding you back through negativity and limiting beliefs? Take a moment to reflect on the people in your inner circle - are they supporting your goals and dreams, or are they hindering your progress? Evaluating your current circle of influence is essential in understanding how it contributes to your mindset and overall wellbeing.

Identifying Positive and Negative Influences

Identifying positive and negative influences within our circle of influence is crucial for personal growth. Surrounding ourselves with individuals who inspire, motivate, and challenge us can greatly enhance our chances of success. On the other hand, negative influences can drain our energy, lower our ambitions, and hinder our progress. It is essential to distance ourselves from toxic relationships and focus on building positive connections.

Identifying positive influences that uplift and inspire us, as well as recognising negative influences that drain our energy and discourage our growth, is key to curating a circle of influence that aligns with our aspirations and values. Look for patterns of behaviour or beliefs that hinder your growth or bring negativity into your life. Pay attention to how you feel after interacting with certain individuals or environments - if you feel drained, discouraged, or limited, they may be negative influences.

Breaking Through Limiting Beliefs and Mindsets

One of the biggest obstacles to personal growth is self-limiting beliefs and mindsets. These beliefs often stem from our upbringing, experiences, and the influence of our surroundings. To overcome them, we must challenge ourselves and reframe our thoughts. Surrounding ourselves with people who have a growth mindset and believe in our potential can help us break through these barriers.

Self-limiting beliefs can manifest in various forms – fear of failure, imposter syndrome, lack of confidence, etc. It is essential to recognise them and actively work towards overcoming them. Surrounding ourselves with individuals who have overcome similar obstacles can be incredibly empowering and motivate us to challenge our own limiting beliefs. Often, our circle of influence can reinforce self-limiting beliefs that hold us back from reaching our full potential. Recognising and addressing these beliefs is essential for breaking free from mental barriers and expanding our horizons.

Cultivating a Growth Mindset for Expansion

A growth mindset is the belief that our abilities, intelligence, and skills can be developed through hard work, dedication, and resilience. Cultivating a growth mindset is essential for expanding our circle of influence. Surround yourself with people who challenge you and encourage you to embrace new opportunities, learn from failures, and persist in the face of challenges. Cultivating a growth mindset within your circle of influence can create a culture of continuous learning, resilience, and adaptability.

Embracing challenges as opportunities for growth and pushing past comfort zones are crucial steps in fostering a mindset that nurtures personal expansion.

Expanding Your Circle of Influence

To expand your circle of influence, you must actively seek out new connections and networks. Look beyond your immediate surroundings and engage with people who have different perspectives, experiences, and expertise. This diversity can broaden your horizons, spark creativity, and provide new opportunities for personal growth. Attend networking events, join professional or interest-based groups, seek mentorship from people you admire, and actively engage in communities that align with your goals. Be open to new connections and perspectives that can broaden your circle of influence.

Seeking Out New Connections and Networks

Deliberately seeking out new connections and networks can introduce fresh perspectives, ideas, and opportunities into your circle of influence. Being proactive in expanding your network can open doors to new experiences and potential collaborations. To diversify your influential relationships, join professional organisations, attend conferences and workshops, and leverage social media to connect with like-minded people.

Seek out mentorship opportunities with experienced professionals who can offer guidance and support in your field of interest. Engaging with individuals from diverse backgrounds and industries can introduce fresh ideas and perspectives, enriching your growth journey. Diversifying your influential relationships by engaging with individuals from diverse backgrounds, industries, and perspectives can enrich your growth journey. Embrace the power of diversity within your circle of influence to broaden your horizons and enhance your potential for success.

Strategies for Elevating Your Surroundings

In addition to diversifying relationships, it is crucial to elevate your surroundings. This can include the physical environment in which you work or live, as well as the digital spaces you frequent. Surround yourself with positive and inspiring content, whether that be through books, podcasts, or social media platforms. Creating an environment that supports your personal growth can significantly impact your journey towards success.

Your Ideal Circle of Influence

To enhance your circle of influence, it is important to create a vision for your ideal network. Determine the kind of people you want to surround yourself with – individuals who are ambitious, supportive, and committed to personal growth. Visualise the positive impact these connections can have on your journey and set goals to actively seek out these relationships. Picture this: your circle of influence as a garden. What kind of flowers, fruits, and plants do you want to see bloom? Envision the positive qualities, values, and ambitions you want in your circle. Having a clear vision sets the tone for the kind of environment you want to create.

Setting Goals for Enhancing Your Environment

To reinforce your vision, set concrete goals for enhancing your environment. This can include attending networking events, seeking out mentors, or joining communities aligned with your goals. Be intentional about the environments you expose yourself to and prioritise relationships that foster growth and personal development. Just like tending to a garden, setting specific, achievable goals is vital for growth. Want more positivity in your circle? Set a goal to engage in uplifting conversations or attend networking events. Goals provide direction and motivation to actively shape your surroundings.

Nurturing Relationships that Foster Growth

Building strong and supportive relationships requires effort and commitment. Nurturing relationships that foster growth involves actively listening, engaging in open conversations, and providing support to others. Investing in mutually beneficial relationships cultivates an environment conducive to personal growth.

To build strong and supportive relationships, it is important to be authentic, trustworthy, and genuinely interested in the wellbeing of others. Actively seek opportunities to provide value and support to those around you. By building these relationships, you create a network that not only supports your growth but also fosters collaboration and shared success. Surround yourself with people who water your growth, not your doubts. Seek out individuals who inspire, challenge, and support you. By fostering strong relationships based on trust and respect, you cultivate an environment where everyone thrives.

Investing in Mutual Growth and Development

Relationships are a two-way street. Offer your support, guidance, and encouragement to others as they do for you. By investing in others' growth and development, you create a symbiotic relationship that fosters continuous improvement and success. To leverage your circle of influence, invest in the growth and development of others. Support their goals, offer guidance, and celebrate their successes. Investing in mutual growth deepens the bonds within your network and strengthens its overall influence.

Dealing With Challenges and Resistance

Influencing your environment is not without its challenges. Resistance and opposition are common hurdles that can hinder your personal growth. In such situations, it is essential to remain resilient, stay true to your vision, and surround yourself with supportive individuals who can provide guidance and encouragement.

Change can be met with resistance, but do not let it deter you. Understand that not everyone may align with your vision or goals. Stay true to your values, communicate openly, and be patient. Over time, persistence can break down barriers and lead to acceptance. When faced with resistance and opposition, approach these challenges with an open mind and a willingness to learn. Seek to understand the perspectives of others and look for common ground. Surround yourself with people who can provide objective feedback and help you navigate these challenging situations. Focus on building rapport, empathy, and understanding with those who may resist your influence. Communicate your intentions, listen to their perspectives, and find common ground to foster collaboration and mutual respect.

Building Resilience in the Face of Adversity

Resilience is a vital trait when it comes to personal growth. Surround yourself with people who have faced adversity and come out stronger. Their experiences and stories can inspire you to persist in the face of challenges, bounce back from setbacks, and continue on your path of personal growth. Influencing your environment is not always smooth sailing. When faced with challenges, focus on building resilience. View setbacks as opportunities for growth, learn from them, and adapt. By staying resilient in the face of adversity, you can navigate obstacles and continue to positively influence your surroundings.

Conclusion

Your circle of influence plays a crucial role in shaping your personal growth and success. By recognising the impact of your surroundings, evaluating your current network, and actively seeking out positive influences, you can break through limiting beliefs and expand your circle of influence. Cultivate strong and supportive relationships, invest in mutual growth, and overcome challenges that come your way. Remember, you cannot rise above your circle of influence, so choose wisely and invest in relationships that will propel you towards personal growth and success.

That we cannot rise above our circle of influence serves as a poignant reminder of the significance of our social environments in shaping our realities. Success, fulfilment, and personal development are not solely determined by individual merits but unduly influenced by the company we keep. By being aware of the dynamics within our circle and actively engaging in its enrichment, we can harness profound opportunities for growth. Therefore, it is essential to cultivate relationships with those who elevate and inspire, as it is through these connections that we can truly aspire to transcend limitations and achieve greatness. In navigating life's complexities, remember that your circles do not merely influence you; they define the very heights to which you can ascend.

As we conclude our exploration of the circle of influence, it is apparent that our surroundings play a crucial role in shaping our reality and potential. By actively assessing and curating our circle of influence, we can unlock new growth opportunities, expand our horizons, and ultimately elevate our lives to new heights. Embracing the power of intentional relationships, beliefs, and environments empowers us to break through limitations, overcome challenges, and create a supportive ecosystem that propels us towards our goals. Remember, you are the architect of your circle of influence. Choose it wisely, nurture it diligently, and watch as it becomes the springboard for your success and fulfilment.

CHAPTER THIRTY-EIGHT

SOMETIMES IT IS BETTER NOT TO KNOW

In an age characterised by unprecedented access to information, the notion of ignorance can be viewed with disdain. Knowledge is typically equated with power, and the pursuit of truth is heralded as a noble endeavour. However, there exists a compelling argument for the idea that sometimes, it is better not to know. This lesson explores the multifaceted implications of ignorance, examining the psychological, social, and ethical dimensions where the absence of knowledge may lead to greater wellbeing, enhanced relationships, and a more harmonious society.

At the psychological level, the burden of knowledge can lead to increased anxiety and stress. The phenomenon known as "information overload" has become increasingly prevalent in the digital age, where individuals are bombarded with a constant stream of news, opinions, and data. Studies in psychology suggest that excessive information can overwhelm cognitive processing capabilities, leading to decision fatigue and emotional distress. For instance, individuals who are acutely aware of global issues such as climate change, political unrest, or economic instability may experience feelings of helplessness and despair. In contrast, those who choose to limit their exposure to such information may find a greater sense of peace and contentment in their daily lives. This selective ignorance can serve as a protective mechanism, allowing individuals to focus on personal growth and immediate relationships rather than being consumed by the weight of global crises.

The social dynamics of relationships can be significantly influenced by the decision to remain uninformed. In many interpersonal contexts, such as friendships, family interactions, and romantic partnerships, knowledge can create unnecessary tension and conflict. For example, uncovering a partner's past relationships or a friend's hidden grievances can lead to jealousy, resentment, or a distorted perception of the present. In some cases, the adage "what you don't know won't hurt you" holds true. Ignorance can preserve the sanctity of relationships, allowing individuals to engage with one another more positively and constructively. Furthermore, the decision to overlook certain truths can foster an environment of trust and loyalty, as individuals choose to focus on the present rather than dwelling on potentially damaging revelations.

Ethically, the question of whether to seek knowledge can be particularly complex. In fields such as medicine, psychology, and even law enforcement, the implications of knowing certain truths can be profound. For instance, consider a patient diagnosed with a terminal illness. While some individuals may prefer complete transparency regarding their prognosis and treatment options, others may find solace in a more optimistic narrative that downplays the severity of their condition. In such cases, healthcare professionals often grapple with the ethical dilemma of how much information to disclose. Striking a balance between honesty and compassion becomes crucial, as the emotional wellbeing of the patient may hinge on their ability to cope with their circumstances. Here, ignorance can serve as a form of emotional protection, allowing individuals to navigate their realities without the added burden of despair.

In the realm of ethics, the decision to remain uninformed can also extend to societal issues such as systemic injustice and inequality. While awareness of social injustices is vital for progress, the emotional toll of constant exposure to such realities can lead to desensitisation or apathy. Activists and advocates often find themselves in a paradox; the more they learn about the depth of societal problems, the more overwhelmed they may become, potentially stalling their efforts to instigate change. In this context, selective ignorance can serve as a strategic choice, enabling individuals to maintain their motivation and passion for advocacy without becoming paralysed by the enormity of the issues at hand.

It is essential to acknowledge that the argument for selective ignorance does not advocate for a blanket approach to knowledge. Ignorance can lead to harmful consequences, particularly when it comes to issues of public health, safety, and ethical responsibility. The challenge lies in discerning when ignorance may be beneficial and when it is imperative to seek knowledge. For instance, ignoring scientific evidence regarding vaccines can have dire public health repercussions. Thus, the decision to remain uninformed must be approached with careful consideration of context and consequences.

Have you ever found yourself in a situation where you were faced with a difficult truth, and you wished you had never found out? It is a common human experience to want to shield ourselves from unpleasant realities, but is ignorance truly bliss? Sometimes, it is better not to know. In a world where information is constantly at our fingertips and the pursuit of knowledge is lauded, the concept of ignorance may seem counterintuitive. However, there is a paradoxical beauty in not knowing, a complexity that challenges our preconceived notions about the value of understanding. In our world where knowledge is power, ignorance often gets a bad rap. But what if sometimes, blissful ignorance is a blessing in disguise? Let us delve into the paradox of ignorance and explore when not knowing might be better.

The Power of Ignorance

In a society that values information and expertise, ignorance is typically seen as a lack of knowledge or awareness. However, we can also view ignorance as a state of not being burdened by unnecessary details or distractions, allowing us to focus on what truly matters. In a world filled with constant change and unpredictability, learning to embrace uncertainty can bring a sense of liberation and serenity. Ignorance can be a powerful coping mechanism. When we are shielded from certain truths, we can maintain a sense of peace and stability in our lives. Ignorance allows us to focus on the positive aspects of our reality, rather than being consumed by negative thoughts and emotions.

Protection from Pain

One of the main reasons why sometimes it is better not knowing is that ignorance can protect us from unnecessary pain and suffering. For example, if you discover that a loved one has been deceiving you, the truth can be devastating and can shatter your sense of trust and security. In some cases, it may be better to remain ignorant to preserve your mental and emotional wellbeing.

Preserving Relationships

Ignorance can also play a crucial role in preserving relationships. There are times when knowing the truth can cause irreparable harm to a relationship, leading to misunderstandings, arguments, and even breakups. By choosing not to delve into certain truths, we can maintain harmony and peace in our interactions with others.

The Information Overload Phenomenon

With endless sources of information at our fingertips, it is easy to fall into the trap of consuming more data than we can effectively process. Information overload can overwhelm our brains and hinder our ability to make clear decisions or find genuine satisfaction.

Cultivating Mindfulness and Acceptance

Practising mindfulness allows us to be present in the moment and accept things as they are, without judgment or resistance. By embracing uncertainty and letting go of the need for control, we can find inner peace amidst life's ups and downs.

Finding Beauty in Mystery and Unpredictability

Rather than constantly seeking answers and explanations, there is a certain magic in embracing life's mysteries and appreciating the wonder of the unknown. By shifting our perspective, we can discover joy in the unexpected and find beauty in the unpredictable nature of existence.

Knowledge Can Lead to Anxiety and Discontent

The relentless pursuit of knowledge can create a sense of inadequacy or FOMO (fear of missing out), fuelling anxiety and dissatisfaction. It is important to recognise when seeking knowledge becomes compulsive and take steps to prioritise our mental wellbeing over the need for constant information consumption.

Letting Go of the Need to Know Everything

In a world where information is constantly at our fingertips, the pressure to know everything can feel overwhelming. But what if we embraced the idea that it is fine not to have all the answers? By letting go of the need to know everything, we free ourselves from the burden of constant seeking and cultivate a sense of contentment in the present moment.

Finding Joy in the Present Moment

When we release the grip of always needing to be in the know, we open ourselves up to finding joy in life's simple pleasures. Whether it is savouring a cup of coffee without checking our phones or relishing a beautiful sunset without googling its exact time, there is beauty in being present and experiencing life without the weight of knowing it all.

Setting Boundaries for Healthy Information

In a world saturated with information, setting boundaries on what we consume is crucial for our mental wellbeing. By being selective about what we expose ourselves to, we can cultivate a healthier relationship with knowledge and avoid the overwhelm that can come from trying to absorb too much.

Ignorance as a Tool for Learning and Growth

Ignorance does not have to be a negative concept. By embracing our ignorance in certain areas, we open ourselves up to the opportunity for selective learning and growth. Rather than trying to know everything about everything, we can focus on deepening our understanding in areas that truly matter to us. Paradoxically, sometimes knowing less can lead to more confident and efficient decision-making. When we strip away unnecessary information and trust our instincts, we can make choices based on what truly resonates with us, rather than getting lost in a sea of endless data.

The Art of Trusting Intuition and Instincts

Trusting our intuition and instincts can be a powerful tool in decision-making. Sometimes, our subconscious mind processes information that our conscious mind may not be aware of. By embracing a bit of ignorance and tapping into our instincts, we can make decisions that align with our authentic selves.

Embracing Humility and Openness

By accepting our ignorance, we embrace humility and openness to new perspectives. Recognising that we do not have all the answers allows us to approach life with curiosity and a willingness to learn from others, fostering growth and connection.

Balancing Knowledge and Respecting Ignorance

In a world that values knowledge and information, finding a balance between seeking knowledge and respecting our ignorance is key. By acknowledging that we cannot know everything and being intentional about what we choose to learn, we can navigate the complexities of the information age with grace and wisdom.

As we navigate the complexities of a knowledge-driven society, it is essential to remember the wisdom in accepting our limitations and embracing the beauty of ignorance. By cultivating humility and openness to new perspectives, we can find peace in the unknown and unlock a deeper sense of contentment in our daily lives. Let us strive to strike a balance between curiosity and ignorance, recognising that true wisdom lies not just in what we know, but in our willingness to acknowledge all that we have yet to discover.

The Downside of Knowing

On the flip side, knowledge can sometimes be a burden. Once you are aware of certain truths, you can never unlearn them. The weight of this knowledge can weigh heavy on your shoulders, causing stress, anxiety, and even depression. In these instances, ignorance may have been the preferable option.

Striking a Balance

While ignorance may offer temporary relief from challenging truths, it is important to strike a balance between knowing and not knowing. Being informed allows us to make better decisions, adapt to changing circumstances, and grow as individuals. However, there are certain situations where ignorance truly is bliss.

Conclusion

That it is sometimes better not to know invites a deeper exploration of the complex relationship between knowledge and wellbeing. While the pursuit of truth is undeniably important, there are instances where ignorance can serve as a protective mechanism, fostering emotional resilience, enhancing interpersonal relationships, and promoting ethical decision-making. As we navigate the complexities of modern life, the ability to discern when to seek knowledge and when to embrace ignorance may ultimately lead to a more balanced and fulfilling existence. In a world saturated with information, the wisdom of selective ignorance may prove to be an invaluable tool for maintaining mental health and nurturing meaningful connections.

Sometimes it is indeed better not to know. Ignorance can act as a protective shield, preserving our mental and emotional wellbeing and our relationships with others. However, it is essential to find a balance between knowing and not knowing to lead a fulfilling and purposeful life. Remember, the choice to remain ignorant should always be a personal decision based on individual circumstances and preferences.

CHAPTER THIRTY-NINE

NO ONE EVER GRADUATES FROM THE INSTITUTION OF MARRIAGE

The institution of marriage has long been an essential aspect of human society, embodying a complex amalgamation of love, commitment, responsibility, and social expectations. While many individuals enter this institution with grand aspirations of happiness and fulfilment, the journey through marriage is far from a linear path of progress leading towards a definitive conclusion.

That no one ever graduates from the institution of marriage epitomizes the notion that marriage is not merely a phase of life to be traversed but rather a continuous journey marked by growth, adaptation, and lifelong learning. This lesson explores the various dimensions of marriage as an evolving commitment, highlighting its challenges, learning opportunities, and the intrinsic importance of ongoing effort within this partnership.

It is crucial to acknowledge that marriage is not a static achievement but a dynamic relationship that evolves over time. Much like an academic institution that offers a multitude of courses, each phase of marriage presents its distinct curriculum, encompassing a range of experiences that foster personal growth. In the early stages of marriage, partners often focus on establishing their bond, negotiating roles, and intertwining their lives. However, as time progresses, marriage partners are faced with new challenges, including parenting, financial pressures, and the inevitable changes that life brings. Each of these experiences necessitates a different set of skills and an ability to adapt, showcasing that the journey of marriage is like a lifelong academic programme with no final examination or graduation ceremony.

That one never graduates from marriage underscores the idea that the institution requires continual commitment and effort. Just as a student must remain engaged in their studies, consistently attending classes and completing assignments, marital partners must actively cultivate their relationship. This might involve open communication, conflict resolution, and mutual support, allowing both individuals to thrive both as partners and as independent entities. Marriage, much like education, demands regular investment; neglecting these aspects can lead to stagnation and discontent. Thus, partners must recognise that the end of one phase does not signal the conclusion of their learning, but rather the commencement of new lessons that will contribute to the evolving nature of their bond.

The unpredictability of life further emphasises the notion that marriage is an ongoing process. External circumstances, such as health crises, unemployment, and loss, can test the strength and resilience of a marital partnership. These challenges serve as unanticipated examinations that can disrupt the status quo and compel partners to reassess their priorities, redefine their goals, and engage in cooperative problem-solving. Rather than a mere test of endurance, these occurrences present opportunities for growth and deeper connection.

Just as scholars often learn more from their failures and challenges than from their successes, married couples often find that navigating adversity can strengthen their relationship and deepen their understanding of each other. It is also informative to consider the perspectives of those who have journeyed through numerous decades of marriage. Many couples will affirm that, despite the passage of time and the accumulation of experiences, there remains an ever-present need for growth and adaptation.

Wisdom gained through years of partnership may foster a profound appreciation for the nuances of cohabitation; however, it does not guarantee immunity to the difficulties that arise. Quarrels, miscommunications, and periodic disconnection can still manifest, suggesting that spouses must continue to engage in their relationship actively.

Long-term partners often highlight the importance of revisiting the foundational aspects of their marriage - such as shared values, goals, and emotional intimacy - demonstrating that ongoing reflection and adaptation remain paramount in the pursuit of a fulfilling partnership. On a broader scale, the idea that no one ever graduates from the institution of marriage reflects a societal recognition of the need for continual growth and education within relationships. In many cultures, the pressures associated with marriage can cast long shadows over the partnership.

Expectations regarding fidelity, support, and partnership can generate excessive stress, leading individuals to feel overwhelmed or inadequate. However, acknowledging that marriage is a lifelong learning experience can alleviate some of these pressures, allowing partners to approach their relationship with a mindset of curiosity and openness. Encouraging a culture of lifelong learning in marriage can empower individuals to become resourceful in developing their relationship skills, seeking workshops, counselling, or community support when necessary to promote growth and connection.

Challenges Faced in Marriage

Marriage, often heralded as a profound union between individuals, stands as both a celebrated institution and a dynamic partnership that encapsulates a variety of challenges. The complexities inherent in human relationships can transform the journey of marriage into an assortment of joys, trials, and tribulations. As couples navigate the intricate landscape of shared lives, they confront numerous challenges that can test the strength and resilience of their bond. Life has taught me that marriages, no matter how good they appear to be on the surface, have almost always faced some primary challenges including communication barriers, financial stresses, differing expectations, and external pressures, while also offering insights into potential strategies for overcoming these hurdles.

1. Communication Barriers

One of the most significant challenges in marriage is communication. Effective communication is the cornerstone of any relationship, and its absence can lead to misunderstandings, resentment, and emotional disconnection. Couples often come into marriage with different communication styles, which may be shaped by their upbringing, cultural background, and personal experiences. For instance, individuals who were raised in families where open dialogue was encouraged may find it difficult to navigate the emotional intricacies of a partner who grew up in a more reserved household. This divergence can result in conflicts where one partner feels unheard or invalidated.

Furthermore, the busy and often chaotic nature of modern life can aggravate communication issues. Couples may struggle to find time for meaningful conversations amid work commitments, parenting responsibilities, and social obligations. As daily interactions become superficial or routine, the emotional depth of the relationship can wane, leading to feelings of isolation. Therefore, establishing consistent and open communication channels is essential. Couples should prioritise regular discussions about their feelings, aspirations, and concerns, thereby fostering a supportive environment where both partners feel valued and understood.

2. Financial Stress

Financial challenges represent another significant obstacle that couples often encounter. The financial landscape is fraught with uncertainties and pressures, from the burden of student loans and mortgage payments to the costs associated with raising children. Disparities in income, spending habits, and financial goals can lead to tension and conflict within a marriage. Furthermore, when couples do not share the same approach to finances, disagreements can intensify. For instance, partners who prioritise savings may struggle to comprehend the viewpoint of a spouse who values spending on experiences and material goods.

In an age marked by economic fluctuations and job insecurities, financial stress can compound existing relational strains. You may find themselves at odds over budgeting issues, leading to power struggles and feelings of inadequacy. You need to engage in open and honest discussions about your financial situation, budget collaboratively, and establish common financial goals. By approaching finances as a shared responsibility and being transparent about your financial status and concerns, you can minimise the potential for financial discord.

3. Differing Expectations

Differing expectations regarding roles and responsibilities can also create substantial challenges in marriage. Couples often enter into marriage with preconceived notions about their roles based on societal norms, cultural backgrounds, and personal desires. These expectations may encompass a range of aspects, such as household responsibilities, parenting styles, and emotional support. Disparities in these expectations can lead to disappointment and frustration if not addressed openly. For instance, a partner may expect the other to take on a dominant share of household tasks, while the latter may feel overwhelmed and unappreciated, leading to feelings of resentment.

To combat this issue, it is essential to engage in candid discussions about your expectations and to negotiate roles based on consensus rather than assumptions. Establishing a clear understanding of shared responsibilities and creating a supportive environment where both of you feel empowered to voice your preferences can significantly reduce conflicts. Flexibility and adaptability are crucial, as roles may evolve over time due to changes in circumstances, such as the arrival of children or career transitions.

4. External Pressures

External pressures can significantly impact a marriage. These pressures may stem from societal expectations, family influences, workplace dynamics, or friends' opinions. For instance, societal norms may impose unrealistic expectations regarding timelines for marriage, parenthood, or financial success, which can inadvertently create stress and anxiety within the couple. Similarly, familial pressure can create tensions, especially in situations where parents or extended family members hold strong preferences regarding aspects such as lifestyle choices or child-rearing practices.

Maintaining a resilient partnership in the face of these external pressures requires us to cultivate a shared identity and reinforce our commitment to each other. We must learn to prioritise our relationship over external opinions and foster a strong emotional bond through mutual support. Setting boundaries with external influences and engaging in discussions about how these factors affect the relationship can also help us navigate challenges as a united front.

Marriage is both a rewarding and demanding journey that requires continuous effort and commitment from both partners. The challenges faced in marriage - ranging from communication barriers and financial stresses to differing expectations and external pressures - demand intentionality and resilience. By fostering open dialogue, collaboratively addressing financial matters, negotiating roles, and maintaining a united front against external influences, we can navigate these challenges and emerge stronger in our partnership.

Recognising and addressing the complexities of marriage is essential for cultivating enduring love and connection. Through proactive engagement and mutual understanding, we can transform challenges into opportunities for growth, thereby enriching our marital experience.

Role of Communication in Sustaining a Marriage

Marriage as a profound union between two individuals is a commitment that extends beyond the mere acknowledgement of love and companionship. At its core, marriage thrives on the intricate dynamics of communication. The ability to convey thoughts, emotions, and needs effectively is not just an ancillary element but a foundational pillar upon which a successful marriage is built.

Communication is undeniably the lifeblood of a marriage. Its role in fostering intimacy, resolving conflicts, enhancing understanding, and nurturing individual and relational growth cannot be overstated. A successful marriage necessitates a commitment to continuous communication, where both partners invest time and effort into expressing their thoughts and feelings candidly. As couples navigate the complexities of life together, the mastery of effective communication serves as a beacon guiding them towards a more fulfilling, resilient, and enduring partnership. Ultimately, those who embrace the power of communication will find that their marriages are not only sustained but enriched, paving the way for a lasting bond fortified by love, trust, and mutual respect.

Communication as the Bedrock of Intimacy

One of the principal roles of communication in marriage is the cultivation of intimacy. Intimacy, characterised by a deep emotional bond and connection, requires vulnerability and openness, which can only be achieved through effective communication. Couples who engage in frequent, honest discussions are likely to share their thoughts and feelings, thereby nurturing a sense of closeness and trust.

Consider the significance of sharing daily experiences, aspirations, and concerns. When partners dedicate time to discussing their day, they not only strengthen their emotional connection but also create a safe space where both individuals feel valued and heard. This exchange can range from trivial matters, such as sharing anecdotes from the day to more profound discussions about hopes and dreams for the future. Such dialogue fosters a mutual understanding and reinforces the notion that each partner is invested in the other's happiness and wellbeing.

The exchange of verbal affection - expressing love, appreciation, and admiration - plays an equally crucial role. Regularly affirming your spouse through kind words and gestures can instil a sense of belonging and security, essential components of lasting marital fulfilment. In contrast, a lack of communication in this area can lead to misunderstanding, feelings of neglect, and ultimately, emotional distance. Therefore, effective communication is critical not only in building intimacy but also in maintaining it.

Conflict Resolution and Communication

Conflict is an inevitable aspect of any relationship, including marriage. How we communicate during disagreements can significantly influence the resolution process and the overall health of our relationship. Communication equips partners with the tools necessary to navigate conflicts constructively rather than destructively.

Effective communication during turbulent times involves active listening, empathy, and a willingness to compromise. When one partner expresses their grievances, the other must listen attentively, seeking to understand rather than to respond defensively. This practice not only validates the speaker's feelings but also fosters an environment where both partners can express their viewpoints without fear of reprisal. Employing "I" statements - phrasing concerns in a way that focuses on one's feelings instead of blaming the other - can further mitigate defensiveness and irritation, paving the way for healthier discussions.

Furthermore, conflict resolution is most productive when we approach disagreements as a team. Recognising that the goal is not to "win" the argument but to reach a mutually beneficial resolution underscores the value of cooperative communication. This collaborative approach not only resolves immediate disagreement but also strengthens the partnership as individuals learn to face challenges together, enhancing their unity.

Enhancing Understanding Through Communication

Beyond emotional intimacy and conflict resolution, communication plays a pivotal role in enhancing mutual understanding between spouses. Each partner brings their unique background, experiences, and values into the marriage, which can lead to differing perspectives and expectations. Communication facilitates the exploration of these differences, allowing couples to navigate potential pitfalls and embrace their diversity.

Open and honest conversations about varying beliefs, cultural backgrounds, and familial expectations can prevent misunderstandings and resentment from arising. For instance, discussing child-rearing philosophies, financial management, and household responsibilities can help you align your expectations and approach as you build a life together. By engaging in these dialogues, you can gain insights into each other's views and priorities, allowing for a more harmonious coexistence.

Continual communication about changing needs and desires is essential for growth within the marriage. As individuals evolve, so too do their perspectives and aspirations. Regular check-ins and discussions serve as a mechanism for couples to reassess and adapt their relationship to better accommodate the evolving nature of each partner. Such adaptability not only fortifies marriage but also inspires an enduring partnership that thrives on exploration and mutual learning.

Nurturing Growth Through Communication

The significance of communication transcends the immediate scope of managing daily interactions; it is also pivotal in nurturing personal and relational growth. Effective communication fosters an environment where both of you feel encouraged to express your ambitions and explore your interests, ultimately enhancing your individuality within the marriage.

Couples who actively encourage each other's pursuits create a dynamic of support and empowerment. Whether it is career aspirations, hobbies, or personal challenges, discussing these facets openly allows you to lend support, offer constructive feedback, and celebrate achievements together. Such dialogues not only reinforce individual growth but also enrich the partnership itself, as both of you bring your evolved selves back into the relationship.

A lack of communication regarding individual goals can lead to feelings of stagnation and resentment. If your partner feels they must suppress their ambitions for the sake of the relationship, it can result in discord and dissatisfaction. Therefore, cultivating a culture of open dialogue regarding personal aspirations is essential for sustaining both your individual and collective growth within the marriage.

Strategies for Nurturing a Lifelong Marriage

Marriage transcends the mere celebration of love between two individuals. It represents a profound commitment to partnership, mutual growth, and shared experiences throughout the vicissitudes of life. While the promise of unconditional love and support serves as the foundation for a marital union, nurturing a lifelong marriage necessitates proactive engagement and effort from you and your partner.

Nurturing a lifelong marriage necessitates a commitment to continuous growth, effective communication, and mutual support. By prioritising open dialogue, cultivating emotional intimacy, navigating conflicts constructively, maintaining individuality, and engaging with family and community, you can create a resilient marital bond that endures the test of time. The journey of marriage is not simply about the destination; it is an evolving partnership that requires effort, understanding, and, above all, an unwavering commitment to each other. As you invest in these strategies, you lay the foundation for a fulfilling, lifelong companionship, enriched by love and shared experiences.

Below are some of the strategies for nurturing a lifelong marriage relationship.

1. Open and Honest Communication

One of the foremost strategies for nurturing a lifelong marriage is establishing a culture of open and honest communication. Effective communication not only facilitates the exchange of thoughts and emotions but also serves as a means of conflict resolution. You and your partner should strive to foster an environment where both of you feel secure in expressing your feelings, desires, and concerns. This entails active listening, wherein each partner gives full attention to the other, validating their feelings without immediate judgment or interruption.

Furthermore, you and your partner need to engage in regular, intentional conversations devoid of distractions. Allocating time each week to discuss your experiences, aspirations, or challenges reinforces emotional intimacy and ensures that both of you remain attuned to each other's needs. By making communication a priority, you can address underlying issues before they escalate into major conflicts, ultimately fortifying the emotional foundation of your marriage.

2. Cultivating Emotional Intimacy

Beyond communication, nurturing emotional intimacy is crucial in sustaining a lifelong marriage. Emotional intimacy encompasses the deep, personal connection shared between partners, characterised by trust, vulnerability, and empathy. To cultivate this intimacy, you and your partner should be willing to share your innermost thoughts and feelings while also being responsive to your partner's disclosures.

Engaging in shared activities, such as hobbies or projects, can significantly enhance emotional bonds. Couples who embark on joint endeavours often discover new facets of each other, leading to personal growth and a stronger partnership. Expressions of affection - such as verbal affirmations, physical touch, and small gestures of kindness - serve to reinforce emotional connections. These practices contribute to an ever-deepening bond that can withstand life's trials.

3. Navigating Conflict Constructively

Conflict is an inevitable aspect of any relationship, and how you address these disagreements greatly influences your marital longevity. Rather than viewing conflict as an adversarial challenge, you should adopt constructive conflict-resolution strategies that emphasise collaboration and mutual understanding. Employing 'I' statements can help articulate individual feelings without casting blame. For instance, instead of saying, "You never listen to me," you might say, "I feel unheard when my concerns are dismissed." Such language promotes responsibility for one's feelings and encourages constructive dialogue.

Moreover, you and your partner should agree on specific strategies to de-escalate tensions during disagreements. Taking time-outs when emotions run high, employing humour to lighten the mood, or seeking the involvement of a neutral third party can facilitate healthier discussions. The objective should remain focused on problem-solving rather than winning an argument, thereby reinforcing the partnership over individual interests.

4. Maintaining Individuality and Growth

While unity is a hallmark of marriage, maintaining individual identities is equally important for a successful lifelong partnership. Encouraging your partner's personal growth and pursuits fosters a sense of autonomy and fulfilment. You and your partner should support each other's dreams and aspirations, allocating space for independent interests and friendships. This autonomy enriches the relationship, allowing you both to bring diverse experiences and insights into the partnership.

Significant life changes, such as parenthood or career transitions, can alter the dynamics within a marriage. You and your partner must actively navigate these changes by communicating openly about your evolving roles and responsibilities. By recognising and adapting to each other's growth, you can avoid feelings of resentment or disconnection that may arise from neglecting individual needs.

5. Commitment to Family and Community

A successful marriage often extends beyond the couple, intertwining with familial and communal obligations. Engaging with family and friends can provide essential support systems that contribute to a healthy marital environment. You and your partner should prioritise family traditions and shared experiences, fostering a sense of belonging not only within the marital unit but also in the larger community. Additionally, participating in community service or joint activities that emphasise teamwork can strengthen your bond and enhance your social network. Setting shared goals - whether financial, personal, or spiritual - encourages cooperation and mutual investment in the relationship. Whether it involves planning a family vacation or working towards purchasing a home, collaborative goal setting fosters a shared vision for the future.

Maintaining Individual Identities in a Marriage

Marriage is a union between two individuals, a partnership built on shared dreams, goals, and emotional support. However, the essence of a successful marriage does not exclusively rest on the union of two lives but also on preserving the individual identities that each partner brings into the relationship. The tension between marital unity and individualism is a complex dynamic that merits careful consideration.

The intricate interplay between individuality and togetherness lies at the heart of any marriage. While married couples often share numerous aspects of their lives, ranging from emotional support to financial responsibilities, both partners must recognise and honour their unique identities. Individuality encompasses various dimensions including personal interests, beliefs, values, ambitions, and social roles. When these individual aspects are acknowledged and respected within the context of a marriage, partners are more likely to experience lasting satisfaction and emotional fulfilment.

One of the primary reasons for preserving individual identities within a marriage lies in the concept of personal fulfilment. Individuals who engage in activities that resonate with their passions and aspirations cultivate a sense of self-worth and confidence. This, in turn, positively impacts the marital relationship. When each partner feels fulfilled in their pursuits, they are more likely to contribute positively to the relationship, fostering an atmosphere of mutual respect and encouragement. In contrast, when one or both partners suppress their individual identities in favour of a singular marital identity, feelings of resentment, frustration, and dissatisfaction can penetrate the relationship. The danger here lies in the potential erosion of self-concept, leading to a breakdown in communication and, ultimately, the relationship itself.

The preservation of individual identities in a marriage can significantly enhance the emotional depth and intimacy of the partnership. Engaging in personal interests often encourages individuals to develop unique perspectives and insights that can enrich conversations and experiences within the relationship. This exchange of ideas and experiences fosters a deeper connection, allowing partners to appreciate each other's differences and learn from each other. In many ways, it is the diversity of perspectives that forms the foundation of a strong marriage, as it equips partners with the tools necessary to navigate challenges collaboratively.

Despite its evident importance, maintaining individual identities within a marriage presents numerous challenges. Contemporary societal norms often espouse a narrative that emphasises unity and togetherness, occasionally at the expense of individuality. This prescriptive notion can create pressure for partners to conform to a collective identity, which may lead to the relegation of personal aspirations and desires. Life transitions such as parenthood, career changes, or relocation can further complicate the balance between individual and shared identities. Partners may inadvertently become enmeshed in their roles, leading to a fusion of identities that might obscure their personal attributes and interests.

In combating these challenges, you can adopt several strategies to promote individual identities within your marriage. One of the most effective methods is fostering open and honest communication. Regularly discussing your individual needs, desires, and concerns encourages mutual understanding and respect. This dialogue can create a safe space where both of you feel valued and supported in your individuality. Moreover, you must establish boundaries that allow each of you to pursue your passions without guilt or fear of judgment. For instance, dedicating time to personal hobbies, friendships, and self-care ultimately enriches you as individuals and as couples.

Creating shared goals that honour individual aspirations can serve as a bridge to a more harmonious partnership. By aligning personal ambitions with collective objectives, you can cultivate a sense of teamwork and shared purpose that also respects personal growth. This could involve supporting your partner's career development while also pursuing joint interests that align with your collective values. Engaging in such practices enhances the recognition that growth as individuals and as a couple is not mutually exclusive but rather an interdependent process that nurtures both dimensions.

You should embrace the concept of continuous growth, recognising that identities are not static but fluid. As life circumstances change and you and your partner evolve, maintaining a dialogue around personal growth becomes imperative. Celebrating successes, whether big or small, in your partner's journey fosters an environment of encouragement and understanding. Approaching marriage with the mindset that both of you will continuously grow and develop allows for a flexible dynamic that adapts to change rather than resisting it.

Maintaining individual identities within a marriage is not merely a personal endeavour but a collective responsibility that significantly enhances the relationship. Acknowledging and honouring your partner's unique attributes allows for emotional depth, personal fulfilment, and mutual respect, all of which are foundational to a successful partnership. While the challenges in achieving this balance are significant, the strategies discussed - such as open communication, boundary-setting, shared goals, and a commitment to continuous growth - can empower you to navigate the intricate landscape of marriage effectively. Eventually, a harmonious marriage thrives not only on shared experiences but also on the rich tapestry of individual identities that each partner contributes to the union.

Cultivating Trust and Respect in Marriage

Marriage is a profound institution that binds the lives of individuals, forming a partnership that necessitates mutual understanding, communication, and growth. At the core of a successful marriage lie the twin pillars of trust and respect. These elements are not only foundational for a harmonious relationship but also serve as the bedrock upon which couples can construct a fulfilling and enduring bond. Cultivating trust and respect in marriage requires intentionality, effort, and an unwavering commitment to each other, attributes that are essential in navigating the complexities of shared life.

The Importance of Trust

Trust is often heralded as the cornerstone of a successful marriage. It is the glue that binds partners together, facilitating open communication and emotional intimacy. In a relationship where trust is firmly established, partners feel secure in expressing their thoughts, emotions, and vulnerabilities. This sense of safety fosters an environment where both partners can thrive, enabling them to confront challenges and conflicts with a united front.

To cultivate trust, you must prioritise transparency and honesty in your interactions. This means engaging in open dialogues about feelings, expectations, and concerns, allowing you to gain deeper insights into each other's perspectives. Moreover, it involves a commitment to keeping promises and being reliable, as betrayal of trust - whether through infidelity, deception, or neglect - can have devastating effects on the foundation of the relationship. When trust is broken, the difficult journey of rebuilding it requires patience and dedication. You must be willing to engage in difficult conversations, confront underlying issues, and, most importantly, demonstrate consistent behaviour that reinforces your commitment to regaining trust.

The Role of Respect

While trust is paramount, it is equally vital to recognise the significance of respect in fostering a healthy marital relationship. Respect entails valuing your partner as an individual, and acknowledging their thoughts, feelings, and boundaries. It goes beyond mere tolerance; it embodies an appreciation for the uniqueness that each of you brings to the marriage. Respect creates a nurturing environment where both of you can pursue your aspirations, voice your opinions, and make decisions collaboratively.

One of the most effective ways to cultivate respect is through active listening. Active listening involves fully concentrating on what a partner is saying, processing that information, and responding thoughtfully. By demonstrating genuine interest and consideration for your partner's views, you can cultivate an atmosphere of respect that encourages open dialogue. It is important to recognise and celebrate your partner's accomplishments and qualities. Regularly expressing gratitude for the small and large things fosters an environment where respect is not just an abstract concept but a lived experience.

Building Trust Through Conflict Resolution

Conflict is an inevitable aspect of any marriage. While disagreements may arise from differing opinions, desires, or stresses, how you handle conflict can significantly impact trust and respect levels within the relationship. You need to approach conflicts constructively, focusing on resolution rather than winning an argument. When disagreements occur, you should strive to express your feelings honestly but respectfully, avoiding personal attacks or derogatory comments. Maintaining a calm demeanour and practising patience during heated discussions can help prevent escalations and promote healthy conflict resolution.

Implementing strategies such as "timeouts" during particularly charged discussions can provide the necessary breathing space, allowing you and your partner to collect your thoughts and re-engage with a clearer mindset. After a conflict has been resolved, the recommitment to trust and respect can manifest through affirming gestures - offering apologies when warranted, acknowledging mistakes, and expressing a desire to understand your partner's perspectives better. These actions reflect a mutual commitment to moving forwards together, reinforcing the bond of trust and respect.

The Mutuality of Trust and Respect

Trust and respect are interdependent; they reinforce and enhance each other. When you and your partner nurture respect, you create an environment in which trust can flourish. When trust is evident, respect deepens, and both of you will feel more secure in your relationship. This cycle of mutual reinforcement fosters a resilient marriage capable of enduring the external pressures that life inevitably presents.

Cultivating trust and respect is a continuous journey. It requires regular maintenance, attention, and adaptation to the evolving needs of both partners. As you grow and change, so will the dynamics of the relationship. Establishing rituals that promote connection, such as regular date nights or weekly check-ins, can help you remain attuned to your partner's emotional state and strengthen your commitment to trust and respect.

Cultivating trust and respect in marriage is essential for building a lasting and fulfilling partnership. These foundational elements enable couples to navigate the complexities of life, continue growing as individuals and partners, and foster a loving environment where emotional intimacy can thrive. By committing to open communication, active listening, and constructive conflict resolution, you can reinforce the virtues of trust and respect in your relationship. As you embark on this continuous journey with your partner, you create not only a robust marital bond but also a legacy of love and understanding that can inspire future generations. In a world increasingly characterised by disconnection, the deliberate cultivation of trust and respect remains one of the most significant investments that you and your partner can make for your marital happiness and overall wellbeing.

Conclusion

The assertion that "no one ever graduates from the institution of marriage" presents a profound and insightful perspective on the nature of romantic partnerships. Rather than culminating in a definitive conclusion, marriage is a journey that demands constant engagement, adaptability, and a commitment to growth. Life's unpredictability and the evolving dynamics of shared responsibilities underscore the necessity for ongoing learning, reflection, and investment in the relationship.

As you navigate the complexities of married life, you are afforded invaluable opportunities to deepen your connection with your partner, cultivate personal growth, and develop resilience in the face of adversity.

Ultimately, the institution of marriage, far from being an endpoint, remains an ever-evolving journey – one that champions the notion of lifelong love and enduring commitment.

CHAPTER FORTY

OUR BEST FRIEND COULD BECOME OUR WORST ENEMY

Friendship is often heralded as one of the most profound human experiences. The bonds formed between friends are typically rooted in trust, mutual interests, and emotional support. However, the inherent complexities of human relationships mean that the very individuals who stand by your side during times of joy and triumph can also harbour the potential for betrayal and conflict. It is an unsettling notion, yet reality persists: our best friend could become our worst enemy. This lesson explores the underlying dynamics of friendship, the potential for rivalry, the impact of jealousy, and the importance of communication in maintaining healthy relationships.

At the heart of any strong friendship lies trust, a fragile yet essential component that fosters intimacy and support. Trust allows us to share vulnerabilities, secrets, and aspirations, creating a safe space where emotional connections deepen. However, this same trust can lead to perilous predicaments when expectations are unmet, or boundaries are breached. The scenario wherein a friend who has been entrusted with personal information, such as fears or failures, intentionally or inadvertently uses this information against you can transform the essence of the relationship. The simple act of betrayal can turn a confidant into a rival, tainting memories of laughter with lingering resentment and feelings of betrayal.

The evolution of competition among friends can further complicate dynamic relationships. In a world that often emphasises achievement and success, it is not uncommon for friends to find themselves vying for the same goals or accolades. The desire to excel can transform into a disruptive rivalry, triggering envy and resentment. For instance, consider two friends who embark on similar career paths; when one begins to receive accolades that elude the other, the latent jealousy may ignite fierce competition. This scenario exemplifies how the desire for personal accomplishment can warp the foundations of friendship, leading to a gradual deterioration of trust and respect. In such instances, the relationship transitions from one marked by friendship to one overshadowed by hostility, revealing how easily friends can become enemies.

Jealousy - one of the most potent emotions - can act as a catalyst for discord in friendships. It manifests when one or both parties feel threatened by the other's successes, relationships, or opportunities. The emotion of jealousy stems from fear and insecurity, often leading to detrimental behaviours. This is particularly evident in circumstances where a friend perceives that they are being overshadowed or replaced. Such feelings can prompt individuals to engage in passive-aggressive behaviour, gossip, or even confrontation, further straining the fabric of friendship. What begins as a sense of friendship can devolve into a battle for recognition, ultimately culminating in a breakdown of mutual support – a transition from best friends to worst enemies, all fuelled by the intensity of human emotion.

While the potential for friendship to turn sour is significant, it is essential to recognise that many of these conflicts can be mitigated through effective communication. Open conversation is crucial in addressing feelings of jealousy, competition, or insecurity before they escalate into deeper issues. For instance, involving direct discussions about aspirations and feelings can clarify misunderstandings and reinforce trust. It is through these conversations that friends can express their concerns and fears, providing a platform for understanding and empathy.

Establishing healthy boundaries is vital to maintaining equilibrium within friendships. Recognising that both individuals are navigating their paths allows each to appreciate the other's journey without resentment. Friends should strive to celebrate each other's achievements rather than view them as threats. This shift in perspective not only boosts individual morale but also strengthens the friendship by fostering an environment of mutual respect and encouragement.

Cultivating emotional intelligence plays an integral role in navigating the complexities of friendship. Developing the ability to recognise one's emotions and effectively manage interpersonal reactions can diminish the effects of rivalry and jealousy. By enhancing self-awareness, friends can work to understand their feelings more constructively, minimising the risk of adverse reactions that could harm the relationship.

Friendships are often seen as pillars of support, sources of joy, and bonds that stand the test of time. However, in the intricate dance of human relationships, there exists a stark reality that our best friend could become our worst enemy. The transformation from trusted confidant to bitter rival is a painful and bewildering experience that many have faced.

Have you ever experienced a situation where someone you considered your best friend suddenly turned against you? It is a heartbreaking experience that many people face at some point in their lives. That your best friend could become your worst enemy holds true in many cases, highlighting the fact that relationships can change drastically over time. But why does this happen, and how can you deal with such a situation? Have you ever experienced the perplexing and often heartbreaking phenomenon of your trusted friend turning into your fiercest enemy? Yes, we are talking about that scenario where your best friend transforms into your worst enemy, leaving you scratching your head and wondering what went wrong.

The Evolution of Relationships

Friendships, like any other relationship, go through phases of growth and change. In the beginning, everything may seem perfect, with both parties sharing common interests and enjoying each other's company. However, as time goes on, people evolve and their priorities shift. What was once a strong bond may start to weaken as differences arise, leading to potential conflicts and misunderstandings.

It is important to remember that no friendship is immune to change. It is natural for people to outgrow each other or drift apart due to various reasons such as conflicting values, changing life circumstances, or simply growing apart. When these changes occur, it is essential to acknowledge them and decide whether the friendship is worth saving or whether it is time to let go.

Defining The Dynamics of Friendship and Enmity

Friendship and enmity might seem like opposites, but the line between the two can sometimes blur, leading to a complex interplay of emotions and behaviours. While friendships are built on trust, mutual respect, and support, enmity thrives on conflict, mistrust, and animosity. Understanding how these dynamics interact can provide valuable insights into the evolution of relationships from friendship to enmity.

Emotional Impact of Falling Out With a Friend

The fallout from a friendship turning sour can be emotionally devastating, like a punch in the gut from someone you once held dear. The sense of betrayal, loss, and confusion that accompanies such a rift can leave you reeling, questioning your judgment, and mourning the loss of a once-cherished connection. Navigating the emotional aftermath of a falling out with a close friend requires resilience, self-reflection, and perhaps a touch of humour to weather the storm.

Signs of a Friend Becoming a Potential Enemy

As the saying goes, keep your friends close and your enemies closer. But what happens when your friend starts exhibiting traits that raise red flags and hint at a potential shift towards enmity? Paying attention to warning signs can help you pre-emptively address issues and potentially salvage the friendship before it spirals into animosity. Below are some of the warning signs:

Lack of Communication

Your interactions become less frequent, and when you do speak, it feels forced or awkward. One of the telltale signs that a friend may be on the brink of becoming an enemy is a noticeable shift in their behaviour and communication patterns towards you. Sudden aloofness, passive-aggressive remarks, or outright hostility can signify underlying tensions that threaten the harmony of your relationship.

Betrayal

Your friend starts spreading rumours about you or betraying your trust in some way. Friends are supposed to have your back through thick and thin, but when loyalty wavers and support becomes conditional or non-existent, it is time to take stock of the dynamics at play. Inconsistencies in how a friend shows up for you in times of need can hint at deeper rifts that may eventually lead to a breakdown in the relationship.

Jealousy

Your friend becomes envious of your success or achievements, leading to passive-aggressive behaviour. Jealousy and competition can poison even the strongest of friendships, breeding resentment and eroding trust. Insecurities lurking beneath the surface can fuel a toxic dynamic where friends vie for validation and success, inadvertently sowing the seeds of animosity.

Constant Criticism

Your friend starts criticising you excessively or putting you down in front of others. Constant criticisms inherent in a toxic friendship can significantly undermine an individual's self-esteem and emotional wellbeing. Such a relationship often fosters an environment rife with negativity, where constructive feedback is overshadowed by excessive judgment and disparagement. Over time, this relentless barrage of harsh comments can lead to feelings of inadequacy and isolation, ultimately impairing one's ability to cultivate healthier connections. It is imperative to recognise the detrimental effects of such dynamics and to seek relationships characterised by mutual respect and support.

Miscommunication and Unresolved Conflicts

Communication breakdowns and unresolved conflicts can act as landmines in friendships, waiting to detonate and shatter the fragile balance between friends. Misinterpretations, unspoken grievances, and pent-up frustrations can snowball into irreconcilable differences that push friends towards enmity.

If you notice any of these signs in your friendship, it is crucial to address the issue openly and honestly. Communication is key in any relationship, and expressing your feelings and concerns can help clear misunderstandings and potentially salvage the friendship.

Preventing Friendships from Souring

While friendships turning sour may seem inevitable at times, there are proactive steps you can take to nurture and safeguard your relationships against the corrosive effects of enmity. By employing effective communication and setting healthy boundaries, you can cultivate strong, resilient friendships that stand the test of time. Clear, open communication forms the bedrock of any healthy relationship, including friendships. By expressing your thoughts, feelings, and concerns honestly and listening actively to your friend's perspective, you can foster understanding, empathy, and mutual respect in your interactions.

Setting Boundaries and Managing Expectations

Establishing boundaries and managing expectations are crucial components of maintaining balanced and harmonious friendships. Clearly defining acceptable and unacceptable behaviours, as well as aligning expectations around support, communication, and boundaries, can prevent misunderstandings and conflicts from derailing your relationship.

Dealing with a Toxic Friendship

If you realise that your best friend has indeed become your worst enemy, it is essential to take steps to protect yourself and your wellbeing. Here are some ways to deal with a toxic friendship:

Setting Boundaries

Establishing and articulating boundaries and expectations in a toxic friendship is essential for safeguarding your emotional wellbeing. It is imperative to clearly define the limits of acceptable behaviour and articulate the consequences of crossing these boundaries. Effective communication, rooted in honesty and respect, fosters an environment where you can acknowledge issues without resorting to hostility. By maintaining transparency regarding personal needs and emotional triggers, you can navigate the complexities of such relationships, ultimately empowering yourself to make informed decisions about your social connections.

Consider Ending the Friendship

Sometimes, the best option is to walk away from a toxic relationship for your mental and emotional health. Remember, it is fine to outgrow friendships and move on to healthier relationships that align with your values and priorities. Your best friend turning into your worst enemy is not a reflection of your worth but rather a natural part of life's journey.

Forgiveness and Closure in Severed Friendships

You know that moment when you finally finish a book you have been reading? It is like a weight lifted off your shoulders. Forgiveness is not just about letting your former friend off the hook; it is about freeing yourself from negativity. Take a deep breath, forgive them, and close that chapter. It is time to turn the page and start your next friendship adventure.

Fostering Positive and Lasting Friendships

Now that you have survived the friendship apocalypse, it is time to put those lessons into practice. Be intentional in your friendships, set boundaries, and surround yourself with people who lift you up instead of dragging you down. Remember, a true friend is like a good cup of coffee – warm, comforting, and always there when you need a pick-me-up. So go out there and be the best friend anyone could ask for.

Conclusion

The dynamic nature of friendships illustrates that the individuals we hold dear can also become sources of conflict and betrayal. This duality is rooted in the complex emotions that bind us - including trust, rivalry, and jealousy. Recognising these dynamics is crucial for navigating friendships effectively. While the potential for a best friend to transform into a worst enemy exists, it is our response to these challenges that ultimately determines the fate of our relationships.

By prioritising open communication, establishing healthy boundaries, and nurturing emotional intelligence, friends can foster resilience against the trials of human emotion, ensuring that their bonds remain strong amidst life's inevitable complexities. In navigating friendships, we must tread with care, for understanding and empathy can be the antidote to the bitterness of betrayal.

That our best friend could become our worst enemy serves as a reminder of the unpredictable nature of relationships. While it may be painful to witness a friendship deteriorate, it is essential to prioritise your wellbeing and surround yourself with positive influences. By recognising the signs of a toxic friendship and taking appropriate action, you can navigate these challenging situations with grace and resilience.

The journey from friendship to enmity is a challenging and emotionally turbulent experience for many. By recognising the warning signs, understanding the root causes, and implementing preventive measures, you can safeguard your relationships and mitigate the risk of friendships souring. While the pain of losing a friend may be inevitable, the lessons learnt, and the strength gained through such trials can pave the way for personal growth and resilience. Remember, in the intricate tapestry of human connections, nurturing healthy friendships and handling strained relationships with grace and understanding are essential steps towards a fulfilling and harmonious life.

Epilogue

As I look back on the journey that life has taken me through, I am filled with a profound sense of gratitude. Each lesson learned, whether through joy or hardship, has shaped the person I am today. Life's experiences have instilled in me the importance of resilience, the power of kindness, and the beauty of connection with others.

Through the pages of this book, I have shared stories that illustrate these teachings, and I hope they resonate with you as they have with me. Life is not merely a series of events, but a tapestry woven with moments of insight, growth, and understanding.

As you close this book, I encourage you to reflect on your own life's lessons. Embrace the struggles, celebrate the victories, and remember that every experience is an opportunity for growth. May you carry forwards the insights gained and continue to explore the depths of your own journey.

Thank you for joining me in this reflection. Here's to a life rich with learning, love, and endless possibilities. What life has taught me is just the beginning; I can't wait to see what lies ahead for all of us.